SHAPERS

OF THE

GREAT DEBATE

ON

WOMEN'S
RIGHTS

Recent Titles in
Shapers of the Great American Debates

SHAPERS
—OF THE—
GREAT DEBATE
—ON—
WOMEN'S
RIGHTS
A BIOGRAPHICAL DICTIONARY

Joyce Duncan

Shapers of the Great American Debates, Number 9
Peter B. Levy, Series Editor

GREENWOOD PRESS
Westport, Connecticut • London

Library of Congress Cataloging-in-Publication Data

Duncan, Joyce, 1946–
    Shapers of the great debate on women's rights : a biographical dictionary / Joyce Duncan.
        p. cm. — (Shapers of the great American debates, ISSN 1099–2693)
    Includes bibliographical references and index.
    ISBN 978–0–313–33869–4 (alk. paper)
1. Feminists—United States—Biography—Dictionaries. 2. Women social reformers—United
States—Biography—Dictionaries. I. Title.
HQ1412.D86 2008
305.42092'273—dc22   2008023050
[B]

British Library Cataloguing in Publication Data is available.

Library of Congress Catalog Card Number: 2008023050
ISBN: 978–0–313–33869–4
ISSN: 1099–2693

First published in 2008

Greenwood Press, 88 Post Road West, Westport, CT 06881
An imprint of Greenwood Publishing Group, Inc.
www.greenwood.com

Printed in the United States of America

The paper used in this book complies with the
Permanent Paper Standard issued by the National
Information Standards Organization (Z39.48–1984).

10 9 8 7 6 5 4 3 2 1

For Jordan,
who will one day shape her own destiny,
and for Jerry and Teresa,
who are always my champions

CONTENTS

TIMELINE OF WOMEN'S RIGHTS IN THE UNITED STATES

1829   Fanny Wright becomes the first woman in the United States to address an audience of both genders; she discusses free love and the abolition of marriage.

1836   Angelina Grimké publishes *An Appeal to the Christian Women of the South.*

1837   Sarah Grimké is the first to compare slavery to the treatment of women.

1838   Sarah Grimké publishes *Letters on the Equality of the Sexes* (1838), the first woman's rights book by an American.

1838   The Congregational Church issues a "Pastoral Letter," denouncing the Grimké Sisters.

1841   Amelia Bloomer founds the *Lily*, the first journal published by and for women.

1845   Margaret Fuller publishes *Women in the Nineteenth Century*, the foundational text for the woman's movement.

1848   The first Woman's Rights Convention is held in Seneca Falls, New York. Organized by Elizabeth Cady Stanton and Lucretia Mott, the convention presents a *Declaration of Sentiments*, calling for equal treatment for women and the right to vote.

1849   Lucretia Mott publishes *Discourse on Woman.*

1850   The first National Women's Rights Convention in Worcester, Massachusetts is attended by more than one thousand.

1851   Sojourner Truth delivers her "Ain't I A Woman?" speech.

1851   Amelia Bloomer begins wearing pantaloons under her dresses, subsequently called "Bloomers."

1853   Antoinette Brown becomes first ordained woman minister in the United States.

1855   Lucy Stone retains her maiden name after marriage and rejects traditional vows.

1903 The National Women's Trade Union League is formed to improve working conditions for women.

1904 Mary Bethune opens Daytona Normal and Industrial Institute for Negro Girls in Florida.

1907 Harriot Stanton Blatch organizes the Equality League of Self-Supporting Women, comprised of over twenty thousand factory, laundry, and garment workers on New York City's lower East Side.

1908 Ida Husted Harper publishes last volume of the *Life of Susan B. Anthony.*

1910 Major suffrage parades are organized in both New York City and Washington, DC and continued periodically until 1913.

1913 Jane Addams publishes satiric "If Men Were Seeking the Franchise."

1913 Alice Paul and Lucy Burns initiate the Congressional Union to work for a federal suffrage amendment.

1913 Inez Milholland Boissevain leads parade of over eight thousand suffragists through the streets of Washington, DC on the eve of Woodrow Wilson's inauguration.

1913 Members of the Congressional Union form the "Silent Sentinels" and picket in front of the White House. Many are jailed for "obstructing traffic."

1916 Carrie Chapman Catt unveils her "Winning Plan" to reenergize the members of NAWSA.

1916 Margaret Sanger opens the first birth control clinic in Brooklyn, New York.

1916 Jeanette Rankin becomes first woman elected to Congress.

1918 President Woodrow Wilson announces his support of a woman's suffrage amendment.

1919 Congress passes the 19th Amendment to the Constitution allowing women to vote after forty-one years of denial.

1920 On August 26th, the 19th Amendment is officially added to the Constitution. Tennessee is the final affirmative vote for ratification.

1920 The Women's Bureau of the Department of Labor is formed.

1921 Margaret Sanger founds the American Birth Control League, eventually renamed Planned Parenthood Federation of America (1942).

1931 Jane Addams becomes the second American and first woman nominated for Nobel Peace Prize.

1935 Mary McLeod Bethune organizes the National Council of Negro Women.

1936 Disseminating information regarding birth control is no longer classed as obscene.

1946 United Nations establishes Commission on the Status of Women.

1948 Universal Declaration of Human Rights, created in part by Eleanor Roosevelt, is accepted by United Nations.

1955 The Daughters of Bilitis, the first lesbian organization, is founded.

1960   The Food and Drug Administration approves The Pill for birth control available to married couples.

1961   President John F. Kennedy appoints Eleanor Roosevelt to head the President's Commission on the Status of Women.

1961   Bella Abzug founds Women's Strike for Peace to fight for nuclear test ban treaty.

1961   Esther Peterson appointed head of Women's Bureau in Department of Labor.

1963   Betty Friedan publishes *The Feminine Mystique* that incites the second wave of feminism.

1963   Congress passes the Equal Pay Act, making it illegal to pay a woman less than a man for the same job.

1964   The Civil Rights Act includes Title VII that prohibits discrimination in employment based on sex.

1964   The Civil Rights Act establishes the Equal Employment Opportunity Commission (EEOC) to investigate complaints.

1964   Fannie Lou Hamer becomes delegate to Democratic Convention, representing the Mississippi Freedom Democratic Party.

1965   Helen Gurley Brown takes over *Cosmopolitan* magazine and changes demographics to appeal to single women.

1966   The National Organization for Women (NOW) is founded by Betty Friedan and others, eventually becoming the largest women's rights association in the country.

1967   Executive Order 11375 expands affirmative action to cover discrimination based on gender.

1967   Pauli Murray aids American Civil Liberties Union in revising policy on gender discrimination.

1968   EEOC rules that separating help wanted advertisements by gender is illegal.

1968   Feminists protest the Miss American Pageant as degrading to women.

1969   California institutes a "no fault" divorce law.

1969   Redstockings, a "consciousness-raising" group, is formed in New York City.

1970   Kate Millett publishes *Sexual Politics,* a critique of patriarchy as socially conditioned.

1970   Alix Kates Shulman publishes "A Marriage Agreement," an essay that advocates that marriage should be the shared responsibility of both genders.

1970   Germaine Greer publishes *The Female Eunuch.*

1970   Lesbians protest against NOW due, in large part, to Betty Friedan's labeling them the "lavender menace" and implying their issues were contrary to the movement goals.

1971   Gloria Steinem launches *Ms.* magazine.

1971   Smaller groups of women activists, divided along racial and sexual orientation lines, begin to form and move away from the predominantly white, middle-class leadership of the second wave.

1971   Gloria Steinem, Bella Abzug, and Shirley Chisholm found the National Women's Political Caucus to encourage women to seek public office.

1972   The Equal Rights Amendment (first introduced by Alice Paul in 1923) is passed by Congress.

1972   Shirley Chisholm announces her candidacy for president of the United States.

1972   Birth control is legally available to single women.

1972   Phyllis Chesler publishes *Women and Madness*, broadening the field of feminist psychology.

1972   Title IX of the Education Amendment prohibits discrimination in schools based on gender, which increases women's participation in athletic programs.

1973   *Roe v. Wade* establishes a woman's right to a safe, legal abortion.

1974   Phyllis Chesler cofounds the National Women's Health Network to offer accurate and unbiased information on women's health care.

1976   The first marital rape law is passed in Nebraska, making it illegal for a husband to rape his wife.

1976   Shere Hite publishes *The Hite Report: A Nationwide Study on Female Sexuality.*

1976   President Jimmy Carter creates the National Advisory Committee on Women.

1977   Bella Abzug gains over a million dollars in federal support to convene a National Women's Conference in Houston, Texas.

1978   The Pregnancy Discrimination Act bans hiring and firing discrimination based on pregnancy.

1979   Susan Brownmiller founds Women Against Pornography.

1980   Audre Lorde publishes the *Cancer Journals,* the first work to address the viewpoint of a lesbian of color and cofounds the Kitchen Table Women of Color Press.

1980   bell hooks initiates a support group for African American women, Sisters of the Yam.

1982   The Equal Rights Amendment fails ratification by the states.

1983   Catharine MacKinnon and Andrea Dworkin are hired to draft city ordinance making pornography a civil rights violation.

1984   Term "glass ceiling" is coined to describe lack of advancement of women in the workplace.

1984   Geraldine Ferraro is the first woman candidate for vice president of the United States.

1985   Wilma Mankiller is elected as principal chief of the Cherokee Nation.

1986   The Supreme Court rules that sexual harassment is a form of illegal job discrimination.

1990   Camille Paglia publishes *Sexual Persona* and criticizes feminists as perpetual victims and man-haters.

1990   Naomi Wolf publishes *The Beauty Myth: How Images of Beauty Are Used Against Women.*

1992   American Association of University Women publishes research on how schools shortchange girls.

1992   Susan Faludi publishes *Backlash: The Undeclared War Against American Women,* showing the media's negative portrayal of women.

1992   Congressional resolution names March as Women's History Month.

1994   The Violence Against Women Act tightens penalties for sex offenders and funds services for victims of rape and domestic violence.

1994   Mary Daly publishes a feminist version of the dictionary.

1994   Katie Roiphe publishes *The Morning After: Fear, Sex and Feminism,* implying that women should be held responsible for their actions instead of crying date rape.

1995   The United Nations Fourth World Conference on Women is held in Beijing and produces list of things yet to be done for international rights of women.

1996   The Supreme Court rules that all-male military schools must admit women or lose public funding.

1999   The Supreme Court rules that a woman can sue for damages due to sex discrimination.

2007   Hillary Clinton was the Democratic front runner for nomination for president of the United States.

AUTHOR'S NOTE

I teach so that others may learn. The courses permit me to immerse my students in issues of inequity, prejudice, and that elusive concept, social justice. Each semester, students are required to create an oral presentation on a historic period and the activist players of that era. And, each semester, I am consistently appalled at how miniscule their understanding of the linearity of history and fear that the adage about "doomed to repeat it" will, indeed, reach fruition. Few have heard of Elizabeth Cady Stanton, Alice Paul, or Margaret Sanger; some are aware of Susan B. Anthony but only because she was featured on a short-lived coin. A small percentage has knowledge that the *Constitution* can be changed but no concept of how those changes are effected or how many changes exist. Across the board, they fail to identify the Nineteenth Amendment.

Early in the term, I ask for a show of hands concerning voting. The majority, if they were of age at the time, voted in the last presidential election but when queried about state elections, hands dropped and when city government was mentioned, only a smattering admitted to selecting city officials. I pay particular attention to the women students, many of whom lament that politics is disinteresting and a waste of their time. As a rule, they are totally unaware of the sacrifices that were made in order for them to be *disinterested*.

Since most traditional-aged college students cannot remember using a typewriter or living without a cell phone and text messaging or suffering through the dog day heat of August without air conditioning, it is not surprising that centuries old ancient history is of little consequence to what they consider important. These young women matured in the Age of Entitlement, when they were told they could be whatever they wanted if they were willing to apply themselves to the task. Although that assumption is still not universally true, their lives are light years removed from their foremothers'. They have no collective memory of an era when women could not own property or money, when they had little decision making power regarding the upbringing of their children, when they were discouraged or forbidden from seeking education or a profession, when they were silenced in public and even in houses of worship, when they were chastised for putting pen to paper or offering their opinion, and when they were powerless to change their destiny because they had no political clout, no power of the vote.

One of my students introduced me to YouTube, the Internet phenomenon that allows anyone to post short video clips. In researching his presentation on women's rights, he stumbled across footage of another young man on a college campus that was encouraging coeds to sign a petition that would abolish suffrage. Most complied, stating they did not feel that women should be allowed to *suffer*.

I realize there is little time in an overburdened K-12 curriculum under constant scrutiny to improve test scores but if students, in becoming globally competitive in math and science, lose all grasp of history, what is to become of us. I do my part, as should we all, to serve as a constant reminder of the persons who fought and were persecuted in order for us to enjoy freedom. I teach so that others may learn and, perhaps, not forget. I send my students forth with hope.

This research has been a grueling, sometimes painful, undertaking. Not because of the subject matter but because of the matter of the subject. It is a simple task to be drawn into the lives of others and to empathize with their undertakings. I came to admire these women for their intelligence, for their persistence, and for their refusal to accept no as an answer. Their strength of will and of character should serve as inspiration to us all. True or not, there is a story that Sigmund Freud, on his death bed, asked, "What do women want?" The answer is simple; women want to be treated with the dignity and respect due all humankind.

SERIES FOREWORD

American history has been shaped by numerous debates over issues far ranging in content and time. Debates over the right, or lack thereof, to take the land of the Native Americans, and the proper place and role of women, sparked by Roger Williams and Anne Hutchinson, respectively, marked the earliest years of the Massachusetts Bay Colony. Debates over slavery, the nature and size of the federal government, the emergence of big business, and the rights of labor and immigrants were central to the Republic in the nineteenth century and, in some cases, remain alive today. World War I, World War II, and the Vietnam War sparked debates that tore at the body politic. Even the Revolution involved a debate over whether America should be America or remain part of Great Britain. And the Civil War, considered by many the central event in American history, was the outgrowth of a long debate that found no peaceful resolution.

This series, *Shapers of the Great American Debates,* will examine many of these debates—from those between Native Americans and European settlers to those between "natives" and "newcomers." Each volume will focus on a particular issue, concentrating on those men and women who *shaped* the debates. The authors will pay special attention to fleshing out the life histories of the shapers, considering the relationship between biography or personal history and policy or philosophy. Each volume will begin with an introductory overview, include approximately twenty biographies of ten to fifteen pages, an appendix that briefly describes other key figures, a bibliographical essay, and a subject index. Unlike works that emphasize end results, the books in this series will devote equal attention to both sides, to the "winners" and the "losers." This will lead to a more complete understanding of the richness and complexity of America's past than is afforded by works that examine only the victors.

Taken together, the books in this series remind us of the many ways that class, race, ethnicity, gender, and region have divided rather than united the inhabitants of the United States of America. Each study reminds us of the frequency and variety of debates in America, a reflection of the diversity of the nation and its democratic credo. One even wonders if a similar series could be developed for many other nations or if the diversity of America and its tradition of free expression have given rise to more debates than elsewhere.

Although many Americans have sought to crush the expression of opposing views by invoking the imperative of patriotism, more often than not Americans have respected the rights of others to voice their opinions. Every four years, Americans have voted for a president and peacefully respected the results, demonstrating their faith in the process that institutionalizes political debate. More recently, candidates for the presidency have faced off in televised debates that often mark the climax of their campaigns. Americans not only look forward to these debates, but they would probably punish anyone who sought to avoid them. Put another way, debates are central to America's political culture, especially those that deal with key issues and involve the most prominent members of society.

Each volume in the series is written by an expert. While I offered my share of editorial suggestions, overall I relied on the author's expertise when it came to determining the most sensible way to organize and present each work. As a result, some of the volumes follow a chronological structure; others clump their material thematically; still others are separated into two sections, one pro and one con. All of the works are written with the needs of college and advanced high school students in mind. They should prove valuable both as sources for research papers and as supplemental texts in both general and specialized courses. The general public should also find the works an attractive means of learning more about many of the most important figures and equally as many seminal issues in American history.

Peter B. Levy
Associate Professor
Department of History
York College

PREFACE

A wave is a seemingly living thing that exchanges certain elements for other elements as it swirls onto the beach and sweeps back into the watery abyss; with each exchange, it deposits new gifts and takes away the old, much as novel theory replaces prevalent thought. As a living thing, a wave also has moods ... sometimes it gently caresses the edges of the world and sometimes, it violently rearranges the landscape. As such, waves create an apt metaphor for the mêlée that produced both the surge and resurgence, both the conflict and change, of the woman's movement as well as denoting its chronological divisions.

The woman's movement, later dubbed feminism, was divided into waves, a term coined by Marsha Lear in the 1960s. To date, the movement splashed through three waves or incarnations as the issues varied and the players changed. Since those waves churned within a historical context, chronology seemed the natural organization for this work. The first-wave activists fought for a constitutional amendment giving women the right to vote; the second wave battled for equity in hiring and salary, for the right of a woman to decide if she wished to give birth and for political acknowledgment of equality; and the third wave, still growing, urged a more inclusive movement to give voice to women of color and lesbians, among other issues.

The problem in creating this work was not deciding whom to include but whom to exclude. In covering a century and a half of any period in history, many persons, leaders and heroes and common folk rise to the surface and within the eras of the woman's movement, that is particularly true. Ultimately, after extensive research, it seemed logical to write about the women who were change agents during their periods but, more appropriately, to introduce the reader to others who resided in the lesser-known shadows of the movement but were equally important in channeling the issues toward resolution. Thus, this volume features recognizable names, such as Susan B. Anthony, Elizabeth Cady Stanton, Gloria Steinem, and Betty Friedan, but also Victoria Woodhull, Margaret Fuller, Amelia Bloomer, Wilma Mankiller, Phyllis Chesler, and Mary Daly as well as their modern counterparts,

Katie Roiphe, Rebecca Walker, and Cherri Moraga, among others. In this, the book differs from other references on the market that tend to emphasize only those names already familiar to the population. All told, the work contains a historic overview of each major period, longer entries on forty-two women and short biographies on thirty-two others. Because it is always an easier task to find information on persons of historical interest than it is on those who are current, the majority of third-wave activists are found among the shorter biographies. As mentioned, the work is divided by the parameters of the waves of the movement. The major entries are historically organized by their dates of activity within the movement. The short biographies are chronologically ordered by dates of birth.

Those selected are rhetoricians, academics, writers, politicians, religious figures, actors, and minor celebrities, diverse in their approaches and their lifestyles but with the common cause of securing a measure of equality and recognition for themselves and their sisters. Regardless of the historical period in the movement, the divisions retained commonalities. The early activists were engaged in organizing activities within their churches, which naturally evolved into the woman's clubs and woman's organizations that would guide the second and third wave. The majority of those involved during each period were educated in some measure and created a network of community through public speaking and writing or both. In the first and second wave, the issues arose in conjunction with other movements, abolition and civil rights, respectively. The third wave, birthed with the advent of technology, continued to network with grassroots movements, edging toward community through the use of the Internet and other media.

This is my second book on women and I am continually amazed by their pluck, their drive, and their indomitable will. In revisiting the period in American history a century and a half ago, I cannot imagine what life would be like without the freedom of choice granted to women in the twenty-first century. It is my hope that this work will serve as a reminder of the sacrifices that were made against great odds, which offer the modern woman the ability to be what she wishes.

PART I

FIRST WAVE: THE WOMAN QUESTION TO SUFFRAGE

INTRODUCTION

At the turn of the nineteenth century and throughout the span of those years, life in the United States was markedly different than it is today, particularly for women of the era. Some historians write off the woman's rights movement as mass pandering to a group of radical, frustrated women who were pushing to voice their inconsequential grievances in public or to gain political power by securing the right to vote, while others elevate those women to idolatrous levels. However, the period and the issues flowing through it were much more complex than merely a drive for the privilege of voting. It was woman's fundamental need for independence and an identity of her own, separate from the men in her life, which thrust the woman's movement forward. The cry for suffrage came only when she realized that political involvement was the most expedient route to attain those goals.

During the 1800s in the United States, before a woman married, she was seldom permitted to leave her father's house and her only social gatherings were within the confines of her family. Once she was married, the woman essentially forfeited not only her legal existence but her existence as an individual. She was forbidden to sign a contract, make a will, or sue in court; if she inherited goods, the money and property went to her husband; if she worked, her husband received her salary; and she was allowed no opinion about how he chose to raise their children. Controlling society's behavior was the Code of Coverture, based on British common law as spelled out by William Blackstone in *Commentaries on the Laws of England,* published in 1765–69, and transferred to America through early immigration. The Code stipulated that the husband and wife were one and that *one* was the husband. In other words, a married woman was *covered* by her husband and, legally, she belonged to him, much as the slaves of the era *belonged* to their masters. According to Blackstone, "the very being or legal existence of the woman is suspended during the marriage, or at least is incorporated and consolidated into that of the husband; under whose wing, protection and cover, she performs every thing." Coverture afforded essentially the same conditions for married women that bound serfs or vassals to their lords during feudalism. A woman was given away by her family and took vows to obey her husband; in other words, she was considered totally devoid of independence or anything of her own.

Woman, then, was relegated to the *woman's sphere;* thus, the extent of her minimal influence was restricted to the home and the family. The nineteenth-century communities were in primarily rural settlements with most families living in small villages or on farms and the vast majority of married women remained at home with little outside contact. In this *sphere,* women were expected to create and maintain a domestic agenda with a day of the week set aside for each major chore, washing, ironing, cleaning, that had to be completed by the time her husband returned home in the evening. If she were lucky enough to be an upper-class wife, she might have servants to take care of the dirtier tasks but it was still her duty to oversee those servants as well as being a charming hostess for her husband's colleagues and friends. Thus, life for woman covered the spectrum from drudgery to doll-ery with few avenues of escape and little patience from others for her personal pursuits beyond the useful ones like needlework or tutoring her children.

Because much of the communal life of the nineteenth century centered on the church, primarily the patriarchal Christian church, women were constantly reminded of their *defective* nature produced by being the daughters of Eve, the archetypal sinner. In addition, the biblical encyclical that women should be quiet in church was reinforced and often followed her to the home. Those who did not employ doctrine to keep woman *in her place* used the medical mythology that woman, by nature, was weak and should be spared the stress and responsibility of a public life. Obviously, they asserted, men were more suited to physical exertion and intellectual pursuits, like those provided by education, work, and politics.

The church, however, became a natural extension of the home and through that affiliation, women could have contact with the community at large. The prescribed role for women was to protect the civilized society, the religion, and the sanctity of the home. They were branded as guardians of the moral fiber of the country; therefore, it was acceptable for them to be involved in the religious upbringing of their children and in the nonprofessional activities of the church. Through this connection, they were often permitted to extend themselves further into the life of the community through social gatherings with other women and, occasionally, through charitable work. If the latter were true, however, and they were permitted to venture outside the confines of their home, a chaperone was required, for a woman walking alone was viewed as lewd and wanton.

Speaking in public was deemed as immoral and speaking to a mixed audience was called promiscuous. Women, even educated women, were not expected to have opinions, particularly if those opinions differed from those of their fathers or their husbands. Thus, it was a reasonable evolution for women to seek the company of other women to express their views on the social and political issues of the day. The logical venue for this expression was, of course, the church, which also became the outlet for social activism. Through these gatherings, women began to build a bond of sisterhood and because the church endorsed their moral superiority to men, they developed a sense of empowerment.

Although education was thought of as wasted on women, it was permitted in limited quantities to those who could afford it, normally through private schooling or tutoring. By becoming educated, usually in religious instruction, a woman would be capable of making herself more suitable to attract a good man to marry or, if already married, to train her male children. Even by the end of the nineteenth century, when more liberal views toward education held sway, women in higher education were discouraged. Because women who were college educated tended to marry later or not at all, higher education was viewed as a subversive threat to the family.

Early professions open to women were teaching and nursing since they were involved with educating children and ministering to the ailing, once again extensions of the *woman's sphere*. Writing was viewed as a hobby, a light, frivolous activity to entertain the wives of the wealthy, harmless as long as they did not attempt to publish their work. Some critics, on the other hand, held that writing, produced frequently as a by-product of thought, would overtire women and perhaps make them ill or insane.

Two outgrowths of the social activism of the church were women's involvement in the abolition movement, calling for the immediate emancipation of the slaves, and the prohibition of alcohol with the subsequent formation of the Woman's Christian Temperance Union in 1874. The movement organizers noted that alcoholism, and the men who used the drug, could subsequently lead to the physical and mental abuse of women and children. The abolitionist movement was endorsed by the church and the latter movement threatened the ideal conditions of hearth and home; thus, women's involvement was a logical evolution. Because of their connection to the activities of the church, women formed a sorority of like-minded opinions and gravitated toward one or the other or both of the issues, even though their involvement was initially on the periphery of formalized associations.

As concerns grew, women found it increasingly difficult to avoid voicing their opinions. When they understood, however, that their assessments would not be validated and that they would be silenced in the formal movement gatherings, particularly among the abolitionists, they realized their lives were, in many ways, not better than those of the persons they were trying to free. The similarities between the condition for slaves in the United States and the condition for women in the United States were overpowering; both were viewed as possessions, both were told to be silent, both had no legal rights, and both were forbidden from helping to elect their governors. Once these facts were realized, it took little impetus to leap from involvement in the issues of the slaves to involvement in the issues of women, thus, the woman's rights movement was born. Suddenly, women were introduced to the possibility of social change; furthermore, they were made aware that they could be the instrument of that change. Using the organizational skills they had acquired as part of the antislavery movement, as well as some of the structure, women began to hold meetings, to speak on the issues, and to encourage the involvement of others.

By 1840, the members of the American Anti-Slavery Association split over the *woman question,* with some adamantly opposed to women being allowed to serve as officers or speakers. They were afraid that women would use their involvement in abolition to promote women's rights. This caused the movement to fragment, eventually splitting into two groups, the radicals and the moderates. The radicals promoted equality for all, including women, while the moderates clung to traditional gender roles. Eventually, the need to fight for their individual rights overpowered their concern for the rights of others, which created a second and inevitable rift with women determined to secure a place of their own.

That same year, two women traveled to London to attend the World Anti-Slavery Convention. The first, an elderly Quaker minister, had been elected as an American delegate to the convention; the second, a young bride, was accompanying her husband to the gathering in route to their European honeymoon. When they arrived, the women were separated from the men delegates, shuttered behind a curtain, and denied the right to speak. Over the days of the meeting, however, they talked to each other, discovered commonalities, and determined to forge new alliances to improve their lot. The two women were Lucretia Mott and Elizabeth Cady Stanton and, although it would be several years before they would meet again to push those plans forward, the seeds of unrest were planted during that encounter.

In July 1848, Mott, Stanton, and others announced the first Woman's Rights Convention would be held in Seneca Falls, New York, and a movement was born. They prepared the "Declaration of Sentiments," modeled on the Declaration of Independence, to shed light on what women wanted. Prior to enumerating their grievances, the women wrote, "The history of mankind is a history of repeated injuries and usurpations on the part of man toward woman, having in direct object the establishment of an absolute tyranny over her." More than three hundred persons, both men and women, attended the meeting and that created enough momentum to launch a nationwide movement.

Even if women could not vote, they could support political candidates who would view their issues in a favorable light and they could lobby through petitions to encourage Congress to adopt their views. They campaigned throughout their home regions and then spread out in a thin line across the country, urging other women to follow in their footsteps. The grassroots organizing began to take hold and Senator Charles Sumner credited their 400,000 signatures on petitions as the impetus in passage of the Thirteenth Amendment. Consequently and ironically, women were instrumental in securing the passage of both the Thirteenth and the Fourteenth Amendments.

The Thirteenth Amendment emancipated the slaves, thus, women were certain that their hour had arrived. They continued to work toward the passage of the Fourteenth Amendment, confident that it would provide universal suffrage and the political power to change the face of legislation in the country. Politicians, however, used the woman's movement to further their own agendas. Republicans accused women of undermining black suffrage to further their own cause and accosted Democrats for supporting women for that very purpose. Having split with abolitionists over the issues, the woman's movement swam in ever widening circles seeking allies.

When the Fourteenth Amendment was passed, women were shocked at the wording. The right to vote had been awarded to former slaves but the second section of the amendment clearly defined the only legal voter as a *male inhabitant* of the country, either born or naturalized in the United States. For the first time, an explicit gender bias was included and women were formally written out of the Constitution. Dramatically, their focus changed from the woman's movement to the suffrage movement.

In 1868, women worked to make suffrage part of the Democratic platform. The Democratic Party needed an issue to differentiate its policy from the Republicans but the antiabolitionists within the Democratic Party made it difficult for some to lend their support to the woman's movement due to the women's previous alliance with abolition. Others considered the movement too radical—what would happen to the framework of the country and the sanctity of the home if women were permitted to flock to the polls.

The suffragists were a diverse group; some were married with many children, some never married. Most were upwardly mobile, through the fortunes of their family or their husband, and the majority was Caucasian. Some were involved in organized religion, particularly those of the Quaker sects, while others refuted religion as institutionalizing patriarchal thinking through biblical misinterpretation. A few had college degrees, primarily in science, while others had only briefly attended grade school or worked with a tutor. Some were primarily writers, using various publications to air their grievances, while others functioned as speakers, traveling constantly and petitioning for the cause. Some were quiet, almost to the point of passivity, while others organized parades, carried banners, and picketed government buildings. Many were arrested and sent to jail. But with all their differences and all the infighting among the various woman's groups, they shared common beliefs: that all men *and women* were created equal; that their lot in life was inherently unbalanced; and that the only way to bring about permanent change was to secure the vote and change the laws. The women noted in this work cover that spectrum.

Not all women, however, believed in the rhetoric of the woman's movement. Many joined the camp of the antisuffragists, a diametrically opposed group, who voiced the opinion that woman's natural frailty would cause her to become fatigued or ill simply by making the trip to the polls. Others felt that women with the vote might jeopardize national security or that women would be inclined to vote more than once or vote only for the most attractive candidate and not for the issues. Some offered that allowing women to express their individual opinion would rend the fabric of family and contaminate politics. At one point, shortly before the passage of the Nineteenth Amendment extended suffrage to women, the National Association Opposed to Woman Suffrage boasted a membership of over 350,000 and was composed of both men and women.

Regardless of whether the women belonged to the faction that advocated a federal amendment for voting rights or the group that believed granting suffrage on a state-by-state level was more appropriate, they were aware that action needed to be taken in individual communities, cities, and states to create awareness. Thus, women took to the open road, spreading out from New England across the United States. The earliest state organizations were in Kansas, Maryland, Missouri, and New Jersey. Some states had given women the right to vote in school elections and in 1869 Wyoming became the first of the United States to grant complete suffrage to women as part of its bid for statehood. By 1895, most of the western states had formed woman's groups. From 1890 onward, the National American Woman Suffrage Association sent paid organizers throughout the country and supported the individual presenters with finances, literature, press releases, and banners. The suffragettes, as they were labeled, tailored their speeches to the audience, employing either the argument that voting should be woman's natural right as a citizen or that it should be an extension of the nurturing of the home since women had more knowledge of societal problems. The final states to form associations were Arkansas, New Mexico, and South Carolina and by the end of 1914, every state that had not yet granted suffrage to women had formed groups to work toward that end.

From its first consideration in the Declaration of Sentiments in 1848 to the passage of the Nineteenth Amendment, the fight for woman suffrage encompassed seventy-two years, spanned two centuries, included eighteen presidents and three wars. It incorporated women who were vilified, spat upon, called names, and sentenced to work houses. Because of the duration of the fight, most of the pioneers of the movement, including Elizabeth Cady Stanton and Susan B. Anthony, did not live to see their dream fulfilled.

As the elder stateswomen of the movement began to fade away, a new, more vocal group emerged led, in part, by Alice Paul and Harriot Stanton Blatch, the daughter of Stanton. Rather than meeting with others in darkened halls or private homes, this new breed took their protests to the streets by mobilizing parades and offering impromptu speeches. Between 1910 and

1913, five major suffrage parades were held in both Washington, DC and New York City. Some of the marchers were on foot, carrying embroidered banners that read, among other sayings: "We Prepare Children for the World, We Ask to Prepare the World for our Children"; "We Demand an Amendment to the Constitution of the United States Enfranchising Women of the Country"; and "More Ballots, Less Bullets." Some pushed babies in strollers with signs noting "Future Voters." Others rode on horseback or on floats that emphasized the history, progress, and future of the movement. The images created by these events engaged the national press and, suddenly, suffrage news leapt from a buried notice in the back of the paper to the front page.

The antisuffragists called this public display unladylike and immature and many displayed their antagonism with physical hostility, tripping the marchers, climbing onto the floats, and striking or spitting on the women. At one point, during the march on the eve of Woodrow Wilson's inauguration, the U.S. cavalry had to be called out to restore order. Later, when Alice Paul's group, labeled by the media as the "Silent Sentinels," undertook an eighteen-month vigil in front of the White House, six days a week, twenty-four hours a day, in all kinds of weather, many of the women were arrested and imprisoned. The mistreatment they received during incarceration, including lack of sanitation and force feeding, was also noted by the media and many across the country were urged to action. And, at long last with public sentiment growing, Congress was forced to propose a suffrage amendment to be sent to the states for ratification.

The final confrontation took place in Tennessee in the summer of 1920. Called the War of the Roses for the boutonnieres worn by each faction, yellow for suffrage and red for those opposed, the State House of Representatives was split almost evenly on ratification with only one vote needed for passage. A first-term congressman and the youngest member of the House, Harry Burns, heeded the request of his mother and changed his vote to yes despite what he feared it might portend for his reelection plans. On August 26, 1920, the Nineteenth Amendment was added to the Constitution of the United States, granting women the right to have a voice in the running of the country. The Nineteenth Amendment stated simply:

Section 1. The right of citizens of the United States to vote shall not be denied or abridged by the United States or by any State on account of sex.

Section 2. The Congress shall have power to enforce this article by appropriate legislation.

The battle had been won and the victor announced; the war, however, would continue for decades.

FRANCES "FANNY" WRIGHT
(1795–1852)

A naturalized American citizen, Frances "Fanny" Wright was the first woman to speak publicly in the United States as well as the first to advocate free public schools and equal rights for women and for slaves. She was so opposed to slavery that she *purchased* a group of slaves, housed them in a communal setting, and provided lifestyle education to prepare them for emancipation.

Fanny Wright was born in Dundee, Scotland on September 6, 1795. Her parents, James and Camilla Campbell Wright, were wealthy aristocrats who died when their three children were young, leaving each child with a fortune. Their son Richard joined the military and was killed at fifteen; while Fanny and her sister Camilla were sent to live with their maternal grandfather and raised by a conservative aunt. The high point of Fanny's youth was visiting her great uncle, James Milne, a professor of philosophy at Glascow College. Through him, she broadened her self-taught education and became well read and fluent in both French and Italian. As a child, she was rebellious, questioning the mannerisms and values of the British upper crust, a class war that would shape her future and lead her to Jeremy Bentham's theory of utilitarianism, the greatest good for the greatest number.

At twenty-three, the streak of rebellion blossomed and funded by her trust account, Fanny left Scotland for the United States, eventually crossing the ocean seven times in her lifetime. Visiting America was an enlightening experience for the young woman and she was intrigued by the freedom offered by democracy. On returning to Europe, she published *Views of Society and Manners in America* (1821), which endorsed society in the United States and offered the theory that life was better for American women than for European women. Even then, she was concerned with the oppression of her gender. Continuing to write, she created a play, *Altorf*, which was eventually produced in New York City, as well as *A Few Days in Athens* that some believe inspired Walt Whitman to construct his epic, *Leaves of Grass*.

While traveling around Europe in 1821, Fanny and Camilla met and were befriended by General Marquis de Lafayette, who would have adopted the sisters if his family had approved. In 1824, they followed Lafayette back across the Atlantic and through his connections, Fanny was introduced to John Quincy Adams, Sam Houston, James Monroe, Thomas Jefferson, and James Madison. Deciding to make the United States her home, she reevaluated American society and emphasizing the country's potential for true equality, she argued for revolution and reform. She was particularly aghast at the institution of slavery as well as the second-class status of women. She was the first woman in the country to argue that men and women should be equal. In 1825, Fanny applied for and was granted U.S. citizenship.

In response to her disapproval of slavery, Fanny used part of her inheritance and the benevolence of her acquaintances, including Lafayette, to *purchase* thirty slaves and 1,940 acres near Memphis, Tennessee. The property lay on both sides of the Wolf River near Germantown. After establishing a board of trustees and hiring twelve white managers, she christened the commune Nashoba, which meant wolf in the Chickasaw language. It was her dedicated purpose to educate the slaves, both morally and intellectually, to prepare them for emancipation; she believed it would be irresponsible to free them without the life skills to make it on their own. It was also her contention that because they were free, the former slaves would work harder, make the cooperative profitable and, thus, allow more persons to join the community. She composed an overview of her theory, entitled *A Plan for the Gradual Abolition of Slavery in the United States without Danger of Loss to the Citizens of the South,* which was presented to Congress. Her emancipation through education plan was watched closely by politicians of the era as a potential model for a national program.

Unfortunately, while she was visiting Europe in 1827, her grand scheme failed miserably. Bouts of malaria and crop failure were bad enough but then she discovered that her overseers had been whipping the men and engaging in inappropriate behavior with the women. Realizing that her vision was in ashes, she chartered a ship, the *John Quincy Adams,* relocated the former slaves to Haiti and gave them their freedom. Her traveling companion on the voyage was William Phiquepal d'Arusmont, with whom she had an affair, later culminating in a disastrous marriage and the birth of her only child, Sylva.

In 1828, she aligned with Robert Dale Owen in New Harmony, a Utopian community in Indiana, to edit the *New Harmony Gazette,* but by the end of the year, both Nashoba and New Harmony had failed. She and Owen relocated to New York and became joint publishers of the *Free Enquirer* that advocated communitarianism, socialism and, some believed, anti-Christianity. Fanny purchased an abandoned church and turned it into a museum, bookstore, headquarters, and lecture hall that seated three thousand.

Using observations she formed in childhood, Fanny began a series of public lectures, consequently becoming the first woman in the United States to address a gender-mixed, called "promiscuous" in those days, audience. The wide-ranging topics of her presentations included free love and abolition of marriage, emancipation of slaves, political rights for workers, free religious inquiry, free public education, birth control, a ten-hour workday, racial equality, and education and equality for women. She attacked slavers, politicians, and religion equally and was one of the first to recognize that knowledge equals power. Men created knowledge, she vowed, in order to control and oppress women.

As a consequence of her opinionated pronouncements, she was immediately under attack. The media called her a "monster female" and her behavior a "disgusting exhibition of female impudence." The clergy branded her the "great red harlot of infidelity." Due to her tirade on the treatment of women, many of the early woman's rights activists were labeled "Fanny Wrightists," considered the ultimate insult, even though she was the first to break ground for the movement. Although she was accused of atheism and worse, crowds flocked to hear her speak. On one occasion, ten thousand were in attendance and since not all received her message favorably, it took the entire New York City police force to protect her.

In 1831, Fanny moved to Paris and married William Phiquepal d'Arusmont, her daughter's father. She continued to write, to lecture, and to travel, while he cared for Sylva and divested the balance of Fanny's inherited estate, which, under the laws of the period, he was entitled to do. After being robbed of most of her money and the majority of her daughter's affection, Fanny returned to the United States in 1835, locating in Cincinnati, Ohio. She attempted to revive her lecture circuit but there appeared to be little interest in her appearances. In 1852, she divorced d'Arusmont. Shortly after, she slipped on a patch of ice in the street and broke her thigh. Complications from the break caused her death on December 13, 1852.

Fanny deeded the Nashoba property to her daughter Sylva who, ironically, testified against woman's suffrage before an American Congressional committee in 1874. Although never a successful organizer and despite her radical ideas, Fanny Wright did much to pave the way for activists who would follow.

FOR FURTHER READING

Bartlett, Elizabeth Ann. *Liberty, Equality, Sorority: The Origins and Interpretation of American Feminist Thought: Frances Wright, Sarah Grimké, and Margaret Fuller.* Brooklyn, NY: Carlson Publishing, 1994; Eckhardt, Celia Morris. *Fanny Wright: Rebel in America.* Cambridge: Harvard University Press, 1984; Wright, Frances. *Biography and Notes of Frances Wright D'Arusmont.* Boston: J.P. Mendum, 1848.

SARAH MOORE GRIMKÉ (1792–1873)

Though an unlikely choice based on her heredity, place of birth, and time period, Sarah Grimké was considered one of the first women in the United States to campaign directly and openly for woman's rights. Beginning, as many of those who would follow her, as an activist for the emancipation of slaves, she was the first to note the similarity between her condition as a woman and the condition of those for whom she was advocating lack of enslavement.

Sarah Grimké was born in Charleston, South Carolina on November 26, 1792. Her father, Judge John Faucheraud Grimké, was a Revolutionary War hero, state senator and, eventually, judge on the South Carolina Supreme Court. Her mother, Mary Smith, sprang from southern aristocracy and gave birth to fourteen children. The family owned not only a home in Charleston but a plantation in nearby Beaufort that was manned by hundreds of slaves.

As a small child, Sarah witnessed a horsewhipping of one of the slaves and, even at five years old, she detected something inherently wrong. Each of the Grimké children was assigned a *constant companion,* a slave child of the same approximate age who was required to serve them. After befriending her assigned servant, Sarah secretly spent her evenings by lamplight teaching the young slave, Kitty, to read, knowledge that was forbidden by the culture and the law. When her father uncovered what she was doing, he told her that she had committed *crimes against the state* and could be sent to prison. Shortly after his discovery, Kitty became ill and died. Sarah adamantly refused to allow her family to find another *companion* for her.

Because of their wealth, the Grimké children were taught by tutors who came to the plantation. Her father, however, took one child, her brother Thomas, under his wing to further his training in law. Sarah was allowed to attend the sessions, learning to debate along with her brother and studying Thomas's lessons in the evenings when no one noticed. She was secretly preparing for college but when her parents discovered her goals, they were horrified. Women in 1804 did not pursue higher education. To cure her unwomanly ambitions, she was forbidden to read and encouraged to study sewing and music instead. When Thomas was admitted to law school at Yale, Sarah was left behind. Feeling cheated, the young woman appealed to her father who remarked that she would have made the greatest jurist in the country, if only she were born a boy.

When Sarah was thirteen, her last sibling, the fourteenth child, was born. Needing meaning in her life beyond daughter of the manor and resenting being treated as "a doll, a coquette, [and] a fashionable fool," Sarah asked to be named the new baby's godmother. Her wish was easily granted since her mother had exhausted her maternal instincts and most of her energy on the previous children. Sarah *adopted* the newborn, Angelina, raised her as her own and spent the rest of her life in her sister's company.

In 1818, when Sarah was twenty-six, her father became seriously ill and moved to Philadelphia in search of a specialist. Much to her surprise, Sarah was selected to be his traveling companion. During his illness, the two became extremely close, what she called her *greatest blessing*. The young woman was given the freedom to wander about the city and for the first time she witnessed life without slavery. She also discovered the Quaker religion. After almost a year of various doctors and no cure, her father decided that sea air might be beneficial to his health. He and Sarah left Philadelphia for the Atlantic coast but it was too late. Judge Grimké died in route in Bordentown, New Jersey.

Following her father's death, Sarah returned to Charleston, turned down two proposals of marriage and was more deeply disturbed than ever concerning the treatment of the slaves. Less than a month after her return, she packed her belongings and, in spite of her family's protest, moved permanently to Philadelphia. She joined the Quaker Society of Friends, lodging with one of their families, and engaged in volunteerism, working with area charities and prisons. In the evenings she studied theology, desperately seeking answers to the injustice she saw in the world. Several years later, Angelina followed, having been converted to Quakerism by her sister.

In 1834, the sisters joined the Female Anti-Slavery Society founded by Lucretia Mott. Revealing much of what she had witnessed on the family plantation concerning slavery, Angelina wrote a letter to William Lloyd Garrison, editor of the radical abolitionist newspaper, the *Liberator*. To her surprise, Garrison published the letter. Almost immediately, the lives of the sisters changed; they were reprimanded by the Quakers, embraced by the abolitionists, and under threat of arrest if they returned to the South. Angelina was asked to become a speaker for the American Anti-Slavery Society with Sarah as her manager. Eventually, under the tutelage of Theodore Weld, editor of the *Emancipator,* both sisters began speaking in private homes about the horrors of slavery. Sarah, however, accepted the task reluctantly, rationalizing the *calling* as her *Christian duty*. They were among the first women to speak publicly in the United States and the only white Southern women to become abolition speakers. In 1835, they addressed over three hundred women in a variety of venues. Sarah's style was direct, forceful and matter of fact and, for the first time since feeling educationally unequal to her brother, she realized the impact of being silenced because of her gender. She noted that "to change the status of one group [the slaves] meant changing the status of all."

Rebuffed again by the Philadelphia Society of Friends, the Grimké sisters relocated in Providence, Rhode Island, among a more liberal group. In 1836, they penned a series of antislavery pamphlets and books. Angelina wrote *An Appeal to the Christian Women of the South* (1836) and Sarah produced *An Epistle to the Clergy of the South* (1836), followed by *An Address to Free Colored Americans* (1837). When *An Appeal* was mailed out to interested parties, it was confiscated and burned in a South Carolina post office. Publication of their work gained more attention and in 1837, Sarah and Angelina began a twenty-three-week tour throughout the Northeast, including New York, Pennsylvania, Rhode Island, and Massachusetts. The sisters paid for the tour themselves and visited sixty-seven cities in the region. Although many were inspired by their antislavery sentiment, others were shocked that women had the audacity to speak in public. From those who favored their message, the sisters collected over ten thousand signatures, calling for immediate emancipation of the slaves; in 1838, Angelina became the first woman ever to appear before the Massachusetts legislature to present their petition.

By the end of 1837, the focus of their presentations was twofold, slavery and woman's rights, a situation *thrust upon* them in order to be heard. Sarah developed a social theory that compared the existence of two systems of oppression, one for blacks and one for women. She was the first to define slavery as having no legal recourse, no access to education, no independent income, and no control over basic lifestyle decisions, noting that this definition applied to women as well. She argued, furthermore, that white women without freedom were exactly like black women slaves.

During the year, the sisters branched out into the public arena, moving from holding meetings in private residences to speaking in more open venues. Over one thousand people attended a Lynn, Massachusetts presentation; most came because they were merely curious that a woman was being allowed to speak to a *promiscuous group,* one composed of both men and women. Although there was resistance from the audience, Sarah launched into a discussion of woman's rights, noting, "whatsoever it is morally right for a man to do, it is morally right for a woman to do." As a consequence of her views, Quakers closed their meeting houses to the women, their posters were ripped down, and they suffered constant verbal abuse and threats of violence. Under attack from the public and the pulpit, Sarah fought back, scheduling meetings in barns or wherever else she could gather a crowd and growing more convinced that her position was correct and her defense of it was the right thing to do.

Ten years before the first Woman's Rights Convention in Seneca Falls, Sarah Grimké published *Letters on the Equality of the Sexes* (1838), the first woman's rights book by an American. The treatise offered her theory on the link between slavery and the subjugation of women and forecast many of the beliefs of the modern women's movement. She called for immediate emancipation of both blacks and women, defiance and, if necessary, revolution.

Shortly after publication of the work, the Grimké sisters were denounced by the Congregational Clergy of New England. The Reverend Nehemiah Adams issued a "Pastoral Letter" to be read from pulpits throughout the region, calling Sarah "unnatural," noting that she had brought "shame and dishonor" to her gender and forbidding church members to attend her speeches. Sarah responded with a series of articles in the *Boston Spectator* comparing the attitude of the church to the witch trials in early American history and countering their arguments point by point. Her knowledge of scripture was likely more refined than most of her contemporaries, including many of those in power in the pulpit. Through her willingness to continue her struggle, others, such as Lucretia Mott, Elizabeth Cady Stanton, and Lucy Stone, were inspired to ignite the woman's rights movement.

In 1838, Angelina married her former speaking coach, Theodore Weld. Weld encouraged Angelina to avoid emphasizing woman's rights in order to concentrate on antislavery but Sarah continued to accept speaking engagements on both topics. To counteract what he considered a split in attention to the issues, Weld attacked Sarah's ability to present herself well in front of a group. Between her undermined self-confidence and the ironic prejudice from the Anti-Slavery Society over her double allegiances, she resigned from the speaker's podium and moved in with her sister and her husband. For awhile, the three operated a school in Eagleswood, New Jersey and Sarah published a translated biography of Joan of Arc to offer inspiration to other women. They agreed to board two freed slaves whom they discovered were sons of one of their brothers, fathered on the South Carolina plantation. One of the young men, Archibald Grimké became the first black student to graduate from Harvard Law School; while the other, Francis, attended the Princeton Theological Seminary.

Reprinting collected newspaper editorials from Southern papers, Sarah, Angelina, and Weld produced *American Slavery as It Is: Testimony of 1000 Witnesses* in 1839. Considered the most important antislavery document then published, the work sold over a hundred thousand copies and became the basis for *Uncle Tom's Cabin,* written in 1852, by Harriet Beecher Stowe.

Although she continued to pursue her own writing, Sarah also became an agent for John Stuart Mill's *The Subjection of Women* (1869), his treatise revealing that the life of women under the law was worse than that of slaves in some countries. Sarah sold the copies from door to door and donated the money to a woman's suffrage journal.

After the Civil War, Sarah and the Welds moved to Hyde Park, a section of Boston, where they opened a coeducational school. On March 7, 1870, when she was seventy-nine years old, Sarah led a procession through a blizzard to the local polling place. She argued that since the Fourteenth Amendment, passed in 1868, granted the right to vote to all citizens, she, as a citizen, should be able to vote as well. Although she was not allowed to enter her ballot and although she and the other forty-three women were attacked in route, she was not arrested because of her age. She continued to campaign for equal rights until her death on December 23, three years later.

Although she was not a member of the woman's rights movement per se, Sarah Grimké believed fully in the equality of all people, whether black or white, man or woman.

FOR FURTHER READING

Bartlett, Elizabeth Ann. *Liberty, Equality, Sorority: The Origins and Interpretation of American Feminist Thought: Frances Wright, Sarah Grimké, and Margaret Fuller.* Brooklyn, NY: Carlson Publishing, 1994.Grimké, Sarah Moore. *Letters on the Equality of the Sexes, and the Condition of Woman.* Boston: I. Knapp, 1838; Lerner, Gerda. *The Feminist Thought of Sarah Grimké.* New York: Oxford University Press, 1998.

ISABELLA BAUMFREE (SOJOURNER TRUTH) (1797–1883)

The only former woman slave to mount the podium to speak against the injustices of slavery and for the rights of women, Sojourner Truth stands alone in the history of the woman's rights movement. She was, perhaps, the most celebrated African American woman of the nineteenth century and unlike many of her contemporaries on the lecture circuit, she was listened to and admired by both men and women of the period.

Born in 1797, in Hurley, New York, in Ulster County, Isabella was the youngest of thirteen children born to James and Betsey, who were the *property* of Colonel Johannes Hardenbergh. As a child, her first language was Dutch due to the community in which they lived and she had no formal education; consequently, she never learned to read or write. Although she came from a large family, she did not know her brothers and sisters since most of them were sold to other slavers while she was still in infancy. At nine years old, she too was sold for one hundred dollars. She passed through multiple owners before being bought by John Dumont of New Paltz, New York. When she turned fourteen, Dumont insisted that she marry an older slave, Thomas, by whom she had five children.

As the date neared, which had been set for liberating the slaves living in New York, July 4, 1827, Isabella learned that Dumont did not intend to grant her freedom. Taking her infant daughter, Sophia, she ran away in 1826, seeking refuge with a Quaker family, the Van Wagenens, whose last name she adopted. She had to leave her other children with their father because they were not legally free until they reached their twentieth birthday. Isabella spent several months with the Van Wagenens, doing light housework for the family, as well as working among the city's poor and acquiring a step toward literacy. During the period, she learned that Dumont had illegally sold her son, Peter, to an Alabama plantation owner. At that time, New York State law forbade the selling of slaves to anyone who lived outside of the state. Fearlessly, Isabella sued Dumont to have her son returned to her. By taking action against injustice and illegality, she became the first black woman to sue a white man and win.

In 1829, Isabella, Peter, and Sophia moved to New York City. She worked briefly with the Magdalene Society, a Methodist mission to reform prostitutes, before joining Robert Matthews' Zion Hill commune. The group believed in the existence of good and evil spirits and attributed power to each to create or cure illness. When Matthews was arrested for murder, however, the group disbanded. Shortly after, her son Peter took a berth on a whaling ship and with the exception of five hurried letters to his mother, he was not heard of again.

Inspired by the Millerites, a religious group that predicted the Second Coming of Christ in 1843, Isabella changed her name to Sojourner Truth, selected as a pseudonym that implied a wandering evangelist who spoke honestly. A self-proclaimed Pentecostal minister, she walked through Long Island and Connecticut, preaching to anyone who would listen. With a powerful singing voice, she often lured crowds with her renditions of old favorites like the "Battle Hymn of the Republic" and then shared her beliefs on religion and slavery with anyone who would listen.

Following the dissolution of the Millerites after the Great Disappointment, when Jesus did not appear as predicted, Truth moved to Massachusetts and joined the Northampton Association, founded by members of the Northampton Association of Education and Industry and organized around a communally owned and operated mill. A Utopian community, the Northampton group was led by George Benson, brother-in-law of William Lloyd Garrison, editor of the antislavery newspaper, the *Liberator*. Through her association with this group, Truth met leaders, such as Frederick Douglass, William Lloyd Garrison, and feminist Olive Gilbert, and was exposed to radical new ideas like emancipation and woman's rights. After the group was dissolved in 1846, she continued to work as a housekeeper for Benson, maintained her association with the abolitionists, and earned extra income by creating and selling portraits with the tagline, "I sell the Shadow to support the Substance."

In 1950, after being persuaded by Garrison, Truth dictated her life story to Olive Gilbert. The work was published as the *Narrative of Sojourner Truth, a Northern Slave, Emancipated from Bodily Servitude by the State of New York, in 1928.* Sales were immediate and impressive, enabling her to purchase a home and giving the abolitionists a powerful tool in their quest for liberation. Based on the name recognition generated by her published work, she was invited to join the abolitionist speakers' bureau through which, using her personal narrative as a presentation tool, she gained a reputation for unsentimental straight talk. Early in her travels, she noted that women, herself included, were considered part of the abolitionist movement but were discouraged from taking part in the proceedings. Based on that observation, she attended her first Woman's Rights Convention in Worcester, Massachusetts.

Inspired by the smaller gathering, Truth attended the national convention that took place in Akron, Ohio in 1851. On the second day of the convention, a group of ministers joined the gathering and began their usual protests concerning the superiority of men, backing up their arguments with select quotes from scripture, and lamenting the sins of the "first mother," Eve. Whether she had planned it or not, Truth rose from her seat and ascended the podium. A hushed silence permeated the room; the audience was awed by the fact that any woman, much less a black woman, was being allowed to speak to the group. After placing her bonnet at her feet, the woman stretched to her nearly six-foot height and countered each of the arguments made by the ministers. Speaking of the sins of Eve, she noted, "If de fust woman God ever made was strong enough to turn de world upside down all alone, dese women togedder ought to be able to turn it back, and get it right side up again." Starting almost every point with "Ain't I A Woman," Truth rallied the audience to her side by asserting that women deserved equal rights because they were equal in capability to men. She ended her presentation by asserting that, although Jesus was a man, a comment introduced by one of the preachers, that he was the offspring of a woman. The discourse assured her place in the woman's movement as well as in the abolitionist movement and in history. Her commanding presence demanded that those in attendance listen to and heed her views. She advocated direct action, urging the women to take the rights they wanted and demanding that the group also consider the needs of black women. In this, she was one of the first to make the connection between abolition and woman's rights, stating that not all slaves were men and not all women were white.

Between 1851 and 1853, Truth was in demand as a speaker; her tour covered most of the East and areas of the West and when she was not traveling, she dictated pieces for inclusion in the *Anti-Slavery Bugle*. In 1855, a second printing of the *Narrative* was offered for sale and did so well that it enabled her purchase of a larger home in Harmonia, near Battle Creek, Michigan. Her speaking tours continued, almost without interruption, until after the Civil War, although most were restricted to presentations in the state of Michigan. In each speech, she underlined the horrors of slavery and her resilience based on faith.

When the Civil War ended, freed blacks flocked to the North, primarily to Washington, DC, seeking employment. The federal government, unprepared for the influx, set up the Freedmen's Bureau to take care of the population. Truth went to Washington to offer aid to the group, while teaching them lifestyle skills. In 1863, she met Abraham Lincoln and reported to him on the plight of the former slaves. While in Washington, Truth took the city's streetcar companies to task by lobbying against segregation. Thanks, in part, to her efforts, a congressional ban was issued against the streetcar companies in 1865 that prohibited them from separating black and white patrons on their conveyances.

While touring in upstate New York, Truth met Elizabeth Cady Stanton in 1867. After meeting with some of Stanton's colleagues, she initiated a job placement program to match poor black freedmen with employers in the region. She clearly saw the economic and educational gap between blacks and whites and was one of the first to discuss reparation, federal payment due to blacks for their enslavement. In 1870, she submitted an unsuccessful petition to Congress to give free parcels of land in the West to former slaves. Although the petition failed to gain congressional approval, she did enable the movement of many blacks to lands in Kansas.

Having met Ulysses Grant, Truth attempted to vote for him in 1872 but was turned away from the polls. She died in her home in Battle Creek, Michigan, on November 26, 1883 after a long battle with skin ulcers. Over a thousand people attended her funeral.

A U.S. postage stamp was issued in honor of Sojourner Truth in February, 1986, and the Mars Pathfinder Microrover was named in her honor. In 2004, Senator Hillary Rodham Clinton introduced legislation to add Truth's likeness to the statue of Lucretia Mott, Elizabeth Cady Stanton, and Susan B. Anthony that sits in the Capitol Rotunda in Washington, DC. Clinton noted that one piece of stone on the statue was never sculpted and that Truth had certainly earned the honor. The bipartisan effort was endorsed by over two hundred national organizations, including the National Political Caucus of Black Women, the National Organization for Women, and the Center for Women Policy Studies, although some believed the blank stone should be reserved for the likeness of the first woman president of the United States. Truth's papers are archived in the Historical Society of Battle Creek, Michigan.

FOR FURTHER READING

Bernard, Jacqueline. *Journey toward Freedom: The Story of Sojourner Truth*. New York: Feminist Press at the City University of New York, 1990; Stetson, Erlene, and Linda David. *Glorying in Tribulation: The Lifework of Sojourner Truth*. East Lansing: Michigan State University Press, 1994.

MARGARET FULLER (1810–1850)

Considered the first feminist pioneer, Margaret Fuller's battles on behalf of woman's rights were equal to any of the other women in the field, although the bulk of her protests were offered through the written word. Even though her life was brief, she "possessed more influence on the thought of American women than any woman previous to her time," according to Elizabeth Cady Stanton and Susan B. Anthony in the *History of Woman Suffrage*.

Born on May 23, 1820, in Cambridge Port, Massachusetts, Margaret Fuller was the first child of Timothy Fuller and Margaret Crane. Timothy Fuller attended Harvard University and practiced law prior to being elected to the Massachusetts Senate and serving four subsequent terms in the U.S. Congress. Although lacking in formal education, Margaret's mother was well read and independent in thought. The Fullers had eight children, six of whom survived to adulthood, but until she was five years old, Margaret was their only child. Detecting an intellectual curiosity in the young girl, her father focused on her education, training her in the classics at an early age. A strict disciplinarian, he was demanding of perfection and Margaret could read classic Greek and Roman authors by age six and Shakespeare by age eight. As a result of this youthful rigor, she suffered from migraine headaches and poor eyesight for the rest of her life. At nine years old, she was sent away to school, attending the Cambridge Port Private Grammar School, the Boston Lyceum, and Miss Prescott's Young Ladies Seminary between 1819 and 1825. Her brilliance gave her an air of superiority that her peers interpreted as arrogance; consequently, she had few friends and was not invited to be involved in the social life of the schools. She did, however, gain admittance to the male-only dominion of the Harvard library to continue independent reading and research.

By the time she finished school, her family had moved to rural Massachusetts, where she spent her time translating the works of Johann von Goethe, the German classical writer, and submitting essays to the Boston newspaper. In 1835, her idyllic state changed dramatically with the sudden death of her father after a bout with cholera. Although she had a financial backer that offered to let her continue her studies in Europe, she turned down the offer to fulfill the role she felt was expected of her; as the oldest child, it was her duty to help alleviate the financial difficulties of the family. To compensate her in some way for her unselfishness, family friends introduced Fuller to Ralph Waldo Emerson, who invited her to visit him and his family for three weeks during the summer.

Through Emerson, Fuller was introduced to the Transcendentalist movement, a group of intellectuals and writers with a Utopian vision of life, and through that movement, she met Bronson Alcott, who offered her a position teaching languages at his progressive Temple School in Boston. Fuller was intrigued by the prospect because the school offered its students not only educational pursuits but spiritual development as well and it was one of the few institutions of its day that was racially integrated.

To supplement her income and the cost of moving her family to a Boston suburb, Fuller initiated a series of "Conversations," or seminars, for women at Elizabeth Peabody's West Street Bookshop. Attendees, social reformers of the day as well as the wives of prominent businessmen, paid twenty dollars each to attend the sessions that were devoted to art, education, and women's rights. Fuller employed the Socratic Method, posing only one philosophical question during each meeting and encouraging dialogue among the women in attendance before adding her own synergistic conclusions. The conversations encouraged the women to think for themselves and most were amazed and pleased by the fact that their opinions had merit and were appreciated. Through the endeavor, Fuller earned enough money to stop working for five years in order to have time to write.

Although she had attended her first Transcendental meeting in 1838, maintained her alliance with Emerson and the other members and was instrumental in the development of Brook Farm Institute, the communal settlement created by and for that group, Fuller did not fully participate until 1840. That year, she and Emerson founded the *Dial,* a humanitarian journal based on the transcendental philosophy. Fuller served as editor and contributor to the publication for two years, publishing her groundbreaking essay, "The Great Lawsuit: Man vs. Men and Woman vs. Women" in 1843.

When her tenure as editor of the *Dial* ended, Fuller was offered a position on the staff of Horace Greeley's *New York Tribune* as a literary and cultural critic. In that role, she became the first woman journalist to work for a major newspaper in the United States. The period consolidated her views on social justice, particularly prison reform, abolition, the plight of the urban poor, educational and political equality for minorities and immigrants and, of course, woman's estate or woman's rights.

In 1845, Fuller enlarged her essay, "The Great Lawsuit," to create the book length, *Women in the Nineteenth Century,* a manifesto that provided impetus for the woman's rights movement and the launch of the first convention in Seneca Falls, New York. Considered the foundational text of the movement, the work was a treatise on stereotyped gender roles with suggestions for altering them. Fuller described woman's oppression throughout history, labeling women as slaves, and advocated equality. Consistently, she penned her belief that men and women possessed a dual nature that could not be separated.

At last achieving her dream of visiting Europe, Fuller was assigned as foreign correspondent for the *Tribune*. She spent some time touring England, Scotland, and France before settling in Italy. During the period, Italy was in a state of inner turmoil because the Italian Unification Movement, headed by Giuseppe Mazzini, was attempting to overthrow the rule of the Catholic Church and the papacy and to restore the Roman Republic. Fuller supported Mazzini's efforts for she was convinced that socialism was the only true way to assure the concept of social justice that should be implicit in democracy. In her view, revolution equaled freedom and human rights for workers and for women; consequently, she was particularly attracted to the Roman Republic's Constitution that guaranteed religious freedom and abolished capital punishment. Her activism was further fueled by her involvement with an Italian nobleman, one of Mazzini's guard, Giovanni Angelo, the Marchese d'Ossoli. While he served the Republic, she worked as a nurse at the field hospital.

Discovering that she was with child, Fuller retreated to the small village of Rieta to await the birth of her son, Angelo Eugene. When the military coup failed after only four months and the pope was restored to power, Ossoli joined her and the family relocated to the safer haven of Florence. Although Fuller sent letters home that she had married, no record of the union existed and some believe she was merely avoiding the chastisement placed on an unmarried mother when she returned to the United States.

Having invested most of their money in the effort to overthrow the government, the couple decided to return to the United States to improve their finances. On May 17, 1850, they sailed from Livorno with their young son. During the voyage, the captain of the ship contracted smallpox and died suddenly, leaving a young and inexperienced officer in command. Miscalculating his position and unaware of an approaching hurricane, the officer struck a sandbar in the early morning hours of June 19. The ship sank near Fire Island, New York, only a few miles from port and most of the passengers, including Fuller and her family, perished in the wreckage.

Hearing of the accident, Emerson sent Henry David Thoreau to the site to retrieve Fuller's body and her manuscripts but only the boy's remains and a few of her love letters could be salvaged. Among the missing documents was her history of the Roman Republic; however, her letters to the *Tribune* on the topic were collected and published posthumously as *At Home and Abroad* in 1846.

Among her many accomplishments, Fuller tried to create a frame of reference for women based on their own reality. Outdistancing many of her peers in intellect, she strove to right the injustices of the world. According to her friend Ralph Waldo Emerson, "she wore this circle of friends, when I first knew her, as a necklace of diamonds about her neck."

In 1902, the Fuller family home was converted to a neighborhood settlement house and still serves over 1,500 people annually, assisting with education, support, outreach, and community services.

FOR FURTHER READING

Balducci, Carolyn Feleppa. *Margaret Fuller: A Life of Passion and Defiance*. New York: Bantam Books, 1991; Bartlett, Elizabeth Ann. *Liberty, Equality, Sorority: The Origins and Interpretation of American Feminist Thought: Frances Wright, Sarah Grimké, and Margaret Fuller*. Brooklyn, NY: Carlson Publishing, 1994; Bell, Margaret. *Margaret Fuller: A Biography*. Freeport, NY: Books for Libraries Press, 1971.

LUCRETIA MOTT (1793–1880)

The flint that ignited the spark of the woman's rights movement was struck by a Quaker minister who inspired others to stand up for what they believed. Called by some the most enlightened woman of the period, Lucretia Mott was a tireless advocate for human rights, as well as for woman's rightful place in the home, the country, and the pulpit. Her involvement in woman's rights was produced primarily by her exclusion as an advocate for abolition and the opposition she encountered when speaking publicly on the issue.

Born in the shipping capital of Nantucket, Massachusetts, the daughter of Captain Thomas Coffin, an East India trader, and Anna Folger Coffin, a relative of Benjamin Franklin, Lucretia had an early introduction to independence. Because the men of the island community were away at sea for long periods, the women became the natural leaders of the daily operation of the village with duties ranging from politics to the economy. The Coffin women, as many others in the region, kept a shop in the front room of the family home, selling wares brought back from Captain Coffin's travels and featuring such exotic items as teas, spices, ivory, jade, and silk. When her mother journeyed to Cape Cod or the mainland to trade whale oil and India imports for necessities, Lucretia was frequently left in charge, not only of the other children but of the shop's clientele as well. Through this interaction with the public, she learned the art of hospitality and conversational skills, which contributed to her precocious maturity. Since the family belonged to the Religious Society of Friends (Quakers), the practice of self-examination and the belief in the equality of all people were also instilled in the children; consequently, as youngsters, they were relatively unaware of the biases present in other regions.

When Lucretia was seven, her father retired from the sea. After having been away from home for over three years and having his ship confiscated in route, he gave up his career as a mariner and accepted a position with a mercantile firm in Boston. Accustomed to the freedom of Nantucket, the Coffin women were unprepared for the restrictive life on the mainland, where education for females was at a minimum and women, other than Quakers, were not permitted to speak in church or in public. Lucretia briefly attended public school where girls were allowed only two hours of study in the afternoon after the boys had left for the day. High school for women was unheard of. Luckily, however, her father was a strong proponent of education and at thirteen she was enrolled at the Nine Partners Boarding Seminary in New York, where she lived for two years. Because she was an exemplary student, Lucretia was offered a teaching position at Nine Partners when she was only fifteen. Although the salary was noticeably less than the male instructors and although it meant being away from her family for several more years, the position allowed one of her younger sisters to attend the school without having to pay tuition, thus, she gratefully accepted the post.

While teaching at Nine Partners, Lucretia met James Mott, another instructor, and even though he was painfully shy and she was overly talkative, the two developed a friendship. When she was eighteen and he was twenty-three, they married and moved to Philadelphia where her family had relocated. James went into the dry goods business with Lucretia's father but a series of circumstances cast a pall on the family finances. During the War of 1812, an embargo was imposed, limiting imports from both Britain and France and making it impossible to procure certain goods the business offered for sale. The war, coupled with the sudden death of Captain Coffin, put a strain on the family economics.

Stretching the budget to care for her mother, her brothers and sisters, and her own five children offered numerous challenges. Although she was capable of working, Lucretia, as most mothers of her era, stayed at home when her children were small but instead of the customary pursuit of sewing, she read extensively, particularly the works of William Penn. She took copious notes on her reading and was capable of reciting long paragraphs. Additionally, during the period, she gained a reputation as a gracious hostess and the Mott home frequently served as a refuge for various reformers of the day. After the children grew older and more independent, Lucretia opened a school and went back to teaching in order to increase the family finances. At inception, the school had only four pupils but within seven months, the student body had grown to forty.

Although she enjoyed teaching, Mott felt a higher calling and at twenty-five, she was determined to become a Quaker minister. The Quakers had no professional preachers; anyone could address the meetings if that person had the *gift* and was recommended by the church elders to become an official speaker. Proclaiming herself more interested in morality than in theology, Lucretia Mott gained her place in the pulpit in 1821 and spent several years traveling from place to place as a speaker without pay. Those who heard her were impressed with her independent thinking and the clarity of her message. She thought the church should take a critical role in shaping public beliefs and was intrigued by the prospect of using her message for cultural change.

Having been exposed to the problem of slavery when she was a student, Lucretia officially declared herself an abolitionist in the 1830s, proclaiming that slavery was a sin and had to be abolished. Although she found arguing over church doctrine irritating, she and her husband followed the lead of Elias Hicks, the springboard of the Great Separation of 1827, who opposed the evangelical and orthodox branch of the Quaker church and who refused to use cotton cloth, cane sugar, and other products produced by slave labor. Although disturbing to some, the views of the Hicksite Quakers were consistent with the Free Thought movement of the era that appealed to many, such as Walt Whitman and Ralph Waldo Emerson. The situation did make it rather awkward for James Mott, however, since his dry good trade was mostly in cotton cloth. He compensated by joining the Free Produce Society, switching to dealing in wool and offering the family home as a stop on the Underground Railroad.

In 1834, William Lloyd Garrison and the poet John Greenleaf Whittier organized the American Anti-Slavery Association in Philadelphia, calling for the immediate emancipation of the slaves. Only four women, Lucretia Mott among them, were invited to attend the meeting as observers. Although the women were not encouraged to speak, Mott, as demurely as possible, made an *unsolicited* presentation, recommending word changes in the charter to add to its clarity. Eventually named a delegate of the association, she subsequently traveled thousands of miles giving speeches for emancipation, in addition to the stagecoach trips she was already making as a Quaker preacher. A few weeks after the initiation of the American Anti-Slavery Association, the Philadelphia Female Anti-Slavery Association, the first in Pennsylvania, was organized and Mott was elected as its first president.

When the Female Anti-Slavery Association held a convention in Pennsylvania Hall in Philadelphia, a mob gathered outside the facility. The protestors threw rocks through the windows, set the building on fire, and rioted in the streets. No police protection was offered to the women primarily because the city's mayor was opposed to abolition. Despite the fact that no one was seriously injured and that Mott remained composed in the midst of chaos, there was a subsequent move by both the Quakers and the abolitionists to stop women from speaking in public. By May 1840, the members of the American Anti-Slavery Association split over the *woman question* with some adamantly opposed to women being allowed to serve as officers or speakers. Others were afraid, and rightfully so, that women would use their involvement in abolition to promote women's rights. This caused the movement to split into two groups, the radicals and the moderates. The radicals promoted equality for all, including women, while the moderates clung to traditional gender roles. As a result of her involvement with the tirade within the movement, Mott was asked to give up her position in the Quaker church and became socially ostracized among its members.

Although many of the male abolitionists viewed women speakers as antagonists, William Lloyd Garrison was not one of them. When the World Anti-Slavery Convention was called at Freemason's Hall in London, England in 1840, Garrison selected Lucretia Mott to serve as the representative of the American Anti-Slavery Association. Traveling from the ship to London across the English countryside, Mott was deeply moved by the lifestyle of the British factory workers and the numbers of the country's poor.

Although not all were delegates, seven women attended the Convention, among them Elizabeth Cady Stanton who came with her new husband, Henry, as part of an extended honeymoon. After an elongated debate, the male convention delegates ruled that the women delegates could not be seated. Some speakers even said that women were constitutionally unfit to serve and their mere presence would negatively affect public concern for the cause of abolition. When the women delegates were refused a place on the main floor, Mott and Stanton were seated in the observer's gallery behind a curtain and required to keep silent. Both were offended by this sight because they were aware that the women delegates were among the most intelligent and educated members present. In order even to be nominated, a woman would have had to prove herself equal to or superior to the men representatives at the meeting.

Indignant that women had no rights, even within the ranks of reform movements, Stanton and Mott were instantly bonded. Throughout their time in London, the two women seldom left one another's company and by the time the convention was over, they determined that the woman's issue was of equal importance to the one of slavery. Mott called the treatment of women, "a second form of enslavement" and noted that her friendship with Stanton "set fire to woman's issues." The two made plans to call a convention for women on their return to the United States.

Although they were enthusiastic about creating a woman's conference, time had other demands and eight years slipped away before Mott and Stanton met again to plan their meeting. With Mott's sister Martha Coffin Wright and Mary Ann McClintock, they placed an advertisement for the conference in the Seneca Falls, New York newspaper. On July 14, 1848, the *Seneca County Courier* announced that, on the following Wednesday and Thursday, a "convention to discuss the social, civil, and religious condition and rights of women" would be held. The event would take place in the Wesleyan Chapel in Seneca Falls. Once committed to a date and time, the women realized they had given themselves only three days to set an agenda. Seated around a mahogany table, later preserved in the Smithsonian Institute, the women penned a Declaration of Sentiments that purposefully paralleled the Declaration of Independence with the opening phrase, "We hold these truths to be self-evident, that all men and women are created equal." The Declaration contained eleven resolutions that demanded redress of grievances, including the inflammatory ninth resolution calling for woman's suffrage. These grievances reflected the severe limitations on women's legal rights in America at the time: women could not vote; they could not participate in the creation of laws that they had to obey; and a married woman's property and wages legally belonged to her husband. Further, in the relatively unusual case of a divorce, custody of children was automatically awarded to the father; access to the professions and higher education generally was closed to women; and most churches barred women from participating publicly in the ministry or in other positions of authority.

When the appointed dates arrived, more than three hundred men and women assembled in Seneca Falls, often called the birthplace of the feminist movement, for the nation's first annual women's rights convention. Mott gave the opening and closing prayers as well as a presentation on the progress of reforms and her husband James chaired the meeting. During her speech on July 20, she added another resolution to the list, providing women with access to the pulpit and other male-dominated professions. Although the suffrage resolution produced discord among the attendees, at the end of the meeting sixty-eight women and thirty-two men signed the final draft of the Declaration. The media had a field day with the meeting and the resolutions. The *Philadelphia Public Ledger* proclaimed that women would not want to vote, adding that "a woman is nobody. A wife is everything." On the other hand, the *New York Herald* noted that Lucretia Mott would "make a better President than some of those who have lately tenanted the White House."

In her published piece *Discourse on Woman* (1849), Mott revealed "There is nothing of greater importance to the well-being of society at large—of man as well as woman—than the true and proper position of woman." She also argued that, in the future, educated women would not be content with the roles that were assigned to the women of her era. As a preacher and a freethinker, she viewed human equality as a divine right.

In 1850, Mott was the key organizer for the Rochester Convention held at the Unitarian Church. During that gathering, resolutions were passed in favor of securing women the franchise, of dropping the word *obey* from the marriage vows, and of helping women secure better wages. Abigail Bush was elected president of the Rochester convention and became the first woman to preside over a public meeting that was attended by both men and women.

After the Civil War, Lucretia Mott was elected as the first president of the American Equal Rights Convention, through which she attempted to reconcile the split between the black and woman's suffrage factions. Although an activist for women for only a short period of her life, Mott is credited with inspiring Elizabeth Cady Stanton, Susan B. Anthony, and others who would carry the fight for equality into the future. When Lucretia Mott died at eighty-seven years of age, twelve years after her husband, no one spoke at her funeral. One of the mourners noted, "Who can speak? The preacher is dead."

FOR FURTHER READING

Burnett, Constance Buel. *Five for Freedom: Lucretia Mott, Elizabeth Cady Stanton, Lucy Stone, Susan B. Anthony, Carrie Chapman Catt.* New York: Greenwood Press, 1968; Gurko, Miriam. *The Ladies of Seneca Falls: The Birth of the Woman's Rights Movement.* New York: Schocken Books, 1974; Mott, Lucretia. *Discourse on Woman.* Philadelphia: W.P. Kildare, 1869; Zink-Sawyer, Beverly A. "From Preachers to Suffragists: Enlisting the Pulpit in the Early Movement for Woman's Rights." *The American Transcendental Quarterly* 14 (September 2000): 193.

ELIZABETH CADY STANTON
(1815–1902)

Although Susan B. Anthony is usually recognized as the primary motivator behind the beginnings of the woman's movement, it is possible that she would have never gained that position without a push from her friend and mentor, Elizabeth Cady Stanton. Dubbed the "mother of the woman's rights movement," Stanton was a critic of social mores, political disenfranchisement, and patriarchal Christianity. With Lucretia Mott, she was responsible for initiating the first Woman's Rights Convention.

In 1815, when this unlikely hero took her first breath, women were viewed either as chattel—property of their father until they married and then, of their husband—or window dressing or inexpensive house labor. Throughout most of the United States, it was considered unwomanly to have an opinion, even if one were fortunate enough to be educated, and utterly outrageous to voice that opinion publicly or to publish it. Higher education was out of the question and some believed intellectual development was detrimental to women, in fact, that too much reading would make them go insane. Women were not allowed to own property, borrow money, divorce their husbands, serve on juries, testify in court, or take any part in the political process. Once married, they forfeited their legal existence. They could not sign a contract, inherit money, or have any say over the upbringing of their children. The *fairer sex* was expected only to manage a household and care for her husband and family. Thus, in early-nineteenth-century America, the birth of a girl child would have gone largely unnoted or, perhaps, even regretted.

Into these narrow confines, Elizabeth Cady was born on November 12, 1815, in one of the most expensive homes in Johnstown, New York, the eighth of the eleven children of Judge Daniel and Margaret Livingston Cady and one of only six siblings who survived into adulthood. Five of her brothers and one sister died between 1810 and 1828.

Elizabeth's father amassed enormous wealth, dabbling in land, while pursuing a career in law and politics. He was elected circuit court judge and state legislator and, eventually, appointed associate justice of the New York State Supreme Court. In her selectively remembered autobiography, Elizabeth Cady Stanton recalled that she was born in the same year that her father was elected to Congress and added that "perhaps the excitement of a political campaign, in which my mother took the deepest interest, may have had an influence on my prenatal life and given me the strong desire that I have always felt to participate in the rights and duties of government."

Her mother, Margaret Livingston Cady sprang from old money and had the pompous attitude that class afforded her. She was the daughter of Colonel James Livingston, a Revolutionary War hero, who was awarded almost six thousand acres in land grants as payment for his military service. Margaret Cady ruled her home and her family with an air of detached superiority and demanded that the children mind the rules of good breeding as she recited them. Elizabeth, however, wanted no part of formality or restrictions. Even as a child, she was spunky, argumentative, and uncompromising in her convictions as well as being compulsively talkative and persuasive. She questioned not only the judgment of her family and the family servants but also the justice system and the dogma of the church. With curly ringlets and cherub cheeks, she attempted, even then, to exert influence on her corner of the world, challenging doctrine, class, and the general order of things.

Since her parents were always preoccupied—her father in his office and her mother involved in the day-to-day management of the home—Elizabeth and her sisters sought refuge in Peter Teabout, a black servant in the household who frequently assumed the role of *nanny* for the children. Whenever Teabout was mentioned in any of Elizabeth's writing, he was referred to as a servant; however, according to the 1820 census, Peter Teabout was a slave, the property of Daniel Cady. Thus, Teabout's role served as one of the many ironies in Elizabeth's life, particularly considering her later involvement in the antislavery cause and her consistent denial of her father's imperfections.

With Peter in charge, Elizabeth and her sisters were permitted to wander freely about the city, a rare treat for young girls of the time. Through these walks, Elizabeth encountered people she would not have met otherwise. She often angered her Scottish nursemaid, Mary Dunn, with her unladylike behavior, like taking pity on the poor, giving cake to a prisoner in the jail, or talking to a young man with a physical impairment. When scolded by the nurse for her unladylike behavior, Elizabeth replied, "Everything we like to do is a sin...I am so tired of that everlasting no! no! no! At school, at home, everywhere it is no! Even at church all the commandments begin with 'Thou shalt not.' I suppose God will say 'no' to all we like in the next world, just as you do here."

Her childhood offered two defining moments. The first noteworthy event was the birth of her sister, Catherine, in 1820. After a long wait, the older children were allowed into the room to see the new baby. Elizabeth overheard several of the adults comment on how pretty the newborn was but followed the compliment with "what a pity it is she's a girl." At only four years of age, it is unlikely that Elizabeth understood the importance of the comment but it evidently lingered in her unconscious since she felt it important enough to write about in her autobiography.

The second and likely more significant occurrence was the death of her brother, Eleazer, the only surviving male Cady child and heir apparent to his father's law practice. Shortly after graduating from Union College in his twentieth year, Eleazer became ill and died suddenly. Judge Cady was heart broken and even his perky little daughter, whom he favored, was incapable of bringing him relief. As her father sat mourning alone in the room next to the casket, Elizabeth crept quietly in and crawled onto his lap. Her father held her for a moment but then groaned, "Oh, my daughter, if only you were a boy." According to Stanton, at that point, she vowed to become like a son to her father even though she still did not have a clear understanding of why there was a difference between boys and girls.

Over the next few months, the young woman did all she could to keep her promise to herself and to her father. She out rode most of the neighborhood boys, strove for academic excellence, and spent her free time snuggled up in her father's office listening to the legal discussions that made up the majority of his day. On one such occasion, an area woman appeared in the office to say that after the death of her husband, the farm they had tended together was handed over to her stepson who knew nothing of farming and was generally considered irresponsible. Daniel Cady told the woman she had no legal claim to her husband's property; the law gave it fully and freely to the male heir. Elizabeth was shocked. When the woman left, the child begged her father to change the law to which he replied, "when you are grown up, you must talk to the legislators...and, if you can persuade them to pass new laws, the old ones will be dead letter."

As she grew older, Elizabeth became convinced that education was the answer, not only to gaining her father's approval but also to finding a means of equal treatment for women under the law. As a fourteen-year-old student at Johnstown Academy, a private coeducational boarding and day school, she excelled in Latin, Greek, and higher math, frequently making higher marks than the boys in the class in the subjects usually reserved for them alone.

In an attempt to make her father proud, she even won a language competition. The prize had traditionally guaranteed admission into Union College but when she told her father, he replied that college for women was out of the question. Instead, in 1831, he enrolled her in Emma Willard's Troy Female Seminary. Although the seminary was one of the finest and most advanced schools for women in the country, Elizabeth still thought she should have an education equal to those offered to young men.

Most of her training as an activist came from her mother's cousin Gerrit Smith, whose home Elizabeth was allowed to visit despite her father's dread that Smith would fill her head with liberal nonsense. Smith was a wealthy abolitionist and Elizabeth was permitted to listen to conversations among such notables as William Lloyd Garrison, Frederick Douglass, John Brown, and others involved in the antislavery movement.

Elizabeth wondered if she might meet a runaway slave during her visits in Peterboro for she had heard rumors that the Smith house served as a stop on the Underground Railroad. Late one evening, cousin Gerrit took her up a winding staircase into an attic room where a fair-skinned black woman, not much older than Elizabeth, was hiding, waiting for transportation into Canada. After hearing the stories of the woman's life, Elizabeth, for the first time in her life, questioned her father's judgment that people had paid good money for slaves and had the right to have them returned. For the first time as well, she realized that only she could determine what was right and what was wrong for her life.

During her time in Peterboro, there were daily guests for dinner. One such guest came with so much advance praise for his speeches and organizational skill that Elizabeth was eager to meet him, certain he must be elderly and wise. When the man arrived in October 1839, she was greatly surprised for, although he was older than she by ten years, he was still quite young and she was attracted not only to his ability but also to the man himself. He, in turn, was charmed by her thirst for knowledge. They went horseback riding across the hillsides, took long walks, and played chess in the evenings. When Elizabeth beat him at the game and he did not appear offended, she knew she had found a man with whom she could have an equal partnership. By the time her visit was over, Elizabeth Cady was engaged to Henry Brewster Stanton, a man she called "the most eloquent and impassioned orator on the anti-slavery platform."

As predicted by cousin Gerrit, her father refused to bless her marriage to Henry Stanton for not only was the man branded as a radical abolitionist, Henry offered no visible means of financial support. As time and space stretched between Elizabeth and Stanton's charm, she too began to doubt her interest and to please her family and friends, she broke the engagement.

Henry Stanton, however, had not gained his reputation for persistence by being easily dissuaded and he sent daily letters. Elizabeth read each one but remained consistent in her resolve not to marry Stanton; that was until the last letter arrived. Stanton had been selected to serve as a delegate to the World Anti-Slavery Convention in London and offered prolonged speaking tours throughout the British Empire and Europe. He wanted Elizabeth to go along as his wife. It was unknown whether it was his proposal or the possibility of travel and work that enticed her but Elizabeth accepted both and the wedding date was set for May 11, 1840. The ceremony was conducted by the Reverend Hugh Maire, a staunch Scot clergyman. When vows were taken, she refused to repeat the word *obey*. The event likely irritated the minister and confirmed her father's suspicions that the marriage was doomed but, to Elizabeth, it equaled a partnership.

The World Anti-Slavery Convention took place on June 12 at Freemason's Hall in London. Women were permitted to attend the convention but they were not allowed to sit with the men, speak, or vote. Elizabeth wrote, "To me there was no question so important as the emancipation of women from the dogmas of the past, political, religious and social. It struck me as very remarkable that abolitionists, who felt so keenly the wrongs of the slave, should be so oblivious to the equal wrongs of their own mothers, wives, and sisters, when, according to the common law, both classes occupied a similar legal status."

Isolated from Henry, Elizabeth sat with Lucretia Mott. Since both were offended by the prejudice displayed against them, the two like-minded women discussed organizing an American woman's rights convention on their return to the United States. Elizabeth was interested in addressing equal educational opportunities and business training, removing the ban on entering the professions, gaining legal rights to inheritance and property, and women's inability to change the laws by voting.

After traveling through Europe, the Stantons returned to New York where Henry was to enter Daniel Cady's law office as a protégé. In order for Henry to be near the judge during his two-year apprenticeship, the Stantons moved into the Cady house. In 1843, Henry passed the bar exam and was offered a position in Boston, Massachusetts.

Even though she was living in Boston, Elizabeth frequently visited her siblings in Albany, primarily because she wanted to take an active part in the discussion of the Married Woman's Property Bill pending in the New York State legislature. The bill would overturn the current law that stated a woman would lose any right to control property that was hers prior to the marriage, nor would she have rights to acquire any property during marriage. Although it took several more years for the resolution to pass, the period could be labeled as the dawn of women's rights activism.

In addition to her involvement in the fledgling woman's movement, her family expanded to three sons and, eventually, to a total of seven children. Henry was absent for the birth of each child. Although he was traveling more than he was home, by the spring of 1847, Henry announced that his health would not permit him to survive another New England winter. Elizabeth hated to leave the social circle of Boston but they moved once again—this time to Seneca Falls in mid-state New York.

In Seneca Falls, Elizabeth received an invitation to visit her old friend, Lucretia Mott. It had been eight years since the World Anti-Slavery Convention in London and eight years since Mott had suggested organizing a woman's convention in the United States. During that time, Elizabeth had been burdened with child bearing and rearing and Mott, with religious and missionary work. Many reformers had appeared during the interim but Elizabeth's version of history revealed Lucretia Mott as the prophet, herself as the foot soldier, and Seneca Falls as the launching point for the woman's movement.

The women renewed their commitment to organize a Woman's Rights Convention and wrote the meeting announcement in one evening. The statement, which was published in the *Seneca County Courier* the next day, read:

> Seneca Falls Woman's Rights Convention—A Convention to discuss the social, civil, and religious condition and rights of woman will be held in the Wesleyan Chapel, at Seneca Falls, N.Y., on Wednesday, the nineteenth, and Thursday, the twentieth of July, current; commencing at 10 o'clock a.m. During the first day the meeting will be exclusively for women, who are earnestly invited to attend. The public generally are invited to be present on the second day, when Lucretia Mott, of Philadelphia, and other ladies and gentlemen, will address the convention.

According to Stanton, it was "the most momentous reform that had yet been launched on the world—the first organized protest against the injustice which had brooded for ages over the character and destiny of one-half the race."

Having essentially put their cart in front of their horse and announced a meeting in only five days for which they were completely unprepared, the women scurried to create an agenda and a platform. Elizabeth suggested writing a Declaration of Woman's Independence but was voted down by the others who considered her proposal somewhat radical. Her next offer, however, was unanimously approved and the Declaration of Sentiments, modeled on the Declaration of Independence, was born. Using statute books, church, and social customs as sources, the group designed eighteen grievances equal to the eighteen points in the Declaration of Independence. The grievances all began with the word *he* and many cited the innumerable sins they felt men had committed, for example: "He has withheld from her rights which are given to the most ignorant and degraded men—both natives and foreigners; He has compelled her to submit to laws, in the formation of which she had no voice; He has endeavored, in every way that he could, to destroy her confidence in her own powers, to lessen her self-respect, and to make her willing to lead a dependent and abject life; and He has usurped the prerogative of Jehovah himself, claiming it as his right to assign for her a sphere of action, when that belongs to her conscience and to God."

After creating their list of grievances, it seemed appropriate to suggest a companion group of resolutions, ways in which the problems could be resolved. The majority of the resolutions indicated that woman was man's equal and should be encouraged to develop her intellect, speak in public, and have a larger sphere of activity, including the pulpit. All went well, with everyone in agreement, until Elizabeth insisted on adding a ninth resolution: "it is the duty of the women of this country to secure to themselves their sacred right to the elective franchise." Although the other women were afraid that asking for the vote would weaken their argument and cast a negative light on the entire proceeding, they eventually agreed and the meeting was set.

Declaration of Sentiments

When, in the course of human events, it becomes necessary for one portion of the family of man to assume among the people of the earth a position different from that which they have hitherto occupied, but one to which the laws of nature and of nature's God entitle them, a decent respect to the opinions of mankind requires that they should declare the causes that impel them to such a course.

We hold these truths to be self-evident; that all men and women are created equal; that they are endowed by their Creator with certain inalienable rights; that among these are life, liberty, and the pursuit of happiness; that to secure these rights governments are instituted, deriving their just powers from the consent of the governed. Whenever any form of government becomes destructive of these ends, it is the right of those who suffer from it to refuse allegiance to it, and to insist upon the institution of a new government, laying its foundation on such principles, and organizing its powers in such form, as to them shall seem most likely to effect their safety and happiness. Prudence, indeed, will dictate that governments long established should not be changed for light and transient causes; and, accordingly, all experience hath shown that mankind are more disposed to suffer, while evils are sufferable, than to right themselves by abolishing the forms to which they were accustomed. But when a long train of abuses and usurpations, pursuing invariably the same object, evinces a design to reduce them under absolute despotism, it is their duty to throw off such government, and to provide new guards for their future security. Such has been the patient sufferance of the women under this government, and such is now the necessity which constrains them to demand the equal station to which they are entitled.

The history of mankind is a history of repeated injuries and usurpations on the part of man toward woman, having in direct object the establishment of an absolute tyranny over her. To prove this, let facts be submitted to a candid world.

He has never permitted her to exercise her inalienable right to the elective franchise.

He has compelled her to submit to laws, in the formation of which she had no voice.

He has withheld from her rights which are given to the most ignorant and degraded men—both natives and foreigners.

Having deprived her of this first right as a citizen, the elective franchise, thereby leaving her without representation in the halls of legislation, he has oppressed her on all sides.

He has made her, if married, in the eye of the law, civilly dead.

He has taken from her all right in property, even to the wages she earns.

He has made her morally, an irresponsible being, as she can commit many crimes with impunity, provided they be done in the presence of her husband. In the covenant of marriage, she is compelled to promise obedience to her husband, he becoming, to all intents and purposes, her master—the law giving him power to deprive her of her liberty, and to administer chastisement.

He has so framed the laws of divorce, as to what shall be the proper causes of divorce, in case of separation, to whom the guardianship of the children shall be given; as to be wholly regardless of the happiness of the women—the law, in all cases, going upon a false supposition of the supremacy of man, and giving all power into his hands.

After depriving her of all rights as a married woman, if single and the owner of property, he has taxed her to support a government which recognizes her only when her property can be made profitable to it.

He has monopolized nearly all the profitable employments, and from those she is permitted to follow, she receives but a scanty remuneration.

He closes against her all the avenues to wealth and distinction, which he considers most honorable to himself. As a teacher of theology, medicine, or law, she is not known.

He has denied her the facilities for obtaining a thorough education—all colleges being closed against her.

He allows her in church, as well as State, but a subordinate position, claiming Apostolic authority for her exclusion from the ministry, and, with some exceptions, from any public participation in the affairs of the Church.

He has created a false public sentiment by giving to the world a different code of morals for men and women, by which moral delinquencies which exclude women from society, are not only tolerated but deemed of little account in man.

He has usurped the prerogative of Jehovah himself, claiming it as his right to assign for her a sphere of action, when that belongs to her conscience and her God.

He has endeavored, in every way that he could to destroy her confidence in her own powers, to lessen her self-respect, and to make her willing to lead a dependent and abject life.

Now, in view of this entire disfranchisement of one-half the people of this country, their social and religious degradation,—in view of the unjust laws above mentioned, and because women do feel themselves aggrieved, oppressed, and fraudulently deprived of their most sacred rights, we insist that they have immediate admission to all the rights and privileges which belong to them as citizens of these United States.

In entering upon the great work before us, we anticipate no small amount of misconception, misrepresentation, and ridicule; but we shall use every instrumentality within our power to effect our object. We shall employ agents, circulate tracts, petition the State and national Legislatures, and endeavor to enlist the pulpit and the press in our behalf. We hope this Convention will be followed by a series of Conventions, embracing every part of the country.

Firmly relying upon the final triumph of the Right and the True, we do this day affix our signatures to this declaration [http://www.nps.gov/archive/wori/declaration.htm]

On June 19, 1848, the Wesleyan Chapel opened its doors to the first ever public meeting of American women concerned with social change. Over three hundred people, both women and men, attended the convention during the two days. Henry Stanton, however, was not among them. Although he supported his wife's activism, he did not approve of her insistence that women needed the vote if they wanted to change the laws.

The twentieth day of June was the date set aside for the reading of the Declaration of Sentiments and the resolutions. None of the women really wanted to be completely in charge of the meeting, thus, Lucretia Mott's husband, James, presided. The resolutions were read and voted on one at a time until Elizabeth approached the platform to deliver the bombshell ninth resolution. When she reached the phrase requesting the vote for women, a gasp of disbelief rose from the audience. Several men and women stood to voice exception, citing everything from *woman's place* to biblical boundaries; however, much to Elizabeth's surprise, the resolution passed, although certainly not unanimously. One hundred of the persons gathered signed the Declaration of Sentiments and then scheduled the next convention for Rochester, New York, a month later.

After the meeting, Elizabeth wrote a series of articles for publication in the *Lily,* the woman's rights paper edited by Amelia Bloomer. Through Bloomer, she was introduced to another abolition advocate, Susan B. Anthony, with whom she formed a lifelong bond. Although the two women were vastly different—Elizabeth was tied to her family, Susan was unmarried; Elizabeth was verbal, Susan was analytical; Elizabeth was political, Susan was spiritual—their relationship blossomed into an interdependence that set the course for the woman's movement. Unable to leave her home for extended periods, Elizabeth aided in writing the speeches that Susan delivered; as Henry Stanton was fond of saying, Elizabeth forged the thunderbolts and Susan threw them.

By 1854, the two women had addressed the New York legislature to demand suffrage and by 1860, Elizabeth had added divorce rights to her agenda. She defined marriage as a civil and not a religious contract, challenged religion's belief in woman's inferior nature, and called for a marriage contract that would be null and void if not honored by either party.

Between 1861 and 1865, the work for woman's rights was put on hold while the country was embroiled in the Civil War. Against Anthony's advice, Stanton believed that if women aided the war effort, they would be rewarded. They created the National Loyal Women's League and collected over four hundred thousand signatures in support of the Thirteenth Amendment, which abolished slavery in 1865. Unfortunately, Anthony was correct about halting the pressure for woman's rights; while they were being passive, New York amended the Married Woman's Property Law, reducing the benefits almost to the level they were prior to its passage in 1848. As a result of this infringement and because slaves had gained independence, the woman's rights movement became a full-fledged suffrage movement following the Civil War.

The first popular test for woman's suffrage took place in Kansas in 1867. Although other organizers, like Lucy Stone, were already in place, Stanton and Anthony's presence was required. They spent weeks traveling across the state by stagecoach, wagon, and mule team, enduring bad food, lice, and bedbugs, only to suffer defeat. During their travels, they encountered George Francis Train, known financier, racist, and conman, who was known for using the woman's movement as a launching pad for his own presidential ambitions. Desperate for financial aid, Stanton and Anthony agreed to go on a speaking tour with Train in exchange for his fronting a newspaper for them on their return to New York.

In 1868, the *Revolution,* funded by Train to forward his own agenda, published its first issue. The masthead proudly proclaimed: "Men, their rights, and nothing more; women, their rights, and nothing less." Shortly after delivering the start-up costs for the paper, Train disappeared, as did his backing, but determined to make the paper a success, Stanton and Anthony began distributing the weekly paper at a charge of two dollars per year. The *Revolution* reported on women farmers, inventors, and sailors and the need for sex education and cooperative housekeeping as well as woman's right to vote. Fueling an old enmity, Lucy Stone initiated a competing paper, *Woman's Journal,* with sound financial backing. Knowing they could not remain afloat and could not compete because of dwindling resources, Stanton and Anthony sold the *Revolution* with Anthony assuming the balance of the indebtedness out of her own funds.

Although the women had lobbied Congress for inclusion on numerous occasions, the passage of the Fourteenth Amendment in 1868 did not mention woman's suffrage. The amendment defined a citizen as "all persons born or naturalized in the United States" but explicitly listed the word "male" in the voting clause. It was the first time there had been an obvious gender distinction in the Constitution and the women considered it an unbearable insult. Despite the fact that two years earlier, the American Anti-Slavery Association and the woman's rights movement had merged to form the Equal Rights Association, "burying the black man and the woman in the citizen," and regardless of the women gathering over ten thousand signatures on a petition supporting the amendment, they were essentially shut out.

By 1869, many of those in the movement, particularly Lucy Stone, were agitated by Stanton's radicalism and by both Stanton and Anthony's association with Train. They were further divided on the method they believed would guarantee success in the quest for suffrage. Stanton and Anthony felt the only way of gaining the vote was to hold out for a Constitutional amendment, while Stone and others thought the most effective course was state-by-state organizing. The movement split on issues, with Stanton and Anthony heading the National Woman Suffrage Association and Stone, the American Woman Suffrage Association.

Between 1871 and 1872, Stanton managed to free herself from her husband and family to join the lecture circuit. During the year, she spent six months in the East and six months in the West, traveled some thirteen thousand miles and presented sixty-three lectures. As a paid lecturer for the New York Lyceum Bureau, she visited thirty cities in six weeks, delivering daily presentations. The three thousand dollars she earned as a yearly salary was set aside to help pay for her children's college education. Although she was frequently accompanied on the tour by Anthony, the two women held different opinions on the subject matter suitable for the presentations. For example, Stanton was firmly behind the presidential candidacy of Victoria Woodhull and continued to attack organized religion, both topics on which Anthony disagreed.

By 1880, Stanton determined to stop talking and start writing. With Anthony and Matilda Joslyn Gage, she penned the history of the woman's movement that eventually filled four volumes. Shortly after the first volume was published, she left for an extended European tour with her daughter Harriot and did not return to the United States until several years later. Her husband Henry, who had been out of her life more than he was in it, died in 1887.

By the turn of the decade, old animosities were buried in the need to work together for the same end and the two woman's associations merged to form the National American Woman's Suffrage Association (NAWSA). Stanton returned from Europe, was elected president of the new group and delivered her finest speech, "Solitude of Self," at the first meeting. She gave the speech three times over a period of three days, including to the House Committee on the Judiciary on January 18, 1892; it was also published in the *Woman's Journal* and in the *Congressional Record*. Susan B. Anthony called the presentation, "the speech of Mrs. Stanton's life." The years in Europe and age had taken their toll, however, and she was extremely overweight and becoming blind. She moved in with her daughter in New York City and continued to write.

In 1895, her most controversial work, *The Woman's Bible,* was published. Although her old friend Anthony was embarrassed by the work, Stanton used the book to attack patriarchal religion and to prove that biblical history had been wrongly translated and misrepresented. The book was branded as heresy and became an immediate best seller. Consequently, in 1896, she was issued an official rebuff from NAWSA for her attacks on religion. She followed that work with *Eighty Years and More,* her highly subjective autobiography, in 1898. While working on two articles for publication, Stanton died in 1902.

Ultimately, the life of Elizabeth Cady Stanton was one filled with irony. She was an abolitionist, while her family owned slaves; she became political in the cause for women, while trying to please her father; she advocated freedom for women, while being homebound with seven children; she is little remembered while Susan B. Anthony, the person she groomed, is lauded as the pioneer for woman's rights; and, perhaps the greatest irony of all, she did not survive to see the completion of her life's work, the passage of the Nineteenth Amendment in 1920. She was a staunch advocate of self-determination and of the individual assuming responsibility as well as rights. Woman, she often remarked, must be the arbiter of her own destiny.

FOR FURTHER READING

Banner, Lois W. *Elizabeth Cady Stanton: A Radical for Woman's Rights.* Boston: Little, Brown, 1980; Clarke, Mary Stetson. *Bloomers and Ballots: Elizabeth Cady Stanton and, Women's Rights.* New York: Viking, 1972; Dubois, Ellen Carol, and Richard Cándida Smith. *Elizabeth Cady Stanton, Feminist as Thinker: A Reader in Documents and Essays.* New York: New York University Press, 2007; Lutz, Alma. *Created Equal: A Biography of Elizabeth Cady Stanton.* New York, Octagon Books, 1974; Stanton, Elizabeth Cady. *Eighty Years and More.* London: T. Fisher Unwin, 1898.

AMELIA JENKS BLOOMER
(1818–1894)

A perceptive social critic of the way of life of her time, Amelia Jenks Bloomer was the owner and editor of the *Lily,* the premier conduit for suffrage news, designed for women readers. Although she became an accomplished journalist, she is best remembered for popularizing more comfortable and functional clothing, pants worn under a shorter skirt that became known as "bloomers" in her honor.

Amelia Bloomer was born in Homer, New York on May 27, 1818, the daughter of Ananias Jenks, a clothier, and Lucy Webb. Because her family included six children and was not wealthy, Amelia received only two years of formal education. At seventeen, she taught briefly in Clyde, New York, before becoming the governess and tutor for the children of Oren Chamberlain in 1837.

While employed by Chamberlain, Amelia met Dexter Bloomer, a law student from Seneca Falls, New York, who owned the *Seneca County Courier,* a weekly newspaper. The couple married in April 1840, notably omitting the word *obey* from their wedding vows. They had no children of their own but adopted two.

After the marriage and the move to Seneca Falls, Bloomer encouraged his new wife to write. In spite of her lack of education, she took his advice and began to add her views to his newspaper on the social and political topics of the day under the pseudonym of "Gloriana."

In 1840, as many of the women of her day, Amelia entered temperance work and expanded her writing opportunities by contributing to the temperance paper, the *Water Bucket.* Since she lived in Seneca Falls and was acquainted with Elizabeth Cady Stanton, Bloomer attended the first Woman's Rights Convention in 1848. She did not, however, sign the Declaration of Sentiments but, instead, accepted a position as an officer in the Ladies Temperance Society.

During the following year, the temperance group decided there was a need for a new paper that would appeal specifically to their women members. As a writer who was married to a journalist, Amelia Bloomer was the natural choice to initiate such an endeavor. The *Lily* was the first journal published exclusively by and for women; in addition, it was the only publication in the United States to be owned, operated, and edited by a woman. Initially, the paper was used as a tool for temperance reform but slowly it began to evolve toward issues wrapped more around social justice. The tone of the pieces changed rapidly, however, when Bloomer's friend, Stanton, under the pen name, "Sunflower," began contributing columns. Within a few months, the *Lily* had reinvented itself as the primary news instrument of the woman's rights movement and featured articles ranging in topic from recipes to morals to activism. Even the masthead that read "devoted to the interests of women" was later altered to advocate woman's emancipation.

Dexter Bloomer was politically active in the region and for his part as a campaign worker, he was appointed postmaster of Seneca Falls. Although it was not customary for women to hold such posts, Bloomer appointed Amelia as his deputy. They used the spare room next to the post office to hold women's meetings. Through her paper, Amelia met most of the activists of the day, including Susan B. Anthony, who was then involved only in abolition and temperance work. One day, while Anthony was visiting Bloomer, the two encountered a group talking on the street. Since she knew each of the women, Amelia introduced Anthony to Elizabeth Cady Stanton, an auspicious encounter that would solidify much of the progress toward woman's rights over the following decades.

In 1850, the state legislature in Tennessee publicly determined that women had no souls, thus, they had no right to own property. Bloomer was up in arms and used her journalistic skill to mount an attack. Realizing that Stanton had been correct all along, Amelia transformed her personal views and the *Lily*'s editorial stance, proudly wearing the title of the first woman's suffrage journal in the United States. The paper began promoting marriage reform laws, higher education for women, and the vote.

Although she did not create it nor was she was the first to put on the costume, Amelia's national notoriety came in 1851 when she began dressing for comfort rather than style. The attire, designed by Elizabeth Smith Miller, the daughter of Stanton's cousin, Gerrit Smith, and first worn by activist Fanny Wright, consisted of Turkish pantaloons worn under a skirt that came above the knee. Equal in shock value to the bra burning of the 1960s, the bifurcated outfit, so called because it was divisible into parts, created stares and jeers as well as hurled eggs and stones. Despite the fact that the garment was denounced by the church, Amelia continued to defend the look in person and in print. Her articles were picked up by the *New York Tribune* and widely published. Because she was associated with the defense of the clothing style, the outfit became known as "The Bloomer Costume," which was eventually shortened to bloomers. The fashion was adopted by many of the forward-thinking women of the era, including Stanton, but eventually abandoned because it was diverting attention away from the movement.

In 1852, Bloomer traveled to a temperance meeting in Rochester, New York, with eighteen hundred others in attendance. She was elected secretary of the group and Stanton was elected president. It was her first venture into public speaking but by the next year, she was making continuous presentations for both temperance and woman's rights.

When her husband purchased another paper, the *Western Home Visitor,* he and Amelia moved to Mount Vernon, New York, to manage it. By that time, the *Lily* had a paid circulation of over six thousand and enabled Amelia to hire a professional typesetter, a woman. In 1855, they relocated once again to Council Bluffs, Iowa. Both publications were liquidated in order to finance the move with Mary Birdsall taking over the *Lily.* Their home became a stopover for the parade of suffragists moving their campaigns to the West. Amelia joined the Iowa Woman's State Suffrage Society, campaigned in both Iowa and Nebraska, became vice president in 1870, and petitioned the Iowa state assembly for state suffrage.

After furnishing the chapter on Iowa for Volume III of the *History of Woman Suffrage* (1887), the opus edited by Stanton and Anthony, Bloomer suffered partial paralysis of her vocal chords. She died on December 30, 1894 of heart failure. Her grave marker in Council Bluffs states simply that she wished to be remembered as "a pioneer in woman's enfranchisement."

FOR FURTHER READING

Bloomer, D.C. *Life and Writings of Amelia Bloomer.* New York: Schocken Books, 1975; Flexner, Eleanor. *Century of Struggle: The Woman's Rights Movement in the United States.* New York: Atheneum, 1974; Gurko, Miriam. *The Ladies of Seneca Falls: The Birth of the Woman's Rights Movement.* New York: Schocken Books, 1974.

SUSAN BROWNELL ANTHONY
(1820–1906)

Called, by some, the Napoleon of nineteenth-century feminism, Susan Brownell Anthony, often single-handedly, marshaled the cause of woman's rights in the mid- to late-1800s and led the charge for woman's suffrage. Through the relentless pursuit of colleagues, funds, and congressional approval, she traveled the length and breadth of the United States as a missionary for equality in an era when women were discouraged from such pursuits. Due in large measure to her lifelong friendship with another suffrage pioneer, Elizabeth Cady Stanton, Anthony edited and delivered speeches both to small groups in rural areas and to enormous gatherings in major cities as well as helping to chronicle the period in the multivolume *History of Woman Suffrage* published between 1881 and 1902.

Susan Brownell Anthony, the daughter of Daniel Anthony and Lucy Reed and the second of eight children, was born in 1820 near South Adams, Massachusetts, where her father built the town's first cotton mill. As part of his Quaker heritage, Daniel Anthony believed in the equality of women, teaching his daughters to be self-reliant and self-supporting and imbuing in them a sense of social responsibility for their fellow human beings. Because his standards also included the value of education, Susan was allowed to attend Deborah Moulson's Academy near Philadelphia. Unlike many of her contemporaries, who voiced displeasure at having to attend institutions designed for women only, Susan Anthony was eager for education in any form, although she suffered from intense bouts of homesickness. Unfortunately, the financial crisis of 1837 caused her father to lose most of his holdings and Anthony was forced to leave school after only one semester to help support her family. Deciding to take up farming, Daniel Anthony purchased acreage near Rochester, New York, with monies technically belonging to his wife. In that era, married women were not permitted to own property or transact business independent of their husbands, thus, the inheritance was held in trust for her by her brother, Joshua.

In 1839, to replenish the family assets, Susan began teaching at Eunice Kenyon's Quaker boarding school, although she had little formal schooling herself. After several years of teaching, she was asked to head the female department at the Academy at Canajoharie, New York, a position she held for three years. While leading that division, Anthony experienced firsthand the unequal wages being paid to men and women that may have caused her later emphasis on economics as a path to equality. In fact, one of her best-known lectures was titled "Woman wants bread, not the ballot." At the Academy, she also abandoned most of her *Quakerisms*, including the formal thee and thou in her speech and the customary black garb of the group.

Her activist spirit was awakened at Canajoharie and she sought an outlet by joining the Canajoharie Daughters of Temperance, for which group she gave her first public speech in 1848. The service allowed her to view the many inequities in her world and, through that, she gained a lasting reputation for uncompromising honesty. Additionally, her time with the temperance movement provided a logical entrée into antislavery and woman's rights activities. Due, in part, to the inevitable stalemate in professional advancement, she left Canajoharie and returned to Rochester to manage her family farm, directing all planting, harvesting, and marketing. There, she joined the local Daughters of Temperance, was elected president of the group and met Amelia Bloomer, the woman credited with popularizing the wearing of pants under long dresses for comfort. Bloomer was editor of the *Lily*, the temperance newspaper of the day, and familiar with many women across the spectrum of activist organizations.

While Susan was working as headmistress, her family took part in the antislavery movement, often hosting meetings at their farm. They also attended a woman's rights rally and spoke favorably of the impression made by organizers, Elizabeth Cady Stanton and Lucy Stone. Based on her family's evaluation, Anthony longed to meet these women, particularly Mrs. Stanton who had initiated the first Woman's Rights Convention in 1848. While visiting Bloomer in Seneca Falls, New York, Susan Anthony encountered Elizabeth Stanton on the street and was introduced. Because Mrs. Stanton was in the company of William Lloyd Garrison and the Englishman George Thompson, contemporaries of her husband and staunch abolitionists, the meeting was short but, nevertheless, historic and one that would dictate the direction of the balance of Anthony's life.

Shortly after that first encounter, Stanton invited Lucy Stone and Horace Greeley to her home to discuss the issue of coeducation and asked Susan Anthony to join them. According to Stanton, the two became *fast friends* at once. It was definitely a complementary relationship, one of constant balance. Anthony was reserved; Stanton was flamboyant. Anthony was unencumbered; Stanton was encased in domesticity. Anthony was analytical; Stanton was rhetorical. Together, they forged a formidable team that would spearhead decades of work toward equal rights.

By January of 1852, Anthony was ready to try her hand in new areas. She was invited as a delegate to a meeting of the Sons of Temperance in Albany. When she arrived, however, she was told that she had to sit with the women and would not be allowed to speak. At last thoroughly convinced that Elizabeth Cady Stanton was correct about the position of women, Susan Anthony organized a counter group, the Woman's State Temperance Society, which met in Rochester in 1853 with the ambition of lobbying the state legislature into limiting the sale of alcohol. Since she was insecure about her own speaking skills, Anthony requested Stanton's attendance at the meeting and asked her to compose a speech. Stanton accepted but not only did she weave her declaration of woman's rights into the temperance speech, she appeared at the meeting wearing bloomers and scandalizing some of those in attendance.

Following that meeting, Susan took to the road—setting a pattern for the duration of her life—fundraising and gathering names on petitions. In many of her confrontations on suffrage, she was told that married men cast votes for their wives. Thus, she called on married women to put their proxy vote to the test and to send their men forth to cast the vote they wished to register. By February of 1854, Anthony had gathered over ten thousand signatures on a petition to present to the New York State legislature on married woman's property rights and suffrage. She funded the printing of fifty thousand copies of Stanton's speech and passed them out. Although the legislators were amused to the point of snickering, they denied the request for suffrage as they would continue to do throughout the decade. Through most of 1854, Anthony was on tour again to Washington, Baltimore and Alexandria, Virginia, in order to present signed petitions once more in 1855. In 1857, she accelerated her work with the American Anti-Slavery Society and began extemporaneous lectures, presenting the material more effectively than she did from written documents.

In January of 1856, Anthony worked closely with Elizabeth Cady Stanton on a coeducational campaign that emphasized their belief that men's access to education dictated their access to work. The women wrote "Educating the Sexes Together," with Stanton supplying most of the ideological flair and Susan adding the tightly scripted wording.

By 1860, word was received at the State Woman's Rights Convention in Albany that the judiciary in New York was recommending a bill for married woman's property rights. After five long years, the bill was adopted, giving married women the right to own property separately from their husbands, to carry on business, to enter into contracts, to sue and be sued, and to have joint custody of their children. Once again, unsatisfied with the less than monumental gain, Stanton insisted that divorce be added to the list, defining marriage as a civil contract and nothing more. She encouraged Susan to work with her in designing a marriage contract that could be rendered null and void if either party broke the bonds.

By the spring of the next year, Susan continued to arrange antislavery meetings, lamenting the fact that the Constitution was proslavery and must be destroyed to end a system that was being enforced through lack of economic power on the part of the slaves. Destroying the Constitution was not well received among her listeners; consequently, she was denied access to gatherings, hanged in effigy, and belted with rotten eggs.

During the Civil War, the Anti-Slavery Society decided it would be best to curtail their activism and the National Woman's Rights Convention of 1861 was canceled. Stanton was in favor for she assumed that if women helped *win the war,* they would be rewarded with citizenship. It was an opinion that angered Anthony for she feared inactivity would cause women to lose the rights they had gained. Her feelings proved to be prophetic. While women passively sewed, knitted, and scraped lint for the war effort, the New York State legislature repealed most of the Married Woman's Property Act, including equal guardianship of children and rights of inheritance.

On July 13, 1862, President Abraham Lincoln delivered the Emancipation Proclamation but, once again, the activists felt it was too little. They demanded that all slaves be freed immediately and their rights guaranteed and protected under the Constitution. To forward this cause, Anthony and Stanton organized the Woman's National Loyal League. In March of 1863, they wrote an appeal to women to demonstrate their loyalty by attending a convention in New York City in May. By August of 1864, the League had five thousand members and almost four hundred thousand signatures. Perhaps moved by such pressure, the House adopted the Thirteenth Amendment that forbade slavery.

By that time, Anthony had become a charismatic leader with many followers who believed in her message. She charted her own course, followed her own rules, and believed in the perfect equality of all human beings. In January of 1865, she went to Kansas to visit her brother, Daniel, who was editor of the *Leavenworth Bulletin.* She had been in Kansas for eight months with no particular plans to return east when she read about the potential passage of the Fourteenth Amendment. The amendment afforded due process, equal protection under the law, defined citizenship, and offered suffrage to all *male* citizens. Thoroughly angered that, once again, women had been given short shrift, she returned to New York to discover the abolitionists with whom she had worked so diligently had aligned with the Republicans to assure passage of the amendment. She knew reenergizing the woman's rights campaign would be difficult.

A week after the antislavery convention in May of 1866, Anthony called the eleventh National Woman's Rights convention. She pleaded that the two societies merge into one national equal rights society but the president of the antislavery group insisted that adding rights for women to the mix would be intrusive because it was the *negro's hour.* Never one to consider no as an answer and despite growing resentment to her challenge of the

Fourteenth Amendment, Anthony, with the aid of Elizabeth Cady Stanton and others, formed the American Equal Rights Association (AERA).

In November of 1867, Kansas was considering two amendments that would grant suffrage to both blacks and women. As corresponding secretary for AERA, Anthony was assigned to oversee the petitions to Congress and wage campaigns to amend as many state Constitutions as possible. In Kansas, the state Republican Party had formed an Anti-Female Suffrage Committee and, although Lucy Stone was already there, Anthony and Stanton's persuasive skills were needed. They raised money for the trip and spent two weeks on a speaking tour of the principal towns. Traveling by stagecoach, wagon, and mule team, the women encountered less than perfect weather, bad food, lice, and bedbugs. They also encountered George Francis Train.

Train, a Democrat, was known as an eccentric financier with the reputation for being unsavory, blatantly racist, and opportunistic. History suggests that the meeting may not have been accidental and that Train was purposely put on the track of the two women to derail their efforts. Anthony and Stanton were familiar with Train's reputation but, at that moment, he appeared to be their last and best hope. Despite all their efforts, the Kansas amendments were defeated but Train offered to finance their trip back east if Anthony and Stanton would join him on a speaking tour. In addition, he promised funding for a woman's rights newspaper, an offer that was difficult for them to refuse. Although everyone advised against the association, calling Train a charlatan, Anthony and Stanton accepted the offer as a means of acquiring a platform for their message. On their way back across the country, the three spoke in Chicago, St. Louis, Louisville, Cincinnati, Boston, and Hartford, while a sinister coalition was being formed against them in New York.

With monies from Train and his colleague David Meliss, the *Revolution* was born on January 8, 1868. The weekly newspaper was a sixteen pager that proudly featured on the masthead: "Men—their rights and nothing more; women—their rights and nothing less." In addition to woman's rights campaigns, the *Revolution* advocated an eight-hour workday and the purchase of American-made products as well as encouraging immigration to rebuild the South, interests that some felt were added to forward Train's agenda. Shortly after the newspaper was launched, Train left for Britain and was subsequently arrested because of his Irish sympathies. Although he sent the women periodic notes of encouragement, no further funds appeared.

Elizabeth Cady Stanton and Parker Pillsbury, a colleague from their abolitionist days who favored women's suffrage, became the editors of the paper, while Anthony served as managing editor, taking care of the business of selling advertising space, soliciting subscriptions, and running the office. The first issue of ten thousand copies was sent to all parts of the country, postage free, under the frank of James Brooks, the Democratic leader in Congress. The newspaper served three areas of interest: (1) economic, advocating women's unions for better wages and working conditions; (2) social, addressing gender status, abortion, prostitution, birth control, divorce, and moral double standards; and (3) political, maintaining the battle cry of suffrage for women. Due to the newspaper's small circulation and because Anthony was particular about what advertising was acceptable, it was difficult to find supporters and profit was never within reach. For two years, however, the *Revolution* was the papered foundation of the woman's rights movement, while featuring good poets, short story writers and journalists, and providing a vehicle for grassroots activism for a variety of causes.

Publishing brought Anthony into contact with women who worked in the printing industry. After gaining access to their lives and noting the conditions under which they labored without protection, she encouraged those women as well as others from the sewing industry to form a trade union, the Workingwomen's Association, in 1868. Due to that encouragement, she became a delegate to the National Labor Congress in 1868 and persuaded the committee on female labor to call for votes for women and equal pay for equal work. The men of the conference, however, deleted the reference to suffrage. She further alienated some by encouraging women to fill positions vacated by striking men and was accused of running a non-Union shop at the *Revolution* and, thus, was branded an enemy of organized labor.

In 1869, due to Anthony and Stanton's association with the Democratic Party and George Francis Train, rumors of financial impropriety and their lack of moderation on certain issues, the women were essentially disowned by Lucy Stone and other moderates. Taking the situation one step further, Lucy Stone and her husband Henry Blackwell formed the American Woman Suffrage Association to avoid the fighting with the Republicans over universal suffrage, asking that the issue be considered on a state-by-state basis. In doing so, they were in direct opposition to Anthony's and Stanton's platform and created a chasm in the movement that would continue for decades and cause dangerous setbacks. As a further insult, Lucy Stone raised ten thousand dollars to launch a competing joint-stock newspaper, the *Woman's Journal,* on January 1, 1870.

The *Revolution,* always merely scraping by, was unable to compete financially with the *Woman's Journal* and within six months, Anthony, then fifty years old, was forced to close the doors and personally assume the balance of the insurmountable debt. To raise those funds, she undertook a western lecture tour and by January of 1872, she had spent six months in the East and six months in the West. Prior to leaving for California in June, she delivered sixty-three lectures in the East, then twenty-six on the way across country, coupled with eighty-two in Oregon and Washington. All toll, she traveled over thirteen thousand miles and earned only a little over four thousand 'dollars, hardly putting a dent in the *Revolution*'s indebtedness.

Testing the parameters of the Fourteenth Amendment, Anthony, three of her sisters, and other women went to the polls in Rochester, New York in November of 1872. When she was arrested for voting illegally, she refused to pay her streetcar fare to the police station because she was traveling under protest. After being arraigned, she also refused to post bail and applied for a writ of habeas corpus in the hope of taking the case to the Supreme Court. Her lawyer, however, paid her bail, thus, denying her the right to appeal. She was eventually convicted but refused to pay the fine because she considered it illegal.

The work continued with Anthony traveling from place to place, persistently gathering signatures and delivering speeches to a variety of groups. In 1876, the U.S. centennial year, celebrations were organized in every city and village of the country. Anthony, of course, refused to participate in any event celebrating political freedom, while it denied that freedom to half of the population. She did, however, request a seat for the Centennial Celebration in Philadelphia on July 4th. When the request was denied, she secured a press pass from her brother's newspaper, wrote a Declaration of Rights for Women, and printed flyers to pass out. She wanted to read her declaration, directly following the reading of the Declaration of Independence but when she stood to approach the podium, she was escorted from the hall. Knowing in advance that would be the case, her supporters built a platform just outside the building and Anthony proudly mounted the construction to read her Declaration.

Despite all she had contributed, Anthony's major challenge lay just around the corner. By August, she and Stanton with the help of Matilda Joslyn Gage were hard at work on the massive *History of Woman's Suffrage.* Pulling together letters, speeches, documents, photographs, and biographical remembrances of women who contributed to the effort, the three intended to compile six to eight hundred manuscript pages. Even without the help of Lucy Stone, who refused to be involved, the work grew until it filled four volumes, the last of which was not published until 1902, with the help of Ida Husted Harper, Anthony's biographer.

Despite the fact that she composed dozens of speeches of her own as well as editing the bulk of those scripted by Elizabeth Cady Stanton, penned a detailed journal of her work and aided in the crafting of the *History,* Anthony was always unsure of her skill as a writer. It is unlikely that she would have ventured onto the printed page in any format without the encouragement of Stanton and others and although a few journal articles are attributed directly to her, the majority of her publications depicted her as a secondary coauthor. Even the final volume of the history that she edited primarily on her own is frequently grouped with the initial three and features Stanton's name first in the byline. Susan was aware that her primary strength lay in organization and in the 1880s, she trained a new generation of women, known as *Susan's Nieces,* that included future activists, such as Carrie Chapman Catt.

After a tour of Europe, Anthony returned to the House and Senate committees in 1884, demanding a Sixteenth Amendment guaranteeing suffrage for women. She reminded the austere body that it marked the fifteenth consecutive year she had asked for such recognition. Having been denied once again, in 1887, Anthony and others organized the International Council to celebrate the fortieth anniversary of the first woman's meeting at Seneca Falls. From March 25 to April 1, 1888, fifty-three organizations and forty-nine foreign delegates were represented at the Council that featured over eighty speakers. President Grover Cleveland held a reception for those in attendance and both factions of the woman's movement were represented. As a peace offering, Anthony enthusiastically introduced Lucy Stone when it was her turn at the podium.

Partly as a consequence of that extension of unity, in February of 1890, the National Woman Suffrage Association and American Woman Suffrage Association that had been separated for nearly three decades joined forces once more. Coinciding with Susan Anthony's seventieth birthday, the new group, adopting the name National American Woman Suffrage Association (NAWSA), elected Elizabeth Cady Stanton as president and Susan B. Anthony as vice president. When Stanton returned to Europe, the presidency was passed to Anthony, an office she held until resigning on her eightieth birthday. When she resigned, some believed the presidency had been earned by Anna Howard Shaw but, on Anthony's recommendation, the reins were passed to Carrie Chapman Catt who carried the movement to victory, at long last, fourteen years later. It was an event that neither Susan Anthony nor Elizabeth Cady Stanton lived to celebrate.

In 1902, Anthony was notified of the death of her dear friend Elizabeth Cady Stanton but in spite of her consuming grief, she carried on. She attended the 1903 NAWSA convention in New Orleans and the International Council meeting in 1904. Having completed the work on the *History,* she gathered her scrapbooks, diaries, and correspondence and donated them to the Library of Congress. Susan B. Anthony died on Tuesday, March 13, 1906 of heart failure. Twelve women dressed in white surrounded her casket as thousands came to pay their respects to the pioneer.

Susan Brownell Anthony was the only one of the original woman's rights activists who never married and had no children. Between them, the other sixteen gave birth to sixty-six. Although she suffered a severe heart condition during the last six years of her life, it was the strength of that heart which motivated others and the movement to eventual success. Her last documented public words were "failure is impossible," a creed that had marked the duration of her eighty-six years.

FOR FURTHER READING

Anthony, Susan B. *The Trial of Susan B. Anthony.* Amherst, NY: Humanity Books, 2003 (repr.); Barry, Kathleen. *Susan B. Anthony: A Biography of a Singular Feminist.* New York: New York University Press, 1988; Dubois, Ellen Carol, ed.

The Elizabeth Cady Stanton-Susan B. Anthony Reader: Correspondence, Writings, Speeches. Boston: Northeastern University Press, 1992; Harper, Ida. *The Life and Work of Susan B. Anthony.* 3 vols. Indianapolis, IN: Bowen-Merrill, 1899 and 1908; Lutz, Alma. *Susan B. Anthony: Rebel, Crusader, Humanitarian.* Boston: Beacon, 1959.

ANNA HOWARD SHAW (1847–1919)

Although she was born in Newcastle-on-Tyne in England on Valentine's Day in 1847, Anna Howard Shaw and her family emigrated to the United States when she was four years old. After being trained as both a theologian and a medical practitioner, she gave up those professional callings to serve as an activist in the temperance and woman's suffrage movements, excelling as a speaker and engaging her audiences through wit and intelligence. Labeled the "Queen of the Platform" and "the foremost orator of her generation," Shaw was a consummate entertainer, using charismatic but often self-deprecating humor to lure her listeners to her cause.

Her parents were descended from wealthy Scottish landowners who, through no fault of their own, had fallen into financial difficulties. After taking his family through several relocations across the British Empire, Shaw's father decided to follow many of his countrymen who had sailed to America in search of a better life. Leaving his family behind, he crossed the Atlantic to seek employment and prepare for their arrival. When, at last, the moment came for Anna, her mother, and her seven siblings to join her father, they encountered rough weather and came close to being shipwrecked. Her father was told that, indeed, the ship had sunk and there were no survivors; thus, when the family arrived, he was not there to meet them and they had to be taken in by local missionaries until the problem was resolved.

After living in New Bedford, Massachusetts for a year, the Shaws relocated to Lawrence, Massachusetts, where at nine years of age, Anna was first exposed to and became interested in abolition. By 1857, her father had saved enough money to purchase a plot of land near Big Rapids, Michigan, and the family traveled to yet another location. At first, the trip was rather pleasant as they moved across the open landscape by train but that ended in Grand Rapids, Michigan, with over a hundred miles yet to go. They rented a wagon to carry their belongings and began the long trek across open country without roads or even paths, a journey that took over a week. On arriving, they found their new home was a one-room cabin deep in the woods with a dirt floor and no windows or doors; on top of that, there was the immediate realization that her father and her two eldest brothers would have to go back East to earn a living for the family. Thus, Anna's mother and the younger children were left to fend for themselves on the frontier with minimal supplies, the nearest store ten miles away on foot and the threat of wild animals and natives. Anna chopped trees, aided in putting down a wood floor and planted a corn crop.

As more pioneers entered the region, a school was opened three miles from the Shaw home and Anna and her brothers and sisters walked there daily. At age fifteen, she was offered a position as a teacher at another school at a salary of two dollars a week to be paid annually from year-end taxes. Since the job was five miles from her home, the school system also added free room and board as part of her reimbursement. By then, the small cabin had grown in size and her mother aided the family finances by taking in boarders from a local lumber camp.

After teaching for a year, Shaw attended high school in Big Rapids. She had long felt a calling to enter the ministry and began preaching in the surrounding area. As a consequence of her growing reputation, she became one of the first women to be licensed to preach by the Methodist Episcopal Church.

In 1873, Anna entered Albion College, arriving with $18 and continuing to preach in order to support her room, board, and tuition. After graduating, she entered Boston University School of Theology, becoming only the second woman ever admitted to the program. After graduating in 1878, she was refused ordination by the New England Conference of the Methodist Episcopal Church based on her gender. However, two years later, she became one of the first women to be ordained in any branch of the denomination through the New York Conference of the Methodist Protestant Church. Although her first assignment was in East Dennis, Massachusetts, through her travels, she became the first ordained woman to preach in such varied venues as Amsterdam, Berlin, Copenhagen, London, and the State Church of Sweden.

Only a few years into the profession she had planned for her entire life, Shaw removed herself from the ministry to enter a new field. At thirty-five, she entered Boston University School of Medicine, hoping that medical knowledge would aid her in bettering the lives of the poor she had met during her ministry. She received her doctoral degree in 1886.

As a pastor, Shaw had noted the influence alcohol played in the lives of her parishioners, particularly the women who were often mistreated by alcoholic husbands. Thus, a natural reaction to this issue was to join Woman's Christian Temperance Union, the group that fought to control the abuse of alcohol and the consequent abuse of women. The organization quickly became aware of Shaw's rhetorical skill and in 1886, she was invited to serve as their national lecturer, presenting hundreds of speeches annually, including 204 in one year in New York alone. As a speaker, Shaw drew large audiences, primarily because she did not *preach* to the people who attended, but instead, won them over through humor, frequently at her own expense. A media favorite, her most frequent presentation was titled "The Fundamental Principle of a Republic." Due to her other interests, she was elected to head the suffrage department of the organization.

As many others of her generation, Shaw was naturally propelled from temperance to woman's rights and in 1887, she was hired by the American Woman Suffrage Association as a national lecturer. After the two woman suffrage groups merged, she was elected vice president of the National American Woman Suffrage Association (NAWSA) in 1892 under the leadership of Susan B. Anthony. It was assumed that when Anthony resigned in 1900, the presidency would go to Shaw but, instead, Anthony named Carrie Chapman Catt as her successor. Although somewhat wounded by that decision, Shaw continued to work for suffrage and when Catt resigned in 1904, she took the organizational reigns she felt should have been hers four years earlier. She served as NAWSA president for eleven years (1904–1915). During her tenure, the association membership grew from thirteen thousand to over two million and with those numbers, the group required diplomatic, political, and administrative leadership, which were not Shaw's long suit. Despite her tendency to use humor, often adopting the role of a humble, country preacher, she was easily angered, argued that men and women were equal in the eyes of God and tended to blame men for the ills of the world. Consequently, she lost support from both within and without the organization and many of the men in her audiences appeared "ready to do murder."

By 1915, Catt was asked to return to the presidency, while Shaw took the position of chairman of the Woman's Committee of the Council of National Defense during World War I, through which she encouraged the government to give women more responsibility. For her humanitarian work during the period, she was awarded a Distinguished Service Medal by the U.S. Congress, the first woman to achieve such an honor.

Following the publication of her autobiography, *The Story of a Pioneer*, in 1915, Shaw continued her speaking engagements on behalf of woman's rights as well as other issues. While on tour in Springfield, Illinois, advocating for the League of Nations, Shaw contracted pneumonia, which subsequently worsened. She returned to her home in Moylan, Pennsylvania, where she died on July 2, 1919, only sixteen months before she would have been allowed to vote.

Anna Howard Shaw never married because she was married to the causes for which she so valiantly fought. She said, "Nothing bigger can come to a human being than to love a great cause more than life itself." In 1985, in her honor, Albion College in Michigan instituted the Anna Howard Shaw Women's Center to facilitate programs "to build a collaborative community in which women's voices are heard and honored."

FOR FURTHER READING

Flexner, Eleanor. *Century of Struggle: The Woman's Rights Movement in the United States.* New York: Atheneum, 1974; Huxman, Susan Schultz. "Perfecting the Rhetorical Vision of Woman's Rights: Elizabeth Cady Stanton, Anna Howard Shaw, and Carrie Chapman Catt." *Women's Studies in Communication* 23 (Fall 2000): 307–36.

LUCY STONE (1818–1893)

Although frequently criticized for her latter-day conservatism and, consequently, overlooked in some histories, Lucy Stone was, nonetheless, a pivotal figure in the early days of the woman's rights movement. Called The Orator or The Morning Star of the movement, Stone is best remembered for her eloquent and persuasive speaking style and her unconventional views on marriage.

Lucy Stone was born on August 13, 1818, the daughter of Francis Stone and Hannah Matthews Stone, and raised on her parents' modest farm near West Brookfield, Massachusetts, a small village in the western part of the state. Descended from British immigrants of the seventeenth century who came to the country seeking religious freedom, Francis Stone ruled his home, his finances, and his wife by *divine right,* the patriarchal view of his faith. As the eighth of nine children, Lucy, even as a child, was deeply troubled by her mother's constant hard physical work and multiple pregnancies. Hannah Matthews Stone lamented after Lucy's birth, "I am sorry it is a girl. A woman's life is so hard!" True to her mother's prophecy, as children, Lucy and her sisters were indoctrinated into the daily chores of farm life. When their time-consuming assignments were completed, the young girls were required to stitch together rough leather shoes that were sold to field hands or traded at the local store to bring extra money into the household.

Lucy's precocious independence developed early. As strict Congregationalists, the family and the religion attempted to reign in the willful young woman with little success. In time, Lucy spiritually withdrew from the life of the church, especially after the minister, as well as her father, supported the "Pastoral Letter" that was written and delivered to attack the work of Angelina and Sarah Grimké as unfeminine behavior. At the time writing was considered a suitable personal hobby for a young woman but if she tried to make her thoughts public, it was considered to be close to blasphemy. Although his young daughter had an active mind and an eagerness to learn, Francis Stone did not believe that women needed to be educated and he refused to pay for his daughter's schooling. Coupling her battle against organized religion with her resistance to her father's views, Lucy determined that higher education was the route not only to freedom but to the truth. She wanted to study Greek and Latin in order to check biblical translations, which she believed to be incorrect, particularly the passages related to man's dominance over woman. Secretly, the young woman devoured the available publications of the Grimké sisters and was particularly inspired by the "Rights of Woman," which confirmed her resolve to "call no man her master."

At sixteen, Lucy Stone was employed as a teacher in one of the district's public schools and began secretly to save part of her salary. By 1839, she had put away enough money to invest the sixty dollars per year required for tuition and she enrolled in the fledgling, progressive Mount Holyoke Female Seminary in South Hadley, Massachusetts. However, after only one term at the school, she realized the schedule of classes available to her would not include the classic education that she wanted. During those years, language training was available only for men students and particularly only to men who were preparing for the ministry. Only one venue was open to Lucy Stone and that was Oberlin Collegiate Institute (Oberlin College) in Ohio, the country's first school to admit both women and African Americans into its programs. Since attending Oberlin would require moving expenses and housing on arrival in addition to tuition, Lucy went back to work. After nine years of teaching, during which time she was continually distressed by the inequality between her wages and those of the male instructors, she had sufficient savings to enroll in the Institute in 1843. But, even then, although she had accumulated enough money to cover the tuition, she did not have enough to cover her daily expenses. Consequently, during her time at Oberlin, she was forced to work in the preparatory department for a few hours each week, in addition to being a housekeeper in the Ladies' Boarding House for three cents an hour, while simultaneously taking classes and attending to her studies. Added to the institution's reputation as one with a progressive admissions program, Oberlin was a keeper of secrets, serving as a stop on the Underground Railroad, a network of private homes and public buildings that offered temporary shelter to escaped slaves. Due in part to her previous teaching experience, Stone became an educator for the runaways, offering what information she could to help with their transition to freedom.

While at Oberlin, Lucy developed a like-minded friendship with Antoinette Brown, who would later become the first woman to become an ordained Protestant minister in the United States. Because Lucy was intrigued by a career in public speaking and Antoinette was preparing for the pulpit, both were shocked when the supposedly progressive institution would not permit women to join the debate team. The Debate Society sponsored frequent public demonstrations for the men students, while the women students were allowed to sit in the audience and cheer the men on. Dismayed by this double standard, the two young women confronted the administration in 1845, demanding the right to participate in the group. Their enthusiasm allowed them to enter one debate but, shortly after, amid much outcry, biblical patriarchy was invoked and their ambition was silenced. Not being one with great respect for authority, Lucy organized a secret debate society for women only, meeting in the woods surrounding the school and posting a guard to watch for intruders.

In 1847, Lucy Stone became the first woman native of Massachusetts to earn a bachelor's degree. As a result of her academic achievement, she was asked to compose a speech for the graduation ceremony. However, after being told she would not be allowed to present the speech herself, that instead it would be read at the assembly by a male student, she turned down the offer. Her future was in public speaking and she would not be denied.

In an attempt to fulfill that destiny, Stone gave her first open talk on women's rights from her brother William's pulpit in Gardner, Massachusetts, shortly after her graduation. It was the winter of 1847, a year before the woman's convention in Seneca Falls and decades before women speaking in public became the norm. As a consequence of her growing reputation as an activist, she was hired as a paid agent for the Garrisonian Massachusetts Anti-Slavery Society in 1848. William Lloyd Garrison, respected abolitionist and publisher of the antislavery newspaper, the *Liberator,* noted that Stone had "a soul as free as the air." But it was that free spirit that eventually caused trouble for her as the representative of the antislavery group for she insisted on inserting women's rights into her impassioned pleas for the slaves. Although Garrison and the society supported the full participation of women, he felt that an emphasis on woman's rights detracted from the primary purpose of the society, securing freedom and voting rights for African American males. On the other hand, Stone was a magnetic and eloquent speaker and her presentations drew large crowds for the cause. When reprimanded, Stone replied that she was a woman before she was an abolitionist. Knowing he was fighting a losing battle but not wanting to lose the momentum Stone had built for his cause, Garrison offered a compromise. Lucy was to work for the society only on the weekends, which would free her during the week to advocate for the rights of women. The society continued to pay her for the abolitionist work and she charged a fee for her presentations on woman's rights, earning a total of $7,000 in three years for her work. In addition to suffrage, Stone advocated temperance, dress reform, married women's access to property rights, and divorce.

As her activist fame spread, she was officially expelled from the Congregationalist church for her radical views and for engaging in prohibited public speaking. Lucy counteracted by joining the Unitarian church and continuing to draw substantial audiences. She also attracted detractors who tore down the posters she had laboriously hammered in with a rock, lobbed prayer books and other missiles at her podium and her person, dunked her with ice water, and burned pepper in the auditoriums and churches where she spoke. On top of the physical abuse, she was subjected to verbal jeers from bystanders as well as prejudice from community ministers who attempted to circumvent her search for appropriate places to speak. In spite of the persecution or perhaps because of it, she continued her mission, lecturing on the Social and Industrial Disabilities of Woman, the Legal and Political Disabilities, and the Moral and Religious Disabilities. She insisted that both blacks and women should have the mandate to vote; that women had the right to their own body; that men should use contraception; and that women needed economic independence, which could be acquired with better educational opportunities and higher paying jobs.

In 1850, Stone helped organize the first National Woman's Rights Convention in Worcester, Massachusetts. Although the Seneca Falls meeting, lead by Elizabeth Cady Stanton and others, predated this gathering, the Seneca Falls group was primarily regional in scope. At the national convention, Stone delivered such a dynamic plea that innumerable audience members, including Susan B. Anthony and later Julia Ward Howe, were drawn to the cause. A printed copy of her lecture submitted to John Stuart Mill and Harriet Taylor inspired Taylor's publication of *The Enfranchisement of Women*, printed in the *Westminster and Foreign Quarterly Review* in 1851.

Although she was determined not to marry, Lucy had not yet met Cincinnati hardware merchant Henry B. Blackwell, brother of Elizabeth and Emily Blackwell, the first women medical practitioners in the country. Seven years younger than she, Blackwell earnestly pursued Lucy for two years, begging for her hand in marriage. That persistence, coupled with his rescuing a fugitive slave from an abusive owner, wore down her resistance and the two were wed in 1855. An advocate for woman's rights as well as the rights of blacks, Henry agreed with Lucy's wish to retain her maiden name in order not to surrender her identity as a person. The couple rejected traditional wedding vows and, instead, wrote their own statement that eliminated the word "obey" and agreed, instead, to an equal partnership. Among other items in the document, the couple stated their disbelief in a husband's custody of his wife's person, a husband's control of and guardianship over the children, a husband's right to own and use his wife's real estate and his undeniable right to monies she earned as a product of her own industry. The Reverend Thomas Wentworth Higginson presided over the ceremony and read their statement to those in attendance; subsequently, with the couple's permission, the minister widely published the declaration. Although Lucy had been scorned before, she was yet to endure the greatest criticism. In choosing to keep her own name, she was shunned not only by the population at large but also by her colleagues in the movement as well. Even Susan B. Anthony scolded that people would not believe Lucy was married and was, instead, advocating free love, a euphemism of the era indicating living together without legal and religious approval. As usual, Lucy turned a deaf ear to the swirling critique. She was, on the contrary, elated to have discovered a soul mate and even happier when her former college ally, Antoinette Brown, married Henry's brother, Samuel, and became her sister-in-law.

For a time, Lucy's pace was slowed down in order to aid her husband in establishing his career as a publisher's representative, first in Chicago and then in Orange, New Jersey, where the couple relocated. In the interim, Lucy gave birth to two children, a son who died in infancy and a daughter, Alice, who was born in 1858. The same year offered a resurgence of the earlier Stone spirit when she refused to pay taxes due to lack of representation in a government in which she could not participate. The seizure of her household goods and furniture as payment for those taxes was applauded as a symbolic gesture on behalf of woman's rights.

As other activists during the Civil War (1861–1865), Lucy Stone halted her touring, partly due to loyalist sympathies and partly due to imminent danger. Although she, as many of the other women in the movement, stitched shirts for Union soldiers, being domestic was not her calling and during the period she helped found the Woman's National Loyal League, advocating full emancipation and enfranchisement for African Americans.

In spite of the fact that she resisted formal groups because they restricted individual thought and were too complicated to produce any real work, Stone aided in the creation of the American Equal Rights Association (AERA), a union of women and abolitionists determined to gain voting rights for both blacks and women during the postwar Reconstruction era.

In 1867, Kansas held the first state Constitutional referendum on enfranchisement for women. Suffragists, including Lucy Stone, went on extended tours of the state, often tramping through mud and slush to campaign from door to door, but the measure failed. It would take two more years before full electoral rights were offered to women in any state.

As Stone had predicted, the framework of the AERA began to fragment as various members held opposite and conflict-ridden opinions on the issues. Even though she had been one of the most radical advocates in her earlier years, Lucy reversed her views, stating that woman's best place was within the family but with economic independence. Slowly, she moved away from the more extreme positions and the persons supporting them, particularly the free love advocacy of presidential-candidate-to-be Victoria Woodhull and those who opposed all but federal suffrage mandates, including Elizabeth Cady Stanton and Susan B. Anthony.

Likely, part of Stone's objection to the free love hype was precipitated by her husband's involvement with another woman, Abby Hutchinson Patton, the wife of a stockbroker. Some theorized that Henry felt threatened by his wife's success, while his sisters blamed Lucy for her over involvement with the movement and Lucy blamed herself for intimate inadequacy. It was true that the other woman was Lucy's diametric opposite: Lucy was pushy, plain, and plump, while Abby Patton flaunted petite and pretty femininity. After continual bouts with migraines, Stone issued an ultimatum. She was enrolling her daughter in boarding school, moving to Boston, and starting a newspaper. Henry could come if he would like.

True to her word, Stone, with her husband accompanying her, moved to Dorchester, Massachusetts in 1867. They formed a joint-stock company, selling shares to wealthy Bostonians, to fund their fledgling *Woman's Journal*. Another major investor was woman's rights advocate, Mary Livermore who merged her Chicago-based reform paper, the *Agitator*, with Stone and Blackwell's new venture and served as editor-in-chief. The *Woman's Journal* was continuously published for forty-seven years, eventually under the editorship of Stone's daughter, Alice.

Considered by many to be the voice of the woman's movement, the *Journal* covered events, history, and personalities of the era. Reflecting Stone's particular views, the coverage shied away from the more controversial issues to concentrate on advocating the vote for women. The well-crafted pieces, many drafted by Lucy Stone, informed women that political power could offer them better protection than could the men in their lives. One series concentrated on the inequality in punishment meted out for sex crimes, particularly rape, and criticism of the legislation in some states that stated that women as young as their preteen years were old enough to be considered *consenting* adults in matters of marriage and sex. The decisive ideological split confronting the movement followed the passage of the Fourteenth Amendment (1868), which, for the first time, provided a national definition of a citizen but noted that males only were part of that definition. Within two years the Fifteenth Amendment was added to the Constitution, granting full enfranchisement to black men. Because, once again, women were overlooked, the amendment created a bonfire that seared one facet of the AERA, while others cheered the inevitability of success. Surely, the latter group thought that women would be next. Disaffiliating with the Republican Party that had supported both amendments, Elizabeth Cady Stanton and Susan B. Anthony formed the National Woman Suffrage Association (NWSA), refusing to recognize any Constitutional amendment that did not include women. Lucy Stone, on the other hand, joined forces with Mary Livermore, Julia Ward Howe, and others to initiate the rival American Woman Suffrage Association (AWSA), dedicated to gaining the vote on a state-by-state basis. Stone's journal continued to take a hard line against supporting striking workers and against the views and presidential candidacy of Victoria Woodhull, while embracing the Utopian Socialism put forth by Edward Bellamy in *Looking Backward* (1888). As a consequence of the separation of views within the woman's movement, the working classes gathered around Stanton and Anthony, while Stone's AWSA appealed to middle- and upper-class activists.

In 1879, a new Massachusetts law allowed women to vote in school elections. However, in an ironic twist, Lucy Stone's own values prohibited her from casting her ballot because she refused to register under her husband's name. Even though she had retained her maiden name, she was required to sign her name as "Lucy Stone, married to Henry Blackwell" on all legal documents.

Despite the growing discord between the two factions of the woman's suffrage movement and among the leaders of each, the two groups realized that more could be accomplished through reunification. Stone, Anthony, and Stanton agreed to an amiable animosity and worked to merge the NWSA and the AWSA in 1890. Stone was elected to serve as chair of the executive committee for the new organization.

In frail health, Stone's last public appearance was at the Congress of Representative Women at Chicago's World Columbian Exposition in May 1893. She died at her home of cancer but refused to make her death the end of the firsts on her list. On her death bed, she whispered her last words to her daughter, Alice. "Make the world better," she offered.

FOR FURTHER READING

Blackwell, Alice Stone. *Lucy Stone, Pioneer of Woman's Rights*. New York: Octagon Books, 1961 (repr.); Burnett, Constance Buel. *Five for Freedom: Lucretia Mott, Elizabeth Cady Stanton, Lucy Stone, Susan B. Anthony, Carrie Chapman Catt.* New York: Greenwood Press, 1968; Kerr, Andrea Moore. *Lucy Stone: Speaking Out for Equality.* New Brunswick, NJ: Rutgers University Press, 1992.

VICTORIA CLAFLIN WOODHULL
(1838–1927)

Almost every time the name Victoria Woodhull is mentioned, it is prefaced by the word "scandalous." One of the most recognized names in America in the nineteenth century, this charismatic, and often outlandish, woman was far ahead of her time, even becoming a candidate for the presidency of the United States in 1872.

Born on September 23, 1838, Victoria, named for the Queen of England, was the seventh of the ten children of Buckman and Roxanna Claflin. Her father was a ne'er-do-well who forced his children to take care of most of the household labor, beating them if they failed; her mother was a spiritual-ist, who had visions and interpreted dreams. Spiritualism was a major move-ment of the time with persons paying large sums of money to attend séances, have their fortunes told, or their dreams explained. Her father, who earned most of his income through first-rate con jobs, decided that Victoria and her sister, Tennessee or Tennie, should support the family by playing on human grief or greed during periods of social and emotional confusion. With his wife's aid, he trained the young women as *spiritualists* and literally took them on the road. Convincingly, they acted as mediums and became adept at falling into mock trances in order to make *contact with the dead*. Whether or not her powers were real, Victoria eventually believed that her physical movements and lifestyle choices were guided by spirits, a conviction that persisted throughout her life, and she seldom made a decision without con-tacting her *spirit guide*, Demosthenes. Although this spiritual connection did provide a means for the young women to gain money, they were essen-tially robbed of their childhood. Unfortunately, as Victoria grew older, some made a connection between her spiritualism and feminism, thus, finding rea-son to discount the latter as mere hocus-pocus.

Due to her constant traveling and her parents' lack of concern, Victoria attended only three years of formal schooling. In addition to those barriers, she also suffered from bouts of rheumatism. She was cared for by

Dr. Canning Woodhull, who was attracted to the young woman even though she was only fourteen and he was much older. In 1853, they married with her parents' blessings, assuming they would be allowed to share in the doctor's income; for Victoria, it was a means of escape from her parents' constant road show. However, she soon discovered the doctor was an alcoholic and that she was far from being the only woman in his life. He left her alone for weeks at a time with no food and no heat in their home. In 1854, alone and frightened, she gave birth to a son, Byron, who, likely as a consequence of her deprivation during pregnancy, had mental deficiencies.

Since she doubted she would be missed, Victoria took the infant and moved to California, working first as a cigar girl in a club and then as a seamstress. One of the people for whom she sewed was the actress Anna Cogswell who saw promise in the young woman and convinced her to try her hand at acting. Her first job in the theatre netted her fifty-two dollars a week.

Once again, her escape was short lived, however, for she was called home by her family and reentered her former life as a spiritualist. Whether or not she had the *gift,* she billed herself as clairvoyant and dabbled in faith healing. Believers came in droves and by 1869, her annual income was over $700,000.

After returning to her marriage, Victoria prayed for another child, one who was normal. Although she was kicked in the stomach by her drunken husband during the pregnancy, her daughter, Zula Maud, born in 1861, was in perfect health. After the birth, Victoria applied for and was granted a divorce. In 1866, she met and married Colonel James H. Blood, commander of the Sixth Missouri Regiment, city auditor of St. Louis, and president of the Society of Spiritualists. Likely for reasons of *marketing,* she retained the name Woodhull.

In 1868, Victoria, Colonel Blood, and her sister Tennie moved to New York City. Through their work as spiritualists, the women traveled in high society circles and were much admired, particularly by railroad magnate Cornelius Vanderbilt. Offering his patronage, Vanderbilt gave the sisters $7,000 to create a stock brokerage firm, making them the first women stockbrokers in history and joint owners of Woodhull, Claflin and Company. By 1869, using funds earned through stock tips from Vanderbilt and her own shrewd management, Victoria began publishing a journal, covering topics from investments to racism to woman's suffrage to banking fraud. The journal, *Woodhull & Claflin's Weekly,* had over twenty thousand subscribers and ran for six years. It was also the first publication to print the *Communist Manifesto* in English.

Victoria was intrigued by the woman's movement, although the views of a self-made woman tended to clash with privileged feminists. When Susan B. Anthony and Elizabeth Cady Stanton met Woodhull at a Woman's Rights Convention in 1869, they were simultaneously attracted to her vitality and repulsed by her otherworldliness. With others in the movement, Victoria observed there was no need for an amendment granting suffrage for women because the Fourteenth Amendment, which granted African Americans the right to vote, also offered that authorization to women as a privilege of citizenship.

Despite that belief, in 1870, Woodhull opened an office in Washington, DC to lobby for woman's suffrage. She quickly discovered that politicians were using the woman's rights issues to polarize the parties. That year, she was the keynote speaker at a national suffrage convention and attempted to put her theory to the test by trying to vote. Never one to back down from a fight, Victoria did the unthinkable; she published a series of papers in the *New York Herald* on politics and finance (later collected as "The Principles of Government") and announced her candidacy for president of the United States.

The following year, she testified before Congress in defense of woman's rights under the Fourteenth Amendment. The House Judiciary Committee denied her request but issued a favorable minority report. Going forward, Victoria claimed the presidential slot on the Equal Rights Party ticket, a political party comprised mainly of laborers, suffragists, spiritualists, and communists, and she selected black leader Frederick Douglass as her running mate. In so doing, she was challenging the popularity of Ulysses S. Grant and newspaper mogul Horace Greeley. The thought of a woman running for the highest office in the land when women were not even permitted to vote was ludicrous to most and Victoria faced an uphill battle in fundraising. She formed "Victoria Leagues" among her supporters and opened her home for meetings. As a last effort, she attempted to sell bonds that could be redeemed once she took office and depleted most of her personal funds.

If being a woman were not enough of an obstacle to her bid for the presidency, Victoria included free love in her campaign platform. She was not advocating promiscuity but believed that marriage should be of the heart and not of the law; in other words, marriage should exist only as long as love existed. Women were shocked and most of those involved in the movement disavowed any support for her position. The media and the clergy accused her of being a witch and a prostitute and of having affairs with married men. Destitute, she was evicted from her home and soon living on the streets.

In 1872, she sought aid from Henry Ward Beecher, a minister and staunch supporter of woman's rights. When Beecher refused his help, Victoria attacked his reputation, exposing his affair with Lib Tilton, the wife of editor, Theodore Tilton. Because she had mounted her accusations in print, Victoria was arrested for libel and spent Election Day behind bars. She was the first woman arrested under the Comstock Act for sending "obscene literature through the mails." Over the next three years, she was arrested numerous times for obscenity and libel with one bail amount set at $60,000.

Eventually, Tilton agreed with her about the affair and took Beecher to court for alienation of affection. A consequence of what was called the trial of the century was Victoria's acquittal but it was too late. By that time, the court costs, the bonds, and the run for the presidency had plunged her into bankruptcy; the trials alone had depleted her accounts of $500,000. After the acquittal, she asked the court to award her a mere $50,000 in restitution but received nothing.

After divorcing Blood, Victoria moved to England and continued to work for woman's rights. In 1883, she married John Biddulph Martin, a wealthy banker. She died on June 9, 1927 in a manor house in Worcestershire, England. In 1871, Theodore Tilton published a biographical sketch of Woodhull, stating "I know of no person against whom there are more prejudices, nor any one who more quickly disarms them."

FOR FURTHER READING

Goldsmith, Barbara. *Other Powers: The Age of Suffrage, Spiritualism and the Scandalous Victoria Woodhull.* New York: Harper Perennial, 1998; Stern, Madeline B. *The Victoria Woodhull Reader.* Weston, MA: M & S Press, 1974; Woodhull, Victoria. *Freedom! Equality!! Justice!!!* New York: Woodhull, Claflin and Company, 1872.

JANE ADDAMS (1860–1935)

In addition to her best-known achievement, the founding of Hull House, Jane Addams helped form both the American Civil Liberties Union (ACLU) and the National Association for the Advancement of Colored People (NAACP). She was committed to both the woman's rights movement and pacifism and was awarded the Nobel Peace Prize in 1931.

Jane Addams was born on September 6, 1860, in Cedarville, Illinois, the eighth child of Quaker parents. Her father John was a miller, a banker, and state Republican senator from 1854 to 1870; her mother, Sarah, died in childbirth, leaving the responsibility of raising Jane to her father. He taught the child tolerance and a strong work ethic and encouraged education. Although they were close, her father was emotionally disengaged. When she was seven, her father remarried.

At seventeen, she entered Rockford Seminary, an educational institution preparing young women to enter the missionary profession, for which her father was a trustee. Jane successfully urged the school leaders to seek program accreditation because she had no interest in mission work and wanted her education to be acceptable in other professions. When she received her bachelor's degree, she was class president, valedictorian, and editor of the school magazine. Briefly considering the medical field, she enrolled in the Women's Medical College in Philadelphia but after only seven months, her father died and she left school. In an attempt to fit her into the mold of the era, her stepmother encouraged her to marry but Jane had other plans. After discovering she could not have children, her family doctor recommended that she take a *rest cure* to recover from her father's death. Thus, instead of marriage, Jane went to Europe where she stayed for eight years. After touring Italy and Germany, she settled for a time in London where she was overwhelmed by the poverty and human misery she saw in the population. Jane realized she wanted to alleviate their pain and improve their conditions.

Having reached that conclusion, she visited Toynbee Hall, one of the first settlement houses, opened in 1884. The concept behind the settlement house movement was to strengthen relationships among the various ethnic and socioeconomic groups in the community by offering a haven where they could meet, socialize, and learn about each other as well as being involved in formal course work. Toynbee Hall featured courses, lectures, art exhibitions, a theatre, and a library. Addams was so impressed that she became determined to open an identical institution in the United States.

Following a short visit to Spain, Addams and her traveling companion, Ellen Gates Starr, moved to Chicago, Illinois in 1889, then the second largest city in America. The site they selected for their social outreach was the former home of architect Charles J. Hull, a massive structure that had somehow escaped the Chicago fire of 1871. Christened Hull House, the settlement house opened in September and a little over a decade later, they were serving over two thousand people each week. It was her intention to keep the enterprise secular in order to draw support from the multireligion neighborhood, to build a sense of community in the neighborhood, and to offer employment opportunities to college-educated young people who wanted to work for social justice. Hull House served as her *social laboratory* to test her theories that character was formed in early childhood and that social classes were interdependent.

Hull House became Addams' home for fifteen years, a haven in the midst of immigrant slums with garbage in the streets, nineteen different nationalities, sweat shops, poor street lighting, and no running water. In examining the neighborhood, she found over a thousand violations of street codes that, when reported, resulted in the transfer of three city employees. She asked for and received one of the positions; it was the only paid job she ever held for which she earned $1,000 a year.

Lack of paid employment was not an issue because Addams was a skilled fundraiser. Each program sponsored by Hull House was fully funded through donations and Addams was known as "Saint Jane" of the "Cathedral of Compassion." Hull House became the center of community life. Combining recreation and education with food and shelter, the center cared for the entire population, infants through the aged, and incorporated a reading circle, a kindergarten, a boys' club, and an art gallery. Employing a changing and adaptable approach to organization, Addams established the first public playground in the city, started a post office and a savings bank, initiated the first juvenile court, and offered bathing facilities for those who had none. In 1891, she formed the "Jane Club," a cooperative for working women, maids, seamstresses, and factory workers, who were residents of the house.

In 1907, Addams attended the first National Peace Conference and, as a consequence, published *The Newer Ideals of Peace,* which became the hallmark of the woman's pacifist movement. The work underscored her belief that international peace could be brought about through social reform.

Addams was an excellent speaker but being involved in politics and reform was not considered a suitable endeavor for a woman at the time. When she was criticized for her efforts, Addams drifted toward the woman's movement and the push for suffrage. In 1909, she published "Why Women Should Vote" in the *Ladies Home Journal*. Like many of her peers, she advocated the expansion of the *woman's sphere* to the community as a means of preserving the home. She asserted that the community streets concerned women more than they did men and that the community was a natural extension of the home. She urged mothers to fight for kindergartens and university women to protest unequal wages.

In advocating for labor and trade unions, she was elected secretary of the Civic Federations' Industrial Arbitration Committee and aided in ending a textile workers strike in 1910. Using her skills in mediation and administration, she tackled the issues of child labor, infant mortality, urban crowding, unsafe workplaces, juvenile delinquency, unemployment, and poverty. Many of her theories graced the pages of her autobiography, *Twenty Years at Hull House* (1910), a work which produced enough revenue to continue her effort for some time.

In 1911, Addams worked for woman's suffrage on a municipal level in Chicago and was elected the first vice president of the newly merged National American Woman Suffrage Association. Diving into politics instead of fighting against it, she campaigned for Theodore Roosevelt's Progressive "Bullmoose" Party in 1912. Although she was a good advocate and was invited to the inauguration, Roosevelt lost the election to Woodrow Wilson.

"If Men Were Seeking the Franchise" was Addams' satiric change of point of view article printed in 1913. In the piece, based on the fictitious assumption that women had the vote and men did not, she accused men of prejudice and warmongering and indicated that, consequently, they should not be permitted suffrage. She wrote, "Would not these responsible women voters gravely shake their heads and say that as long as men exalt business profits over human life, it would be sheer folly to give them the franchise."

Known by some as "the most dangerous woman in America" because of her pacifism, Addams was against World War I. In addition to being opposed to war on principle, she believed that as long as the world was violent, women would be considered inferior. She pleaded with President Wilson not to enter the war and was, consequently, accused of being pro-German and placed on the Senate blacklist. During the war, she helped found and worked for ACLU that grew out of the Union Against Militarism.

Addams was deeply concerned about working conditions for children. After she approached the head of the Illinois Bureau of Labor, he proposed regulations to change the situation in factories in the state. Because Hull House had been so successful in bringing together various nationalities, race was another area of interest for her. She helped form NAACP, which irked her critics even more than her pacifism. She was accused of being a socialist, an anarchist, and a communist; was threatened by Ku Klux Klan; and chastised by the military for her criticism of chemical warfare.

In 1915, over three thousand attendees unanimously elected her chair of the Women's Peace Party, a group calling for arms limitations and mediation. She was also president of the National Peace Federation and served as their delegate to Holland for the International Congress of Women conference. Subsequently, *Women at The Hague* (1915), penned by Addams and others, reflected the inner workings of the group and chronicled Addams's visits to heads of state throughout Europe, attempting diplomacy to avert war.

On returning to the United States, Addams became disillusioned with the woman's movement because she believed they were kowtowing to politicians, trading their defense of the war for possible support for suffrage. She was also expelled from Daughters of the American Revolution for her stance against the war. Regretting that her notoriety was overshadowing the accomplishments of other women, Addams retreated to Hull House in 1917 to write. Her isolation was short lived, however, for she was called back to Washington by Franklin Delano Roosevelt to serve as a consultant for many of his social programs during the Great Depression.

In 1922, Addams published *Peace and Bread in Time of War,* a reminiscence of her experiences during and after World War I. In it, she discussed her views on the damage that war did to human relationships as well as the physical and emotional well-being of those who participated.

By the 1930s, the activist was once again urging women to become involved in their community, to enter city government, and to assume civic responsibility. Only the second American and the first woman to do so, Addams was nominated for the Nobel Peace Prize in 1931. Unfortunately, she was too ill to travel to Oslo, Norway, to accept the award. Following six operations, spinal difficulties, removal of a kidney, and heart trouble, she died of cancer on May 21, 1935 and was buried in Cedarville, Illinois, her childhood home. Over fifty thousand supporters attended her funeral.

In addition to her other accomplishments, Jane Addams wrote ten books, received fifteen honorary degrees, including the first one offered to a woman by Yale University, and was awarded the Greek medal of military merit. Called a pacifist, a socialist, an anarchist, a communist, and an enemy of the state, this small, soft-spoken woman with a congenital curved spine was one of the most manipulative and charismatic leaders of the late-nineteenth and early-twentieth centuries.

FOR FURTHER READING

Addams, Jane. "If Men Were Seeking the Franchise." *Ladies Home Journal* (June 1913): 104–7; ———. *Twenty Years at Hull House: With Autobiographical Notes.* Boston: Bedford/St. Martin's, 1999; Brown, Victoria Bissell. *The Education of Jane Addams.* Philadelphia: University of Pennsylvania Press, 2004.

MARGARET SANGER (1879–1966)

Censured for trafficking in obscene literature, criticized as publicity hungry, accused of racism and eugenist leanings, and jailed as a "public nuisance," Margaret Sanger never lost sight of her quest for an affordable and legal means of birth control for economically disadvantaged women.

Margaret Louise Higgins was born on September 14, 1879, in Corning, New York. Her mother, Anna, a devout Catholic, was pregnant eighteen times in twenty-two years and gave birth to eleven children, none of whom weighed less than ten pounds. Margaret was profoundly affected by her mother's weakened state brought on by excessive childbearing. When Anna Higgins eventually succumbed to tuberculosis, her life as well as her death furnished motivation for her daughter's life's work. That motivation was coupled with youthful molding in activism, imparted by her father, Michael Higgins, a stonemason, who was a reputed free thinker and outspoken radical. Early on, Margaret noted the economic disparity in their community and, even as a young woman, she drew connections between family size and prosperity.

With funds supplied by her sisters, Margaret attended Claverack College and the Hudson River Institute, one of the oldest coeducational institutions in the United States. When she became homesick or discouraged, her father sent her books with strong women role models, such as Helen of Troy and Cleopatra. After graduating, she was offered a first-grade teaching post in New Jersey. Margaret enjoyed her brief stint in the school system even though the majority of her pupils were the children of immigrants, most of whom did not speak English. Unfortunately, her career was short-lived for she was summoned home to help care for her ailing mother.

Only forty-nine but weakened by multiple pregnancies and ravaged by tuberculosis, Anna Higgins died. Believing that if she had a more thorough knowledge of medicine, she could have prevented her mother's death, Margaret decided to become a doctor but funds were not available to send her to medical school. She opted for the next best thing and enrolled in a rigorous nursing training program at White Plains Hospital in New York.

In 1902, Margaret met and married William (Bill) Sanger, an architect and aspiring artist. While expecting their first child, Stuart, Margaret was diagnosed with tuberculosis, likely a dormant strain contracted through the close-contact exposure she had when caring for her mother. After a short stay in a recuperative sanatorium, the disease was cured and, in 1910, the Sangers moved to the avant-garde section of Greenwich Village, considered the heart of Bohemian radicalism. The area and the attitudes reflected Bill Sanger's passion for the arts, while Margaret was quickly drawn into the political activism vibrating through the community. Her first venture into aggressive involvement was with the labor movement and in 1912 she joined the International Workers of the World, an organization with a reputation for advocating revolution and anarchy. Sanger marched with textile mill workers who were on strike for higher wages and, subsequently, testified before Congress on their behalf.

Recalling her mother's physical pain coupled with her leftover youthful belief in the direct line between economic incapacity and family size, Sanger was intrigued when invited by the *Call,* the newspaper of the Socialist Party, to create a column pertaining to social problems, such as sexual issues, contraception, and venereal disease. In 1915, discussion of such topics was considered highly inappropriate, especially by a woman, and those who violated the taboo were labeled as social outcasts, a stigma against morality. Undeterred, Sanger eagerly penned and published the series, "What Every Mother Should Know" and "What Every Girl Should Know." The columns ran for three or four weeks until one Sunday morning when the headline read simply: "What Every Girl Should Know: Nothing, by Order of the Post Office Department." Sanger was accused of nine counts of violating Section 211 of the postal law, prohibiting distribution of vulgar material. Basically, the column was a challenge to the Comstock Law, initiated in 1873 by Anthony Comstock, the creator of the New York Society for the Suppression of Vice. Passed by Congress, the law incorporated the suppression of trade in, and circulation of, obscene literature and articles for immoral use. Part of the campaign to legislate public morality, the law censored printed materials considered lewd, including any information on contraception or sexually transmitted diseases. Comstock preached that contraception would promote promiscuity.

With her writing curtailed, Sanger returned to the nursing profession, taking a position as a public health nurse and midwife in the low income areas of New York City's lower east side. In her autobiography (1938), Sanger reflected that "Below Fourteenth Street I seemed to be breathing a different air, to be in another world where the people had habits and customs alien to anything I had ever heard about." While working in that community, Sanger perfected her theory that repeated pregnancies were a product of poverty and that uncontrolled breeding was the central social problem affecting the poor. Frequently, she observed long lines of women waiting for their turn to visit a five dollar abortion clinic; while those who could not afford the procedure turned to self-induced solutions, such as herb tea, turpentine, slippery elm, or knitting needles. One such patient, Sadie Sachs, begged Sanger for advice on ways to control pregnancy, which the nurse was prohibited from supplying; consequently, in an attempt to end yet another pregnancy, Sachs died. That event served as the final motivator for Sanger who put on the cloak of a crusader committed to the class struggle.

In 1913, the Sangers moved to France in order for Bill to study and pursue his art. While in Europe, Margaret buried herself in research, devouring volumes of manuscripts in dusty libraries, to discover the secrets of childbearing management long practiced in other countries. Although Bill elected to remain, Margaret and the children returned to the United States in 1914, where she became determined to publish the information she had discovered. In March, the first issue of the *Woman Rebel* graced the newsstands. Written primarily for the working classes, the newspaper advocated a woman's right to own and to control her own body. The masthead defiantly proclaimed: "A woman's duty: To look the whole world in the face with a go-to-hell look in the eyes; to have an ideal; to speak and act in defiance of convention." The paper featured the newly minted term, birth control, coined by Sanger with the aid of Otto Bosien to avoid the popularly accepted phrases, family limitation or others.

Only six months elapsed before history was repeated. The *Woman Rebel* was shut down, the landlord was ordered to evict her from her offices and Sanger was indicted for obscenity. Visualizing the birth control movement as a first amendment test case, Sanger begged the court for a continuance in order to have time to prepare her case. The plea was denied based in part on the district attorney's accusations that Sanger was advocating bomb throwing and assassination and facing a thirty-year prison term.

Knowing she needed more information before addressing the court, Sanger made a decision. She enrolled the children in boarding school, completed writing the pamphlet, "Family Limitation," found a printer, and contacted potential distributors. She kept two of the pamphlets and enclosed them in the letters she addressed to the judge and the district attorney. Having completed those steps, she boarded a train for Canada, where she assumed the name Bertha Watson because felony charges would make extradition possible, and found passage to England.

Propelled by the twin engines of finding fuel for her defense and providing answers for the women she had adopted as her charge, Sanger immersed herself in research, spending full days at the British Museum poring over archival documents, including the works of Thomas Robert Malthus, an early essayist in overpopulation studies. In London she met Havelock Ellis, member of the socialist debating society, the Fabians, and supporter of sexual liberation. Ellis focused her reading and encouraged her to continue her work on a more moderate level. Not content with the material she found in the British Museum, Sanger traveled to the Netherlands, where birth control movements had been in place for years. Returning to London, she created three treatises on birth control methods in France, in England, and in the Netherlands.

Although she was not completely satisfied that she had explored all avenues of research, Sanger's work was interrupted in 1915 by word from her husband that he had been arrested. A man, pretending to be in need, entrapped Bill Sanger by asking for a copy of his wife's publication, "Family Limitation." When Sanger offered the pamphlet, the man identified himself as an agent of the New York Society for the Suppression of Vice. Once again, the judge in the case said the writing was not only indecent, but immoral. He continued that too many women were advocating women's suffrage, when they should be focused on bearing and raising children.

Realizing that Bill's arrest was a lure to pull her back to the United States, Margaret left her studies and secured passage home. After she notified the court of her return, she began planning her defense but in the middle of her preparation, her four-year-old daughter, Peggy, became ill and died. Other like-minded activists, public sympathies, and the media were aroused by the case and the government, wishing to squelch any further publicity for the woman, dropped the charges.

Since venues for publication were closed to her, Sanger opted for public appearances and arranged a speaking tour. She tailored her speeches to her audience, hoping to gain support from various groups like the woman's suffrage movement, the socialists, and others. The women's movement found Sanger's views too controversial and asked her to wait until the vote was granted. The socialists begged for more time until they could gather more support for their positions. She contacted the National Birth Control League, an organization she started that had been reorganized in her absence, but was told they were too busy trying to change the laws to lend support to someone who was so fond of breaking them. Consequently, she was constantly forced to reinvent herself to gain whatever tidbits of support she could.

Wherever she went on tour, demonstrators screamed that she was immoral and a sinner. Men were particularly agitated by Sanger's message that contraception was a woman's problem and it was up to her to deal with it. This revelation constituted an ideological power shift and urged women to look at other power constructs in their lives, which was considered as good as a threat. The situation was complex and contradictory; birth control was available for the upper classes who could order devices from Europe and doctors furnished condoms to men as preventatives for disease. But justice for the downtrodden women of the poorer neighborhoods was simply unavailable. Not only had she raised the ire of the government and most men, Sanger confronted religion head on. The Catholic Church, long an opponent of any form of birth control, mounted a campaign against her and even set up a Washington, DC office to lobby politicians. In 1921, the archbishop of New York City even arranged to shut down her presentation at the Town Hall. After the building was closed and she was arrested, free speech advocates, the media, and the newly formed American Civil Liberties Union sprang to her defense. For Sanger, it was free advertising; when the speech was rescheduled, over three thousand people were turned away due to lack of seating.

In 1916, Sanger opted for a more direct approach, opening a clinic in Brooklyn, New York, for treatment and counseling with a secondary purpose of testing the laws. Although doctors refused to help her, the clinic was staffed by Sanger, her sister Ethyl Byrne, a registered nurse, and two other women. By the time the clinic had been in operation for ten days, streams of women, some from as far away as Massachusetts, Pennsylvania, and New Jersey, were wrapped around the block. Gently advising that control was better than abortion, which she considered murder, Sanger told the women what she had learned in Europe.

On the eleventh day, the clinic was raided by the vice squad, led by a woman officer, Margaret Whitehurst. It was debatable which fact outraged Sanger more—the closure itself or the fact that a woman was in charge for she had always viewed women as a group with shared interests and common causes. Vice confiscated over 460 case histories that were never returned. The court cited the establishment as a "public nuisance" to which Sanger remarked that, in the Netherlands a clinic was called a public benefaction, while in the United States, it was a public nuisance. The clinic doors were bolted and Sanger and her sister were each sentenced to thirty days in the workhouse. While a prisoner, Sanger's sister Ethyl attempted a hunger strike but wanting to keep publicity at a minimum, her jailers inserted a tube in her throat and forced her to swallow food. She was the first, but not the last, woman to be treated in that manner.

After her release, Sanger grew more desperate for support, both ideological and financial, and turned briefly to the eugenists. Eugenics was a social philosophy that insisted that hereditary traits could be improved by intervention, birth control, selective breeding, and genetic engineering. The theory was so accepted that it was taught in high school and college curriculums and in the early 1900s, involuntary sterilization for the homeless, orphans, epileptics, the blind, the deaf, and the *feebleminded* was widely practiced in the United States. Using her tendency to chameleon-like behavior, adopting whatever belief she felt would forward her cause at a given time, Sanger wrote *The Pivot of Civilization* (1922), linking birth control to eugenics. In 1921, Sanger organized the first American birth control conference.

Noting that they had lived apart more than they had together, she and Bill Sanger were divorced. The following year, she met and married millionaire James Henry Noah Slee, inventor of Three-in-One oil. Using his fortune as backing, Sanger smuggled contraceptive devices into the United States and Slee agreed to use one of his factories to produce spermicidal medicines.

Sanger traveled extensively over the next few years, establishing the first birth control clinic in Japan in 1922 and becoming the first foreign woman to address the Japanese national legislature in 1954. In 1927, she attended the first World Population Conference in Geneva, Switzerland and in 1935, after meeting Mahatma Gandhi, she was encouraged to open clinics throughout India. While in the United States, she formed the National Committee on Federal Legislation for Birth Control, remaining its president until 1937, and lobbied Franklin Delano Roosevelt for support, pointing out that birth control would help reduce Depression welfare by allowing married women time to work. She was advised to change her course to working to change laws that would give doctors the right to dispense birth control to anyone who requested it.

In 1936 that direction proved successful when the U.S. Circuit Court of Appeals amended the Comstock Law to allow doctors to distribute contraceptives across state lines. Eventually, physicians were awarded the ability to dispense birth control for the general well-being of their patients. At long last, Sanger crossed the line from obscenity to legitimate medical and scientific researcher. Ironically, in 1942, the Birth Control Federation of America, Sanger's offspring, changed its name to Planned Parenthood because the members considered the term "birth control" too controversial.

Having arrived at a plateau from which she could operate without fear of being arrested, Sanger, with suffrage leader Katherine McCormick, began funding the research of Gregory Goodwin Pincus, a geneticist at the Worcester Foundation for Experimental Biology in Massachusetts. Sanger was convinced that an oral contraceptive, The Pill, was the best course for women. When the pill was finally marketed in 1959, she was over eighty years old.

In 1965, the Supreme Court issued a directive that states could not prohibit married couples from using birth control. Although she was incapacitated by several heart attacks and dependent on the painkillers and sleeping pills prescribed for her as a consequence, Sanger heard the news later in the same year that the court had declared the use of contraception a Constitutional right (*Griswold v. Connecticut*). Jubilant, she sat up in bed and drank champagne through a straw. Giving way to age and illness, Sanger died on September 6, 1966 and was buried in Fishkill, New York. Gloria Steinem, activist and publisher, in writing about Sanger, noted that the "Constitutionally guaranteed right to privacy [became] as important to women's equality as the vote."

Some of her contemporaries and later historians attempted to discredit Sanger and her work as motivated by publicity seeking or disapproved of her because of her connection to eugenics, which was, unfortunately, employed by later users as a means of ethnic cleansing. However, science fiction author H.G. Wells penned in 1931: "When the history of our civilization is written, it will be a biological history, and Margaret Sanger will be its heroine."

FOR FURTHER READING

Chesler, Ellen. *Woman of Valor: Margaret Sanger and the Birth Control Movement in America.* New York: Simon & Schuster, 1992; Katz, Esther. *The Selected Papers of Margaret Sanger, Vol. II.* Champaign: University of Illinois Press, 2007; Sanger, Margaret. *Margaret Sanger: An Autobiography.* New York: W.W. Norton & Company, 1938.

FRANCES ELIZABETH WILLARD
(1839–1898)

Called the most eloquent and respected voice of the women's social justice movement in the late nineteenth century, Frances Willard brought a broad and innovative vision to the movement. An educator, a lobbyist, a speaker, and an expert in public relations, Willard produced greater numbers of colleagues to fight for woman's suffrage than any other single person. As president of the Woman's Christian Temperance Union (WCTU), she was the leader of thousands who were eager to change their communities and their world.

The middle child of Josiah Flint, a farmer, and Mary Thompson Hill, a schoolteacher, Frances Willard was born in Churchville, New York, a small farming community near Rochester, on September 28, 1839. When she was three, the family moved first to Oberlin, Ohio, then to a farm near Janesville, Wisconsin. In 1848, Josiah was elected to the state legislature in Wisconsin. The family was dedicated to having their children educated but due in part to their rural location, the children were home schooled with neighbor children through high school. As a child, Frances idolized her brother Oliver and spent most of her free time following him around and engaging in the same pursuits. She also kept a daily journal to improve her writing skills.

On reaching college age, Frances attended the Female College of Milwaukee for a year then transferred to the Evanston College for Ladies in Illinois. In 1859, she was graduated with a bachelor's degree in science as the class valedictorian. She worked several years as a teacher for the Pittsburgh Female College in Pennsylvania and the Genesee Wesleyan Seminary in New York. Although she received several proposals during the time, she rejected marriage and children, feeling that both deserved protection but refusing to surrender her independence.

Following a three-year world tour, financed by the wealthy father of her friend Kate Jackson, Willard accepted the presidency of her alma mater, Evanston College for Ladies, in 1871. When Evanston merged with Northwestern University, she became the dean of women at the university as well as serving as a professor of aesthetics. In that position, she created an innovative approach to women's education by permitting women students to enroll in courses on the main university campus and in designing a plan to affiliate with Radcliffe and Barnard Colleges. She wanted the young women to be well educated, self-reliant, and politically astute. In addition to her administrative and faculty duties at the university, Willard contributed articles to the *Chicago Daily Post* and in 1873, she became a founding member of the Association for the Advancement of Women that encouraged placing more women into traditionally male professions, such as police work.

In 1874, Willard resigned her university post to become the national corresponding secretary of WCTU, which she helped found. Many of the early women activists were involved in temperance work, assuming that part of the treatment of their gender was attributable to excessive alcohol consumption and its effect on the men in their lives. At the time there were no legal limits on the percentages of alcohol content in beverages, no limits on how much a man could drink and, for women and children, there was neither protection from abuse nor any system of public welfare. Willard had personal reasons for affiliating with the WCTU; her brother and childhood idol was an alcoholic as were his sons for whom she assumed responsibility after his death. The only money she earned from the position was what she generated herself through speaking engagements; consequently, she traveled constantly, crossing the Atlantic several times to give presentations in Europe as well as within the continental United States. Throughout the journeys, she became known for her ability to compromise.

Because of her success in the position, Willard was elected president of the WCTU in 1879, at the time the largest organization of women in the United States with over two hundred thousand members gracing the roles and including participants in every state. Under her direction, the women followed parliamentary procedure, took leadership roles, and gained a sense of independence. The meetings appealed to the sight as well as to the ear and featured banners, flowers, music and, of course, speeches. Through carefully selected emotional appeals, called manipulation by some, she converted many to the cause of suffrage as a means of *protecting the home.* Although there were those who initially objected on religious grounds, Willard saw no division between faith and feminism. She declared that voting would bring empowerment and believed that although men and women had different skills, they should be allowed to cross gender lines if they had something to offer. On the other hand, she also contended that women were morally superior to men.

Under the auspices of the WCTU, Willard campaigned for changes in the laws regarding prostitution, primarily because girls as young as seven were being commissioned; worked for the development of Traveler's Aid to assist women in retaining purity, while seeking employment away from home; and encouraged the development of abuse shelters and mothers' clubs, the forerunner of Parent Teacher Associations. She also promoted sports for women and urged physical education for girls, illustrating her commitment by taking her own bicycle tour across Europe. While on that tour, she worked with General Booth of the Salvation Army to aid Armenian refugees who had escaped from Turkey.

Meanwhile, the main goals of the WCTU were going forward. In the early days of the organization, prohibition was not a primary aim; instead, it was a quest to maintain sobriety by educating people about the issues involved in excessive alcohol consumption and by providing clean drinking water near saloons as an alternative for working men. Although it was not her intention, the powerful liquor lobby was propelled to fight against any forwarding of woman's rights issues because of Willard's association with both prohibition and suffrage.

During the mid-1880s, Willard expanded the WCTU to a worldwide scope and served as president of a wider block of women activists, initiating a "Do-Everything Policy" that expanded the scope of the organization to include topics like labor, peace, and arbitration. She also joined the American Woman's Suffrage Association under Lucy Stone and served as associate editor of the *Woman's Journal*. Mounting a virtual army of thousands of women, she sent them into the field to collect signatures on suffrage petitions. Through the sheer numbers her call could assemble, she added respectability to the movement. She urged organization on the local level, reminding her charges that their votes could keep liquor under control in their communities and improve the overall morality.

Willard was also active in prison reform, advocating separate facilities for men and women. Continuing to convert her beliefs into publication, she published *Woman in the Pulpit* (1888), supporting woman's right to preach, and her autobiography, *Glimpses of Fifty Years* (1889). In 1895, Susan B. Anthony introduced Willard to a U.S. Senate committee as "a general with an army of 250,000."

In 1898, Willard suffered a fatal bout of influenza while visiting New York City. She died on February 17, 1898 and was buried in Chicago. Over thirty thousand people viewed her coffin in one day and a New York newspaper obituary noted, "No woman's name is better known in the English speaking world than that of Miss Willard, save that of England's great queen." She was the first woman to be featured on a statue in the U.S. Capitol Rotunda's National Statuary Hall, representing the state of Illinois.

FOR FURTHER READING

    Bordin, Ruth. *Frances Willard: A Biography*. Chapel Hill: University of North Carolina Press, 1986; Gifford, Carolyn, ed. *Writing Out My Heart: Selections from the Journal of Frances E. Willard, 1855–96*. Champaign: University of Illinois Press, 1995; Willard, Frances E. *Woman and Temperance: The Work and Workers of the Woman's Christian Temperance Union*. New York: Arno Press, 1972 (repr.)

CHARLOTTE ANNA PERKINS GILMAN (1860–1935)

Called the most influential woman thinker during the era before World War I, Charlotte Perkins Gilman had a direct influence on the woman's movement. Although not personally involved in the quest for suffrage, she was a keen observer and theorist of the social order and forced other women to question their lot in life. A prolific writer, she produced six works of nonfiction, eight novels, two hundred short stories, and hundreds of poems, plays, and essays.

Born on July 3, 1860, in Hartford, Connecticut, Charlotte had early exposure to diametrically opposing viewpoints. Her parents were both from prominent Rhode Island families that had contrasting opinions on the social and political issues of the day, including polarized views of the roles of women. Her father, Frederick Beecher Perkins, a librarian and magazine editor, sprang from the liberal Beecher heritage, while her mother Mary Fitch Westcott came from generations of conservatives. Her father left the family in 1859, providing only periodic financial support, and her mother was disengaged and emotionally distant. Thus, Charlotte spent much of her younger years in the company of her aunts, Harriet Beecher Stowe, Catherine Beecher, and Isabella Beecher Hooker, three of the most progressive women thinkers of their time. She spent her childhood observing these role models and happily painting and drawing. However, in 1874, her mother moved the family into cooperative housing with a group of divorced women. The women shared the household tasks and the care of their children, a situation which may have inspired Charlotte's later recommendation of communal living.

Pursuing her interest in the arts, Charlotte attended the Rhode Island School of Design from 1878 to 1883. To help fund her education, she gave private art lessons and created designs for advertising companies. After completing school, she worked as a greeting card artist. In addition, she was one of the first women to advocate physical training for women and participated in weight lifting, gymnastics, and running. For her, the effort to control her body was an effort to control her life. In 1884, she met and married a fellow artist, Walter Stetson, although she feared marriage would force her to give up her creative ambitions.

In 1885, Charlotte gave birth to a daughter, Katherine Beecher Stetson. Immediately following the event, she sank into total despair. Modern medicine might diagnose her condition as postpartum depression but in the nineteenth century, such reactions to motherhood were either unheard of or not discussed. She was put into the care of Doctor S. Weir Mitchell, who disapproved of strong-willed women and prescribed a rest cure. His prescription included total lack of stimulation, suppression of thought, and positively no writing for the balance of her life. After nearing insanity, produced by the cure and not by the disease, Charlotte concluded her illness was a direct result of her marriage and motherhood and removed herself from the situation.

She attended her first suffrage convention in 1886 and was stimulated by the intelligence of the women she met, particularly admiring Lucy Stone. Thus inspired, she contributed a suffrage column to the newspaper, *People,* over the next year. In 1892, her experience with postpartum depression shaped her short story, "The Yellow Wallpaper," an often anthologized piece that essentially began the canon of feminist fiction. Shortly after publication of the story, she obtained a divorce from Stetson and moved to Oakland, California.

Ducking out of the public view for four years, the author created the work that would guide the balance of her career and secure her place in the woman's movement. *Women and Economics,* published in 1898, solidified many of her social theories. She expounded that economic inequity created a condition for women that was equal to servitude. Because man was seen as the provider, he was the primary economic supply; thus, money equaled power and power equaled *power over.* Marriage, then, became a quid pro quo institution with women exchanging housework and favors for material support. In making domesticity less romantic, she implied that women were industrious but were compensated only through the good graces of man. Because women were traditionally opposed to tyranny and injustice, she believed that they should set the norms for society and objected to the idea that women who chose not to marry were seen as "unable to get a man." The work became a best seller and was translated into seven languages.

Based on the success of the book, Charlotte was offered a variety of public appearances as well as becoming active in organizing social reforms and feminist groups. Even though she was untrained as a social scientist, she was honored as one. She lectured across the United States and Britain, always pointing out that women had to live with the conflict between being independent and being acceptable. Men, she asserted, did not care for strong women. Her presentations included woman's perspective on work and family. Far ahead of her time, she concluded that men and women should share household chores and that women should be financially independent through working themselves. Advocating a socialist or communal approach to solutions, Charlotte endorsed doing away with nuclear families. She believed that if people lived in groups, sharing housework and child rearing, that each individual would be economically and emotionally independent and would feel validated.

While she was touring on the lecture circuit, her ex-husband married her best friend, Grace Ellery Channing, and the couple asked Charlotte to give up custody of her daughter, Katherine, which she did. Hearing of her action and of her daughter's resentment of the *abandonment,* the media attacked, creating a scandal. The negative press did not affect her speaking engagements, however, and she was on the road for most of the next five years. Everywhere she went, she saw women who were unfulfilled in their roles and presented herself as an organizer for self-respect and economic independence, qualities she considered a woman's basic rights.

In 1900, she married her first cousin, George Houghton Gilman, an attorney in New York City, who was supportive of her work. She started a feminist magazine, the *Forerunner,* in 1909, although she objected to the label *feminist* because it was a word created by men. The magazine had a paid circulation of almost 1,500. As the only author in the periodical, she focused her editorial content on raising the economic and social standards for women, including her forward-thinking theory that housewives should be paid for their work. Lasting until 1916, the magazine also serialized several of her novels, including the Utopian work, *Herland,* featuring a society populated only by women who reproduced without the aid of men. The book was likely influenced by her belief in Nationalism, a reform movement based on Edward Bellamy's Utopian socialist romance, *Looking Backward.* While continuing to write, Gilman cofounded the Women's Peace Party with activist Jane Addams.

Gilman believed that if children were socialized differently, gender roles would not be so limiting. In other words, if young men were not given toy soldiers and plastic guns to play with and if young women were not given dolls and easy bake ovens, their perceptions of the societal expectations for their adulthood would be different. In anticipating modern feminism, she continued to question the impact of biological differences on gender.

After her husband's death in 1934, Gilman was diagnosed with inoperable breast cancer. Having spent the majority of her life attempting to be in control of her actions, she committed suicide by covering her face with a rag soaked in chloroform rather than facing a pain ridden death. Her final note stated simply that she preferred chloroform to cancer.

She had penned her autobiography in 1925 with the understanding that it would be published only after her death. *The Living of Charlotte Perkins Gilman* (1935) showed her public image as a role model for all women, while her diaries revealed her self-doubt. Carrie Chapman Catt called Gilman, "the most original and challenging mind which the movement produced."

FOR FURTHER READING

Gilman, Charlotte Perkins. *The Living of Charlotte Perkins Gilman: An Autobiography.* New York: D. Appleton-Century Company, 1935; Lane, Ann J. *To Herland and Beyond: The Life and Work of Charlotte Perkins Gilman.* Charlottesville: University Press of Virginia, 1997.

OLYMPIA BROWN (1835–1926)

Olympia Brown was one of the first women to be awarded a college degree (1863), one of the first women ordained as a Universalist minister, and one of the few original suffragists who lived to vote in the 1920 election.

Born in Prairie Ronde, Michigan, Brown was the daughter of Asa B. Brown and Lephia Olympia, farmers, who firmly believed in the power of education for their children. She was admitted to Mount Holyoke Female Seminary in Massachusetts in 1854. However, feeling that the school placed too many restrictions on her personal freedom, in 1856, Brown transferred to Antioch College in Yellow Springs, Ohio, one of the first coeducational institutions in the country. Antioch was progressive in a variety of ways, inviting a variety of innovative speakers to campus. One of those speakers was Antoinette Brown, the first publicly recognized woman minister, who inspired Olympia to follow in her footsteps.

Having thus determined her path, Olympia investigated admittance to schools of theology and was accepted at St. Lawrence University in Canton, New York. Although she excelled at her course work and completed the program, the school refused to ordain her as a minister because she was a woman. Not without controversy, she ultimately gained ordination through the Northern Association of Universalists in 1863, the first woman in the United States to receive the full approval of a denomination. A year later, Brown was given her first full-time ministry in Weymouth Landing, Massachusetts. To secure her position and improve her profession, she studied public speaking, acquiring a reputation for her pulpit rhetoric.

In 1866, Brown met Susan B. Anthony and attended her first woman's rights meeting. After becoming a charter member in the association, she adopted an active role in the woman's rights movement and, on leave from her parish, she became an integral part of the state suffrage campaign in Kansas in 1867. Despite traveling for twenty to fifty miles a day in harrowing weather conditions, hostile reception on her arrival, and very little rest, she presented more than three hundred speeches for suffrage during the tour.

The amendment was defeated but Brown was not. On returning east, she cofounded the New England Suffrage Association.

In 1873, Brown married John Henry Willis, a businessman and publisher, but retained her maiden name. The couple relocated to Wisconsin, where she invested time in the state's suffrage campaign. Wisconsin had granted women the right to vote on matters pertaining to education but Brown encouraged her confederates to attempt voting in other elections. When her vote was declined in a city election in 1887, she filed a civil suit that was ultimately dismissed.

As opposed to many of the others in the movement and in the nation, Brown viewed her work with the church and her work for women as inseparable and without conflict. However, attempting to balance both professions and the demands of her family became burdensome and in 1887, she resigned from the ministry to devote more time to the woman's movement, where she served as vice president of the National Woman's Suffrage Association and founded the Federal Suffrage Association in 1892 to push for a federal amendment.

Believing that education was the key to gender equality, she worked tirelessly to encourage higher education institutions to admit women. She was also vocal about temperance and the consequent crime as a result of alcoholism as well as the repeal of capital punishment. As an activist, she demonstrated with the Woman's Party and discouraged by Woodrow Wilson's lack of attention to the issue, she publicly burned his speeches in front of the White House.

Once the suffrage amendment was secure and she had cast her first legal vote, Brown became one of the founding members of the Women's International League for Peace and Freedom. She died in Baltimore, Maryland, at the home of her daughter, on October 23, 1926.

FOR FURTHER READING

Brown, Olympia. *Acquaintances, Old and New, among Reformers.* Milwaukee, WI: S.E. Tate, 1911; Greene, Dana, ed. *Suffrage and Religious Principle: Speeches and Writings of Olympia Brown.* Metuchen, NJ: Scarecrow Press, 1983; Zink-Sawyer, Beverly A. "From Preachers to Suffragists: Enlisting the Pulpit in the Early Movement for Woman's Rights." *The American Transcendental Quarterly* 14 (September 2000): 193.

MATILDA JOSLYN GAGE (1826–1898)

The third member of the "triumvirate of the radical wing," Matilda Joslyn Gage served as one of the editors of the six-volume opus, *A History of Woman Suffrage*, with Elizabeth Cady Stanton and Susan B. Anthony and first published in 1887. She was also one of the founding members of the National Woman Suffrage Association (NWSA) and served as an officer in the New York State branch of that organization.

Born in Cicero, New York on March 24, 1826, Gage was the only child of Hezekiah Joslyn, a medical doctor, and Helen Leslie. Her father was an abolitionist and a suffragist and the young woman was exposed to activism at an early age. The family home was not only a meeting place for the intellectuals and radicals of the era but also a stop on the Underground Railroad, which provided safe passage into Canada for escaped slaves. Her father provided her early education until she was enrolled in the Clinton Liberal Institute in New York. In 1845, she married Henry H. Gage, a dry goods merchant, with whom she had five children.

Gage joined the woman's movement in 1852, when she gave her first speech on the lack of legal rights for women at the third National Woman's Rights Convention in Syracuse, New York. By 1869, she was vice president of NWSA and secretary of the New York State suffrage group. Primarily a writer, Gage's work focused on the omission of women's accomplishments in the histories of the day and emphasized the number of inventions created by women.

In the 1870s, she became a champion against the unjust treatment of Native Americans; consequently, she was adopted into the Wolf Clan of the Mohawk Indians and renamed "Sky Carrier." She wrote of the superior government featured in the Iroquois Confederacy where men and women were considered equal.

From 1878 to 1881, she owned and edited the *National Citizen and Ballot Box*, which became the vehicle to deliver the message of the NWSA; the paper also serialized *A History of Woman Suffrage*. In 1880, when the NWSA concentrated on acts of civil disobedience, Gage attempted to vote for Ulysses S. Grant in the 1872 presidential election and although she was unsuccessful in that endeavor, she did become the first woman to vote under a state law that permitted women to participate in school board elections.

In 1885, Gage aided Stanton in the creation of *The Woman's Bible,* the gender-reversed interpretation of scripture. She was noted for her pioneering work on the origin of woman's oppression, believing that prehistoric matriarchies were replaced through the advent of Christian patriarchy and that religion was instrumental in denigrating women. By the late-1880s, she had launched a frontal assault on the church, forming the Woman's National Liberal Union. Considered the most radical woman's group in the country at that time, the group was closely monitored by the federal government, including the screening of all their mails. The work she considered her most important, *Woman, Church and State,* was published in 1893.

Unlike many of her contemporaries, Gage viewed the vote as merely a stage in the fight against oppression. She expressed the belief that only correcting the underlying causes of inequality could ever result in true equality. Due to her views and her attacks on organized religion, she spent the majority of her latter years estranged from those who had been her friends and colleagues. Gage died in Chicago, Illinois on March 18, 1898, while visiting her daughter Maud Baum, the wife of *Wizard of Oz* creator, L. Frank Baum.

FOR FURTHER READING

Brammer, Leila. *Excluded from Suffrage History: Matilda Joslyn Gage, Nineteenth Century American Feminist.* Westport, CT: Greenwood Press, 2000; Gage, Matilda Joslyn. *Woman, Church and State.* Amherst, NY: Humanity Books, 2002 (repr.)

MARY ASHTON RICE LIVERMORE
(1820–1905)

Dubbed the "Queen of the American Platform," Mary Livermore was one of the key speakers for the early woman's rights movement. As many of her contemporaries, she came to the realization that all persons deserved to be free through her work with the abolition of slavery.

Born in Boston, Massachusetts on December 19, 1820, Mary was the daughter of Timothy Rice, a day laborer, and Zebiah Vose Glover Ashton. As Calvinist Baptists, her parents were strict and structured and much of her childhood was spent thinking about the consequences of sin.

At only fourteen years of age, the young woman attended a Baptist Female Seminary in Charlestown, Massachusetts, and took a position there as a teacher two years later. However, under the influence of abolitionist, Angelina Grimké, Mary resigned her post in Massachusetts, traveled south to tutor children on a Virginia plantation, and witnessed the mistreatment of slaves first hand. The experience ignited her pull toward activism, becoming first a radical abolitionist and then, a suffragist.

In 1845 she married Daniel Parker Livermore, a minister of the Universalist faith who was noted for his liberal views, and relocated with him to Chicago, Illinois. By the time of her marriage, she had published one book, *The Children's Army* (1844), and continued her writing career, penning *A Mental Transformation* in 1848. The latter novel contained semiautobiographical elements as it featured a woman protagonist who renounced her strict Calvinist beliefs. In addition to her fiction, Livermore served as associate editor for her husband's Universalist paper, the *New Covenant*. As a representative of that paper, she was the only woman reporter at the Republican national convention in 1860. In addition to her writing, she was instrumental in establishing a Home for Aged Women, a Hospital for Women and Children, and the Home for the Friendless that cared for poverty-stricken women and children.

While she and her husband, Daniel, were living in Chicago, a citywide cholera epidemic broke out and rather than leaving the region like many others in her community, Mary became one of the principal organizers for removal of the healthy and arranged for medical treatment for those who had the disease. As a consequence of her newly acquired managerial skills, she was recruited as a coordinator for the U.S. Sanitary Commission during the Civil War, where she mobilized volunteers, lent support to Union soldiers, and conducted fundraising campaigns for the Commission. In 1862, her leadership skills lead to her appointment as an agent of the Northwest Commission that incorporated six Midwestern states. In that position, she taught fundraising and bandage rolling skills to women members of over three thousand aid societies.

During the war years, Mary gained awareness of how little the opinion of women held sway on political issues. In 1868, she attended her first woman's suffrage convention in Chicago and by 1869, she had become the editor of the suffrage newspaper, *Agitator* that eventually merged with the *Woman's Journal.*

Having been successful in other ventures, Mary Livermore took to the lecture circuit, where she served as a mainstay for over twenty-five years, speaking with no manuscript or notes. Her most popular presentation was entitled "What Shall We Do with Our Daughters?" that encouraged women to look to the younger generation for progress. She served as the first president of the Association for Advancement of Women in 1873, the first president of the American Woman's Suffrage Association in 1875, and as president of the Massachusetts Woman's Christian Temperance Union for twenty years.

Livermore died in Melrose, Massachusetts, on May 23, 1905.

FOR FURTHER READING

Livermore, Mary Ashton Rice. *The Story of My Life: or, The Sunshine and Shadow of Seventy Years.* Hartford, CT: A.D. Worthington, 1899; Venet, Wendy Hamand. *A Strong-Minded Woman: The Life of Mary Livermore.* Amherst, NY: University of Massachusetts Press, 2005.

CARRIE CHAPMAN CATT
(1859–1947)

More than any other woman, except perhaps Susan B. Anthony, Carrie Chapman Catt served as the catalyst that secured woman's right to vote. Labeled the "New General" of the movement following her success in the Colorado referendum, Catt reaped a bountiful harvest of firsts for women, including being one of the first women in the country to be appointed as a superintendent of schools, one of the first to work as a newspaper reporter, and one of the first to establish formal training programs for woman's rights activists.

Born Carrie Clinton Lane, Catt was the second of the three children of Lucius Lane and Maria Clinton of West Potsdam, New York. Both of her parents were graduated from high school, which was an almost unprecedented achievement for that era. Coupled with her parents' respect for education, Carrie demonstrated a hereditary disposition toward independence, a gift, perhaps, from her great grandmother Abigail who had left an abusive husband, decades before such behavior was heard of much less tolerated. Shortly after their wedding in 1855, the Lanes migrated west, settling first in Cleveland, Ohio, where Lucius purchased a partnership in a coal business. Deciding quickly that the pace of city life was not for them, the family relocated to a farm in Ripon, Wisconsin and, eventually, settled in Charles City, Iowa, when Carrie was seven.

Self-sufficient by the time she was eleven and a voracious reader, Carrie attended elementary school in a one-room schoolhouse. As a young woman, her favorite pastime was debating the issues of the day and she loved to listen to her father and two brothers discuss politics, frequently begging to attend campaign rallies with them. When she was thirteen, she watched as her father and his friends prepared to go to the polls to cast their ballots in the presidential election. Noting that her mother was not getting dressed to accompany them, she asked why; loud laughter from the men was her response. Her father informed her that voting was man's work and woman's work was in the kitchen.

After accelerating through the curriculum in only three years, Carrie was graduated from high school in 1877. During her time there, she cultivated many of the ideas that would guide her later path; she was particularly captivated by the theories of Charles Darwin and embraced the philosophy of evolution. As a young idealist, she envisioned the species evolving toward a free and peaceful society and would later emphasize the evolutionary progress of the relationship between men and women.

Even though her parents were in favor of education, her father refused to pay for her to attend college. Undeterred and determined to continue her training, Carrie invested a year in teaching for the public school system in order to save enough money for tuition at Iowa State Agricultural College. As a bonus, she received college equivalency hours for her work in addition to the tuition monies she earned. Once enrolled, she sustained her previous academic excellence, while earning her way through school by shelving books in the library and cleaning in the college kitchen for eight cents an hour.

Iowa State offered a program for men students, which was comparable to the modern Reserve Officers' Training Corps (ROTC). Since the elective course focused on leadership and problem solving, Carrie believed the training would benefit women students as well as their male counterparts. She convinced the administration to initiate an equivalent program for women. Company "G," standing for "Girls," became the first of its kind in the country; in fact, women were not universally accepted into ROTC programs until 1972. In 1880, Carrie was awarded a degree in science, was class valedictorian and the only woman among the eighteen graduates.

Initially wanting to practice law, Carrie worked part time in an attorney's office in Charles City, while simultaneously teaching high school in Mason City, Iowa, to provide enough money for law school. In the interim, however, she discovered she enjoyed teaching more than law and altered her career path. Eventually, she was appointed principal of the school and in 1883, she was elected superintendent of all the schools in Mason City, one of the first women in the country to hold such a post.

In 1883, Carrie wandered into the newspaper office of the *Mason City Republican,* seeking a venue in which to publish her students' writing. She was ushered into the office of the paper's editor, Leo Chapman, who agreed to run the students' work in the paper, although he was obviously more impressed with their teacher. Only two weeks after their initial meeting, the two were engaged. In 1885, after she and Chapman were married, Carrie was forced to resign from teaching because, at the time, married women were discouraged from following a profession; instead, they were expected to assume the time-honored duties of wife and mother. Carrie, on the other hand, became her husband's business partner, assistant editor, and contributor to the paper. As a columnist, she penned "Woman's World," a weekly advice column that, despite the title, did not feature recipes or homemaking hints; her focus was on gaining rights for women in general and, in particular, woman's right to suffrage. Matching his wife's enthusiasm for tackling sensitive issues, Leo Chapman was sued for libel, following a cruel attack on a local politician. After losing the case, he was forced to liquidate his assets, including selling the newspaper, and subsequently journeyed to San Francisco to seek work. Carrie left to join her husband in 1886 but on the train in route to California, she received a telegram that Leo had contracted typhoid fever and before she reached her destination, a second telegram informed her that he had died.

Seeing no future in returning to Iowa without work or her husband, Carrie boarded with an aunt in San Francisco. She quickly found employment as the first woman reporter for a local paper but resigned after being sexually harassed by a male coworker. While she was deciding what to do next, she bumped into George Catt, a college friend from Iowa, who was working as a civil engineer in his own bridge building firm. Catt encouraged Carrie to consider public speaking as a career and, after hearing of her recent experience, he suggested she do something to aid other women in the same predicament. After taking Catt's advice and preparing a series of lectures on "Great Women in History," Carrie returned to Iowa. At that time, the only venues open to women speakers were local churches and although the doors were opened to such gatherings, the presentations were frequently viewed with contempt. Often, before Carrie began her presentations, the local minister would offer his regrets about his decision to allow her to speak and lead vocal prayers that God would grant the congregation the inability to believe what they were about to hear.

As many of her contemporaries, Carrie joined the Iowa branch of the Woman's Christian Temperance Union (WCTU), the largest organization of women in the nineteenth century, and was appointed to head its section on woman's suffrage. Although some of the members of the WCTU disapproved of the tactics of the suffragists, most believed that gaining the vote would aid in eradicating the misuse of alcohol they considered primarily responsible for spousal and child abuse. Using her writing, oratorical, and organizational skills, Carrie urged a universal approach to the widely scattered fragments of the two movements. In 1889, she was elected secretary of the Iowa Woman Suffrage Association and in 1890 she served as a delegate to and speaker at the National American Woman Suffrage Association (NAWSA) in Washington, DC, shortly after the two organizations, one previously headed by Lucy Stone and Henry Blackwell and the other under the auspices of Elizabeth Cady Stanton and Susan B. Anthony, were reconciled and reunited.

While engaged in the work within the suffrage organizations, Carrie corresponded with George Catt, who had been transformed from college chum to mentor to persistent suitor. After some negotiation, they were married in Seattle, Washington, in June 1890. The negotiation produced a prenuptial agreement, which guaranteed Carrie two months in the spring and two months in the fall to travel to various spots where there was an interest in promoting woman's suffrage. Catt also agreed to help finance the reform efforts since the majority of the work Carrie did for the groups was unpaid. Consequently, immediately after their honeymoon, she joined Susan B. Anthony in South Dakota, where they bucked a powerful liquor lobby in order to be heard. Antagonistic public sentiment that suffragists and temperance advocates were closely aligned caused liquor manufacturers, distributors, and sellers to feel threatened by both.

Between 1892, when the Catts moved to New York, and 1895, Carrie was on the road more than she was home, despite the prenuptial agreement that afforded her four months to travel each year. In 1892, Susan B. Anthony asked Carrie to address Congress regarding the proposed suffrage amendment. She prepared a carefully crafted speech for the Judiciary Committee of the House of Representatives but despite her rhetorical skill, the men made no effort to suppress yawns and a few even fell asleep. The next year, she toured the mining camps of Colorado. Notwithstanding the ruggedness of the terrain and the accommodations, Carrie felt more welcome there than she had in Washington, DC. Even the men in the camps, mostly immigrants, understood her predicament and applauded her enthusiasm for change. Through her efforts and the efforts of others, Colorado became the first state to pass a public referendum that gave women the right to vote, predated only by Wyoming (1890) where statehood was granted with that provision. Based on the Colorado campaign, Catt was labeled "the new General" of the movement.

On the heels of that victory, Carrie was placed in charge of all field organizing for NAWSA. Although there was great opposition from those involved in vice, liquor sales, and big businesses that exploited child labor and underpaid women, she marshaled the cause in untiring fashion. In the South, the site of much of the antisuffragist sentiment, she organized clubs and appointed delegates to the convention in Atlanta. To secure that stronghold, she initiated formal classes for women to teach methods of grassroots organizing. She stated that "agitation for a cause is excellent; education is better; but organization is the only assurance of final triumph."

By 1900, she had traveled thirteen thousand miles and visited twenty states. That year, Susan B. Anthony retired as president of NAWSA and in an unexpected move, she nominated Carrie Chapman Catt as her replacement. Catt accepted the offer, noting there could be no true *leader* except Anthony. She served in that capacity for four years. When George Catt became seriously ill in 1904, Carrie resigned in order to care for the man who had generously allowed her to be *married to the movement* for so long. After his death, she lived with her friend and fellow suffragist, Mary Garrett Hay.

Over the next few years, Carrie's mother and brother also passed away, followed closely by the death of her mentor, Susan B. Anthony. Overcome with grief and depression, Carrie was encouraged to travel abroad, which she could afford thanks to the generous amount of money George had left her in his will.

In 1911, she undertook a world tour through Europe and Asia, founding suffrage organizations and observing the conditions of women in various countries. After attending the International Woman Suffrage Congress in Budapest, Hungary in 1913, Catt founded the International Woman Suffrage Alliance with affiliates in Australia, Denmark, Germany, Great Britain, Holland, Norway, Sweden, and the United States. As the first president, she served until 1923 and inaugurated a series of world conferences every two years.

Having garnered so much success internationally, Catt returned to New York to reinvigorate the push for a national amendment that would secure woman suffrage. She established a school to train volunteers in organizing, public speaking, parliamentary procedure, and the history of the movement. In 1914, wealthy publisher and a dedicated admirer of Catt's work, Mrs. Frank Leslie, left Carrie two million dollars in her will. Although the will was contested throughout eight years of court battles, Carrie ultimately claimed a large percentage of the original bequest. With the inheritance, she opened a school for suffrage workers in Canton, New York, and initiated the Leslie Woman Suffrage Commission, Inc. to create a media barrage that subsequently assured victory in New York State.

In 1915, Catt was pressured to resume the presidency of NAWSA, which was in danger of splitting into factions once again. Ironically, the divergent opinions were the same as those that had caused the initial riff in the group: those who believed with Catt that the most effective strategy was to work in individual states to alter opinions one state at a time and those who sided with Alice Paul, who advocated working only at the federal level. Although Carrie acquiesced and accepted the appointment, she was torn between her interests in suffrage and her work for world peace. Despite Carrie's diplomatic efforts, Paul and her contingent left NAWSA, forming the Congressional Union, later the Woman's Party. In an attempt to merge her areas of interest, Catt helped to establish the Woman's Peace Party in 1915, believing that the potential for peace would be greater once women had the vote.

In 1916, Catt convened an emergency meeting of NAWSA in Atlantic City, New Jersey to unveil her "Winning Plan" campaign that mandated working for suffrage on both the state and the federal level, simultaneously. Interest in the group was lagging and she knew it was imperative to raise morale and inject new energy into the movement. Her carefully crafted speech employed the word "victory" fourteen times and repeated the phrase "the woman's hour has struck" five times. The presentation was applauded as a tactical masterpiece that would assure victory in securing a federal amendment as the only way. At the conclusion of the presentation, Catt called for one million dollars to support the year's work, nearly all of which was pledged before those attending vacated the hall.

In one of the ultimate ironies of her life, considering that she was an avowed pacifist, Catt announced the Association's support of President Woodrow Wilson and World War II and offered her members as volunteers for the cause. It was a strictly political move; if the woman's movement had opposed the war, they would have been viewed as unpatriotic by the president and Congress. The maneuver bore fruit for when the war ended in 1918, the Congress of the United States, at long last, passed the Nineteenth Amendment awarding women the right to vote.

The work was not done, however, for the Amendment needed to be ratified by thirty-six states in order to become law. Anticipating passage, Catt created the League of Women Voters to hand out bipartisan political information during NAWSA's Fiftieth Anniversary "Jubilee Convention" in St. Louis in 1919. On August 26, 1920, Tennessee, by a slim margin, became the thirty-sixth state to ratify the Nineteenth Amendment, granting the franchise to twenty-seven million women. The battle had been won, seventy-two years after the first Woman's Rights Convention in Seneca Falls, New York. By the time victory was assured, Catt had logged over one hundred thousand miles and had delivered more than seven thousand speeches.

Having achieved victory on one front, Carrie devoted the remainder of her life to her other primary passion, world peace, working for pacifism and disarmament. In 1925, she established the Committee on the Cause and Cure of War and served as its chair until 1932. Her pacifism irked many and, although she was likely unaware of the surveillance, her work was under scrutiny by the fledgling Federal Bureau of Investigation (FBI) between 1927 and 1929. Comprising fifty-seven pages, the documents noted her associations as radical, unpatriotic, and a threat to the nation's welfare.

Following World War I, Catt campaigned for the U.S. participation in the League of Nations and was a strong advocate of the Kellogg-Briand Pact. Also called the Pact of Paris, the Kellogg-Briand, finalized in 1928, was an international treaty renouncing war that was signed by sixty-two nations. In 1933, when Adolf Hitler became chancellor of Germany and opened the first concentration camp, Carrie helped establish the Protest Committee of Non-Jewish Women Against the Persecution of Jews in Germany and lobbied Congress for asylum for Jewish refugees. As a consequence of that work, she was the first woman to be awarded the American Hebrew Medal.

When she was eighty-eight years old, Carrie Chapman Catt died of a heart attack at her home in New Rochelle, New York. Ironically, the turmoil that swirled around her during her life, including being accused of communism by members of the Daughters of the American Revolution and being investigated by the FBI, continued long after her death. In 1995, her alma mater, Iowa State University, dedicated the newly renovated Botany Hall in her name. A group of students, called the September 29th Movement, protested the action based on some of Catt's writing, which they interpreted as being racist, xenophobic, and elitist. Under intense media scrutiny, the protests continued for some months until Iowa State's administration stated that the argumentative statements were taken out of written and historical context and that the name of the building would stand. Somewhere, Carrie Chapman Catt smiled.

FOR FURTHER READING

Burnett, Constance Buel. *Five for Freedom: Lucretia Mott, Elizabeth Cady Stanton, Lucy Stone, Susan B. Anthony, Carrie Chapman Catt*. New York: Greenwood Press, 1968; Huxman, Susan Schultz. "Perfecting the Rhetorical Vision of Woman's Rights: Elizabeth Cady Stanton, Anna Howard Shaw, and Carrie Chapman Catt." *Women's Studies in Communication* 23 (Fall 2000): 307–36; Keller, Kristin Thoennes. *Carrie Chapman Catt: A Voice for Women*. Minneapolis, MN: Compass Point Books, 2006.

ALICE STOKES PAUL (1885–1977)

Perhaps the most vocal and charismatic of the suffragists, Alice Paul followed the British model of highly visible public protest, organizing rallies, marches, and vigils, primarily in Washington, DC. Arrested and incarcerated for her efforts, she was likely responsible for swaying public opinion to the side of the woman's rights movement as well as applying the consequent political pressure to amend the Constitution in favor of woman's right to vote.

Alice Paul was the firstborn child of William Mickle Paul, a banker and businessman, and Tacie Parry of Moorestown, New Jersey. Her parents were Hixsite Quakers, thus, firm believers in gender equality and education for women. In fact, her mother was involved in the early phases of the woman's movement and frequently took the young girl with her to suffrage meetings.

After graduating at the top of her class from the Friends (Quaker) School, Alice attended Swarthmore College, an institution founded by her grandfather. She was graduated in 1905 with a bachelor's degree in biology and was awarded a College Settlement Association fellowship to attend graduate school at the New York School of Philanthropy (now Columbia University). Following a year in New York, Paul transferred to the University of Pennsylvania and earned a master's degree in sociology in 1907. While in Pennsylvania, she was offered a scholarship to study social work at the Woodbrooke Settlement and the University of Birmingham in England.

In England, Paul met Christabel Pankhurst, the daughter of the radical British feminist, Emmeline Pankhurst, both of whom advocated "taking the woman's movement to the streets." Joining their ranks, Paul participated in public protests, including hunger strikes. She was arrested multiple times and served three terms in the English penal system, each of which only reaffirmed her militancy. Although she was working with various charitable organizations in London and other cities, she continued to participate in woman's rights demonstrations and joined the Women's Social and Political Union.

In 1910, Paul returned to the United States determined to add fire to the quest for the ballot. She joined the National American Woman Suffrage Association (NAWSA) and was appointed head of the Congressional Committee, although there was no office, no budget, and minimal support. On March 3, 1913, the eve of Woodrow Wilson's inauguration as twenty-eighth president of the United States, Paul and others organized a parade from the Capitol to the White House. Over eight thousand women, both professional and working classes, marched down the street or rode on floats, each wearing white, brandishing banners and calling for the vote. Around the parade there flowed almost one-half million people, including both genders, who responded to the protest with verbal harassment and occasional objects lobbed at the marchers. Washington police did nothing to establish crowd control or to stop the mob attack and finally federal troops had to be called in to restore peace. Although it took the women six hours to complete the route of a few blocks, they persisted without breaking rank. Despite evidence to the contrary, Paul labeled the parade a success, particularly since it shifted the publicity focus away from the inauguration and generated new national sympathy for the cause because of the way the marchers had been treated.

Enough public and press attention was paid to the march to initiate a meeting with President Wilson merely two weeks after he assumed office. Although he professed empathy, Wilson told Paul that the time was not right for initiating a discussion on woman suffrage. Not one to consider no as an appropriate answer, Paul scheduled another parade on April 7, the opening day of congressional sessions.

Although the majority of her efforts were directed toward organization during the period, Paul found time to earn a Doctor of Philosophy degree from the University of Pennsylvania in 1912 as well as a later Doctor of Civil Law degree from American University (1928). In 1914, Paul resigned from NAWSA, although some viewed the resignation as involuntary because the majority of organization members did not approve of her methodology. She, allied with Lucy Burns, formed the Congressional Union for Woman Suffrage, which became the Woman's Party in 1915 and was comprised of predominantly young, white, middle- and upper-class women. The group targeted other women, primarily in Western states, who had already gained the vote and encouraged them to use their political clout to hold Democrat politicians accountable and vote them out of office in the next election. Although her method produced results, campaigning against the current administration instead of seeking approval from both political parties was not necessarily the most expedient means of gaining support. The next year, the Congressional Union and the Woman's Party merged to create the National Woman's Party, loudly demanding that politicians address a Constitutional change for woman suffrage that Paul labeled the Susan B. Anthony Amendment.

In 1917, Paul and her cohorts began picketing in front of the White House. The Silent Sentinels, as they were tagged by the media, stood wordlessly by the gates, holding purple, white, and gold banners that offered such phrases as "Mr. President, what will you do for suffrage?" and "Mr. President, how long must women wait for liberty?" The women were the first persons in the country to wage a campaign of nonviolent civil disobedience and were the first political protest group to picket the White House. On the initial day of the picket, twelve women took up the banners but as the protest stretched out over eighteen months, more than a thousand stood by the gates, winter and summer, each night and day, except Sunday.

When the United States involvement in World War I appeared imminent, Paul and the National Woman's Party posed the question of how the president could fight to help disenfranchised people in Europe when there were still disenfranchised persons in the United States. Patriotic fervor reignited the antiprotestors and spectators once again assaulted the suffragists, both verbally and physically, accusing them of lack of patriotism. As usual, the police took no action to halt the hecklers; instead, in June, they began arresting the picketers for *obstructing traffic*. Initially, charges were dropped and the time the women spent in jail was short but as their activity continued, the situation changed. On October 20, 1917, Paul was arrested and sentenced to seven months confinement in the Occoquan Workhouse in Virginia. Thirty-three of her confederates were also convicted and joined her there where they were offered worm-infested food, no contact with the outside world, dirty blankets, and open toilets.

As the known instigator of the protests, Paul was separated from the other women and placed first in solitary confinement and then in the psychopathic ward. The guards deprived her of sleep, hoping to discredit her as insane from the *mania of persecution*. Paul reacted by refusing to eat, leading to a twenty-two day hunger strike and to the guards force-feeding her by pushing a tube down her throat and pouring raw eggs and other liquids into it. Once news of her treatment spread, public sentiment shifted to the plight of the women. Under the growing public outrage, politicians reneged and the women were released in November. The Court of Appeals overturned all convictions.

In 1918, President Wilson announced his support of an amendment guaranteeing women the right to vote. The resolution eased through the House of Representatives but was defeated in the Senate. Paul renewed her campaign to urge women voters to remove all antisuffragists from Congress in the fall election. When the resolution was presented a second time, it passed through the Senate, winning approval by one vote, and was sent to the states for ratification.

A tireless advocate, Paul was not content in winning suffrage in the United States. In the 1920s, she organized the World Woman's Party for Equal Rights in Geneva, Switzerland and worked closely with the League of Nations and the United Nations to garner universal rights for women. Although it did not reach Congress until 1970 and failed to win ratification, Paul penned the original Equal Rights Amendment (ERA) in 1923. Unfortunately, some of the ideas expressed in the ERA alienated many of her former supporters, among them African American and working women. In her later years, Paul was responsible for the UN Commission on the Status of Women in 1946 and active in the Peace Movement. At seventy-nine, she lobbied to add a gender discrimination clause to Title VII of the Civil Rights Act of 1964; hers was the only organization to do so.

Never married, Paul passed her elder years in a nursing home but still managed to attend protest rallies, including those against the war in Vietnam when she was in her eighties. In 1974, a stroke left her disabled and she died on July 9, 1977 of heart failure at age ninety-two.

In 2004, the recounting of Paul's efforts was moved into the arena of popular culture through the release of the HBO film, "Iron Jawed Angels," which recounted the era of White House protests and incarceration, including the graphic unfolding of the force-feeding of prisoners. Her memory was further preserved when Swarthmore College dedicated a dormitory in her name in 2005. Due in part to fundraising efforts by the National Museum of Women's History, a statue Paul commissioned of Mott, Anthony, and Stanton stands strong in the Rotunda of the Capitol in Washington, DC.

FOR FURTHER READING

Adams, Katherine. *Alice Paul and the American Suffrage Campaign.* Urbana: University of Illinois Press, 2007; Borda, Jennifer L. "The Woman Suffrage Parades of 1910–1913: Possibilities and Limitations of an Early Feminist Rhetorical Strategy." *Western Journal of Communication* 66 (Winter 2002): 25–52; Butler, Amy. *Two Paths to Equality: Alice Paul and Ethel M. Smith in the ERA Debate, 1921–1929.* Albany: State University of New York, 2002.

JEANETTE RANKIN (1880–1973)

Every period needs a transitional figure and for the history of the woman's rights movement, Jeanette Rankin filled that role. Because of her longevity, spanning nearly a century, she was prominent in both first- and second-wave feminism. In addition, she was the first woman elected to the Congress of the United States, several years before women were even allowed to vote.

Born in Grant Creek, Montana, near Missoula, on June 11, 1880, Jeanette was the eldest of eleven children. Her father, John, was a rancher and lumber merchant and her mother, Olive Pickering, was a former schoolteacher. The young woman's early years were spent on the ranch before the family relocated to Missoula. In 1902, she was graduated from Montana State University with a bachelor's degree in biology. Before deciding on her career path, she spent time as a school teacher, a seamstress, and a furniture designer. However, when her father died in 1904, he left her enough money to be self-supporting for life.

Her professional indecision disappeared while she was visiting one of her brothers, a student at Harvard University, in 1904. While touring the city of Boston, Jeanette was deeply moved by the poverty and dismal standards of living in the slum areas and was inspired to go into social work. To prepare for the field, she took an ethnographic approach and deciding to examine the problem firsthand, she moved into a San Francisco settlement house as a patron. After four months of close observation of the living conditions at the institution, she entered the New York School of Philanthropy (now the Columbia School of Social Work) in 1908 to pursue an advanced degree. In 1909, she traveled back to the west coast and spent a few months as a social worker in a children's home. Deciding that children were not her calling, she briefly enrolled at the University of Washington in Seattle.

In 1910, however, a new interest changed her educational plans for Rankin was introduced to the woman's movement. She worked as a movement organizer for four years, first in Washington State and then in California and Montana. In 1915, during a prolonged visit to New Zealand, she repeated her previous research tactics and worked as a seamstress to gain personal knowledge of social conditions for factory employees. While in New Zealand, she was surprised that women were allowed to vote, a right having been granted in 1893.

Following her return to the United States, Rankin moved to New York and joined the New York Woman Suffrage Party. In 1912, she was elected field secretary for the National American Woman Suffrage Association (NAWSA) and participated in the 1913 suffrage march in Washington on the eve of Woodrow Wilson's inauguration.

By 1914, Rankin determined her service would be more beneficial inside the political system rather than outside. She resigned from NAWSA, returned to Montana, and mounted a political campaign. In 1916, she was the first woman in the country to be elected to the U.S. Congress as well as the first woman elected to a national legislature in any western democracy. Ironically, her election came four years before women were even allowed to vote; interestingly, that fact indicated that she was elected by men, even though she campaigned for prohibition, child protection, health care for women and, of course, woman's right to the ballot.

After taking her seat in Washington, Rankin's first act was to introduce a bill that would allow women to have citizenship independent of their husbands. She drew on her notoriety to work for peace, woman's rights, and child welfare, using a weekly newspaper column as her forum. Four days after taking office, she voted against the U.S. entry into World War I. Consequently, she was criticized by her former colleagues in the woman's movement, particularly Carrie Chapman Catt. Catt noted that Rankin, as a national figure, was now speaking for all women and a vote against war would label them all as too sentimental. Suffrage groups canceled her speaking tours and the media questioned her decision-making ability. When she lost her bid for peace, Rankin joined the war effort by selling Liberty bonds to raise money and voted in favor of the military draft. In 1917, Rankin opened the congressional debate on the Susan B. Anthony Amendment, which was passed in the House of Representatives but defeated in the Senate. Over the next two years, she introduced legislation to appropriate funds for health clinics, for midwife education, and for home nurses to reduce infant mortality.

When the time came for reelection, the Montana Republican Party showed no interest in supporting her return to Washington, likely as a consequence of her pacifism. After losing the support of her party, she attempted to mount a campaign as an independent candidate but lost the election. Refusing to accept defeat, Rankin returned to Washington and spent the majority of the next twenty years as a lobbyist, representing factions such as the Women's International League for Peace and Freedom (WILPF), the National Consumers' League for mother and child health care, and the American Civil Liberties Union. After the war ended, she successfully campaigned for the Maternity and Infancy Protection Act (1921), the Independent Citizenship Act (1922), and the Child Labor Amendment (1924).

Having succeeded in aiding the passage of legislation she believed important, Rankin purchased a farm in Georgia and worked as field secretary for the WILPF. She formed the Georgia Peace Society and lobbied for an antiwar Constitutional amendment as well as for cooperation with the world court. She was offered a position as chair of peace studies at a Georgia College in 1935 but the media, after examining her political past, fought her nomination, calling her a communist. She sued the *Macon* newspaper for libel and won.

In 1939, Rankin returned to Montana and once again threw her hat into the political ring. She was reelected in 1940 on an antiwar ticket. By that time, there were six women in the House of Representatives and two in the Senate. Following the attack on Pearl Harbor, Congress was required to vote on whether or not the United States should enter into World War II. Rankin was the only delegate to register a negative response. As the representatives filed out of the chamber, they were met by a crowd of spectators and she had to hide from the mob in a telephone booth and be escorted home by police.

After 1943, having decided not to run for reelection, Rankin traveled extensively, visiting Turkey and India, where she met Mahatma Gandhi. On returning to the United States, she founded a commune for women on her Georgia farm, turning the property into a self-sufficient cooperative. On May 15, 1968, at eighty-seven, she led over five thousand women in a march on Washington to demand the U.S. withdraw from the Vietnam War. The group, known as the "Jeanette Rankin Brigade," marched again in 1970 with Rankin, then ninety years old, leading the crew.

Rankin died on May 18, 1973 in Carmel, California of natural causes. Her body was cremated and scattered over the Pacific Ocean. She willed her Watkinsville, Georgia farm to provide seed money for mature, unemployed women workers. The will established The Jeanette Rankin Foundation that offered annual educational grants to low-income women all across the United States.

When once asked the accomplishment of which she was most proud, Jeanette Rankin replied that she wanted to be "remembered as the only woman who ever voted to give all women the right to vote." In 1985, a bronze statue of her was added to the U.S. Capitol Statuary Hall, a permanent reminder of her conviction.

FOR FURTHER READING

Lopach, James J., and Jean A. Luckowski. *Jeanette Rankin: A Political Woman.* Boulder: University Press of Colorado, 2005; Smith, Norma. *Jeanette Rankin: America's Conscience.* Helena: Montana Historical Society Press, 2002.

PART II

SECOND- AND THIRD-WAVE FEMINISM: CIVIL RIGHTS TO THE INTERNET

INTRODUCTION

History does, indeed, repeat itself or it is, at the very least, cyclical. Some might even say it goes in circles. Although issues were varied, means were dissimilar, faces and certainly attire were altered in the decades between the first and second wave of feminism, activism and activists of the periods had many commonalities.

Following the passage of the Nineteenth Amendment in 1919 and its subsequent ratification the following year, many of the women who had fought so valiantly for the vote moved out of the public arena, content with their victories. A few lingered to assure their gains would be protected and to push for the passage of an Equal Rights Amendment (ERA) but, for the most part, women settled into silenced contentment, contributing to their families' and communities' welfare and doing their part for the war effort during the turbulent years of worldwide confrontation. During the war years, however, manpower shortages in factories and other fields opened traditionally male occupations to women who filled those vacancies. When the men returned from military service, many of those working women were forced to fight to retain their jobs and many had no desire to return to domestic tranquility.

In the early years of the 1960s, several events merged to create space for the surge of the second wave of feminism. In 1961, President John F. Kennedy, inspired by feminist Esther Peterson, created the Commission on the Status of Women and named former first lady Eleanor Roosevelt as Commission chair. The Commission's report, published two years later, revealed that gender discrimination existed in all quadrants of American life. On the other hand, the report also noted that equality should be based on the acknowledgment of fundamental biological differences between the genders and it recommended against passage of the ERA.

The same year the committee report was issued, a suburban housewife, Betty Friedan, rose from middle-class obscurity to pen and publish *The Feminine Mystique* (1963), considered by some to be the primary trigger for the reinvention of feminism. While attending a Smith College reunion in 1957, Friedan discovered that the majority of her former classmates were less than content in their white picketed fence captivity. Although the societal expectations and popular culture representations of the deliriously happy, crisply starched stay-at-home wife and mother were deeply ingrained in the imagination of the era, most women were simply not buying it.

In 1964, the Civil Rights Act was passed with Title VII prohibiting discrimination in employment on the basis of sex. Grouped together, these three events should have been sufficient to recharge activism but, interestingly, it took one last impetus to reinvigorate the feminist movement. As abolition and the lack of inclusion in the movement served as the springboard for the first wave of women's activism, the Civil Rights Movement and the Anti-Vietnam War Movement of the 1950s and 1960s provided inspiration for the second wave. Although women were active participants and organizers in both groups, the recognized leadership was predominantly male, and women were largely excluded from having an active voice in either policy or politics.

Implying that the first wave of the woman's movement ended after the vote was granted in the 1920s, the term "second wave" was coined by Marsha Lear in the mid- to late-1960s. As opposed to the suffragists, the new wave was less unified and the issues were less solidified; however, in similarity to the suffragists, the movement was centered in the northeast primarily among upper- or middle-class Caucasian writers, publishers, and academics. Although the group sought political solidarity, the issues were scattered, covering everything from "equal pay for equal work" to "no fault" divorce to reproduction and abortion to gendered language. The movement was truly as feminist foremother Alice Paul had labeled it decades earlier: "the great mosaic."

The latter category of gender-specific language became the focus of much of the writing and the academic discussion of the era. It was believed that language affected perception and that the pronoun-based English language illustrated male domination and the inferior status of women. Prior to the period, the pronoun *he* was interchangeable with *one* but in the latter half of the twentieth century, pronoun use was rapidly changed to the awkward *he/she* of the politically correct age as were other alterations, such as mankind to humanity and history to history/her/story, and a variety of professional titles, like stewardess to flight attendant and mailman to postal worker, underwent dissection. Accompanying the alteration of the language was a shift in power between genders and subsequent confusion about roles and identities. The second-wave feminists, most of whom worked outside of the home, demanded that men take more responsibility for the housework and the care of children. Critics, primarily men, screamed reverse discrimination.

Finally, an element of cohesion was added to the *new* movement. The National Organization for Women (NOW) was founded on June 30, 1966 during the Third National Conference on the Status of Women held in

Washington, DC. Borrowing their organizational structure from the National Association for the Advancement of Colored People (NAACP), NOW expressed concern in achieving pay equity and securing a spot for women in the political mainstream. The twenty-eight founders elected Betty Friedan as president of the group and she hurriedly scribbled a purpose for the organization on one of the meeting place's paper napkins: "to take action to bring women into full participation in the mainstream of American society now, exercising all privileges and responsibilities thereof in truly equal partnership with men." Although the critics immediately accused the organization of being antimale, male-bashing, and being a bunch of lesbians, NOW boasted over a half-million members by the beginning of the twenty-first century and worked through political channels to eliminate discrimination and sexual harassment and to secure social justice. The most beneficial facet of NOW was that it provided the media with a centralized organization and spokespersons to deliver the *official* position on movement issues.

As with the woman's groups that came before, ideological splits were inevitable. Many felt that NOW was too conservative and that wanting to be welcomed within the political status quo was not equivalent to change. The first splinter group was the New York Radical Women, formed in 1968, followed by the Redstockings and WITCH, an acronym for Women's International Terrorist Conspiracy from Hell. Much as their foremothers had, the groups scheduled public protests geared to attract media attention. Unfortunately, in the newsworthy latter 1960s, the women had to compete with a daily dose of Vietnam, political corruption and student revolt, thus, their protest efforts had to be spectacular to merit coverage.

To facilitate that attention, the New York Radical Women confronted the undisputed bastion of American beauty standards, the Miss America Pageant. In 1968, roughly 150 feminists from various cities gathered in Atlantic City, New Jersey to protest the event, shouting slogans and proclaiming that the pageant was equivalent to a livestock show. Demonstrating on the boardwalk in front of the Atlantic City Convention Center where the pageant was held, the women underscored the livestock metaphor by crowning a live sheep as their candidate of choice for "Miss America" and tossing other symbols of their oppression—girdles, high heels, bras, and eyelash curlers—into the Freedom Trash Can. Although it was suggested and touted by the media as fact, the offending undergarments were not burned; nevertheless, the feminists came to be known as "bra burners" in the popular culture of the day. Following the event, protest photographs graced the front pages of newspapers nationwide and the phrase "women's liberation" reverberated from coast to coast in positive and not so positive terms.

Appropriately, WITCH scheduled their outlandish escapades on Halloween. Combining theatrics with militancy, the WITCH members' first action in 1968 was to race down Wall Street in New York in order to *hex* the financial community. Ironically, perhaps, the Dow Jones industrial average dropped five points the next day. That *success* was followed by the group dancing around the Federal Building in Chicago and staging coven meetings outside various bridal showers across the country.

The Redstockings, so named as a play on bluestockings, a negative nickname given to intelligent women, were the most active of the splinter groups and had the most longevity. Founded in 1969 in New York City, the group was known for its innovative approach to problem solving through consciousness-raising, a psychosocial type of internal processing. Inspired by the Chinese communist practice of "speaking pain," the group began as a study group to understand how sexist oppression had shaped their lives by discovering what person or what group would benefit from that oppression. The group was founded in the hope that women would share their individual experiences and feelings, while discovering a common ground and a universality of experience that would eventually push them toward a collective political solution. In other words, the belief was that changing themselves would eventually lead to change in society. Through this process, it was assumed that theory would be created. Group meetings were held in rounds, requiring each participant to speak for an uninterrupted amount of time. There were no leaders or facilitators, thus, everyone was validated and no one story was viewed as more important than another. When the teller was finished, the group discussed the elements of commonality found in their own lives. This method built self-confidence and trust, developed "sister solidarity," and created the motto of the group, "the personal is political." The methodology was integrated into the National Women's Liberation Conference in Chicago and the founders urged the formation of local consciousness-raising groups, nationwide.

Obviously, the call was heralded because there was ultimately a group formed in every major city with New York alone boasting hundreds of separate groups. University and even high school women clamored for membership. By 1973, the Redstockings claimed more than 100,000 members and promoted their work as one of the largest education/support groups of its kind ever created for women. Viewing male supremacy as an act of oppression of one human being over another, they advocated the overthrow of a male-dominated world where women were seen not so much as sex objects but rather as beauty *prizes*.

Paradoxically, the Redstockings complained that NOW and other moderate groups had not addressed the issues of race and class and offered wider nets for membership. However, that caveat became one of the major criticisms of the Redstockings and consciousness-raising, especially by third-wave activists who would follow. Criticism came from both within and without the movement. Women of color expressed their concern that the group was exclusionary and that they failed to build coalitions across color and class lines. Some of the third-wave criticism offered that the "me too" moments of consciousness-raising were successful only if others in the group could identify with the story and the teller; that the method did not recognize power imbalances based on race, class, and economics among the women themselves; and that the emphasis on unity alienated women of color whose experiences were quite different from the majority group. Others within the movement offered that preoccupation with individual experience caused women to sacrifice the universal fight for political gain, while those outside the group simply referred to the gatherings as "hen parties" or "bitch sessions."

In 1968, the Equal Employment Opportunity Commission ruled that placing help-wanted advertisements separated into jobs for men and jobs for women was illegal; however, by 1970, women were still earning only fifty-nine cents for every dollar that men earned, frequently for the same type and amount of work. During the same time period, only 7 percent of the nation's medical doctors were women and only 3 percent were attorneys. Additionally, when lists were compiled of America's most admired women, they were customarily listed as Mrs. So-and-so and never by their own name unless they were unmarried.

By 1969, a new faction appeared in the women's liberation movement. There had always been those who believed that the women's movement(s) were too "white and patrician," not inclusive of women of color and with little regard for the working class. But the new contingent expressed the view that many of the groups, NOW in particular, were too conservative and purposely excluded women of color and lesbians from the fold. Consequently, other women's groups were formed to focus on the multiple issues of class, race, and sexual orientation. The first of these groups was formed in 1971 by college students; Hijas de Cuauhtemoc served Chicana or Latino issues and The Asian Sisters was formed to give voice to women of Asian descent. Other groups followed, such as Women of All Red Nations for Native Americans; The Third World Women's Alliance, an outgrowth of the Student Non-violent Coordinating Committee, for African American young women; and the National Black Feminist Organization, formed in 1970 to serve all African American women's issues.

The problem was that, although the varied groups felt some kinship with the goals of feminism, they also felt separateness because their sense of oppression sprang from a deeper well. External critics had, early on, labeled the "libbers" as lesbians and this, too, produced internal discord as women were forced to acknowledge their sexual orientation. Interestingly, lesbian and Jewish women were the first to acknowledge that the white women leaders in the movement were often the oppressors and well as the oppressed. NOW was under attack for not addressing lesbian issues and in response, Betty Friedan asserted that lesbians and lesbian issues were a "lavender menace," causing all feminists to be regarded as man-haters or as wishing to be *men*. As a consequence of her statement, an informal group, brandishing anti-Friedan banners, struck the Second Congress to Unite Women in

New York City on May 1, 1970, notable because the protest was not against the status quo or against patriarchal oppression but against a corollary group supposedly fighting for a common cause. Decked out in lavender T-shirts and after noting that no lesbian was on the program, the women took over the podium and would not be silenced. The event marked a turning point in the movement and in 1971, NOW reversed its position, stating lesbianism was a *legitimate* concern of feminism.

In 1972, a pivotal year for women's causes, two events occurred that many felt would turn the tide of liberation. Although birth control, "The Pill," had been available for married women for some time, it had remained an illegal purchase for those who were unwed. When that decision was reversed and the pill could be legally prescribed for single women, it heralded a period the media branded as the "sexual revolution" or "sexual liberation." Some felt the pill marked an era of freedom, while others feared rampant promiscuity and a few noted the period as a field day for men who would no longer bear the responsibility for unwanted pregnancies.

That same year, Congress passed ERA, first penned and proposed by suffragist Alice Paul in 1923 nearly fifty years earlier. Simply stated, the amendment, that would be called the Alice Paul Amendment, guaranteed that "equality of rights under the law shall not be denied or abridged by the United States or by any state on account of sex." With pressure from grassroots organizers, the ninety-second Congress pushed the legislation through, setting a seven-year time period for ratification. Any amendment required approval of a percentage of the states, in this case thirty-eight, before it could officially become law. Unfortunately, the ordinary folk who were behind the grassroots movement for passage were no match for the amendment's detractors. Opponents, notably conservative and family values advocate Phyllis Schlafly, formed militant resistance to the amendment, proclaiming that passage would subsequently lead to unisex lavatories, women in combat, and gay marriage, among other objections. Others felt a gender-specific amendment was simply not necessary. When the 1982 ratification date expired, the amendment was three states short of the number required for passage. From 1982 onward, the legislation was reintroduced annually and some believed that the original vote would stand and if three negatively voting states would change their views and finally agree, passage was still viable.

Television, always the mirror image of societal popular culture, leaped on the feminist bandwagon. In the late 1960s, Marlo Thomas as "That Girl" became the first *liberated* woman to be featured in a prime-time sitcom, taking on the world on her own. "That Girl" was followed closely by Mary Tyler Moore and Valerie Harper as career women, living in their own apartments in a city and having self-supporting careers. Those shows paved the way for "Murphy Brown" in the 1990s, that spawned a national debate when then-vice president Dan Quayle questioned the morals of having a child out of wedlock, and the more recent "Sex and the City," which some believed was the natural evolution of moral decay.

Publishing, which was traditionally a vehicle for the dissemination of information on women's issues, gained a wider field. Created in 1969, Cell 16 Female Liberation, so called because they were only "one cell of an organic movement," published *No More Fun and Games: A Journal of Female Liberation* and *The Second Wave Magazine: A Magazine for the New Feminism*. Noting that feminism had transformed the criticism of patriarchy into an attack on masculinity, both publications offered a wide variety of viewpoints. On the other hand, the primary forum for issues of concern to the second wave was *Ms.* magazine, founded in 1972 with activist Gloria Steinem as editor in chief. As a consequence of the periodical's popularity, "ms." became a nonidentifying, neutral middle ground form of address for those women who preferred not to use the Miss or Mrs. title. Her work as an editor brought Steinem to the forefront of the movement and she became one of the most recognized faces and favored speakers for feminism.

Reproductive rights and abortion rights were part of the woman's movement from its outset but in the early 1970s, an unmarried, pregnant woman in Dallas County, Texas turned the world's attention to her plight and permanently changed American society. Jane Roe, a pseudonym akin to John Doe, mounted a court case against the State of Texas for "abridg[ing] her personal right to a medically safe abortion." The case wended its way through the legal system until it finally reached the U.S. Supreme Court in 1973. In a 7-2 decision, the Court ruled that the "right to decisions regarding one's reproductive system was consistent with the right to privacy under the Fourteenth Amendment." The ruling legalized abortion in all states and effectively polarized the American public for decades. That polarization subsequently led to extremists bombing abortion clinics and threatening medical professionals and to politicians lending rhetorical support to pro-life or pro-choice advocates in their campaign platforms.

Although the 1980s featured two World Conferences on Women and a 1984 article in *Adweek* that initiated the term "glass ceiling," referring to unwritten organizational policies that prohibited job advancement for women, the feminist movement became more fragmented. Despite the fact that the seeds of unrest were germinated between 1963 and 1974 as more women noted the exclusion of women of color and lesbians from mainstream feminism, the advent of the third wave is usually fixed at the beginning of the 1980s. Others, however, report that the third wave evolved from the Riot Grrl Movement of the early 1990s, a grassroots gathering composed primarily of artists, performers, and writers who held annual conventions to discuss woman's identity. Some noted that the conventions were so commercialized, they were like "trade show[s] for entrepreneurs."

The new *wave* marked a generational change and the acknowledgment that the second wave had run its course. Led by young women in their twenties and thirties, the third wave offered to cloak the intersection between feminism and racism. Because many of these women had other interests and other areas of activism in addition to feminism, the movement became more individualistic with scattered groups and issues. Wedged between the collectivist action of the government and the feminism-is-dead philosophy of the postfeminist movement, the third wave felt no need to mobilize and looked at "a wider range of topics through a feminist lens." Those topics included everything from arts and culture to major national issues; it was like feminism with Attention Deficit Disorder.

Added to their individualistic approach to organization, the third wave, by virtue of their youth, came to the movement as feminists with an accompanying sense of entitlement. Because the world was smaller and the media was pervasive, they also viewed issues in a more global context than their foremothers. Although it removed the personal from communication, the Internet served to connect the disjointedness of the movement with many women's groups wired together through listservs and blogs, a virtual form of consciousness-raising.

The third wave railed against the second wave for concentrating on a hegemonic interpretation of history that emphasized the domination of one group over another, primarily men over women, and for creating the image of women as victims. Victims, they noted, are incapable of taking responsibility and are self-sacrificing. In addition, they added that the second wave preached that women were inherently better than men because they were nurturing and peace loving and that they perpetuated the myth that women preferred cooperation rather than competition. One third waver noted that feminists had replaced direct action with bragging about their superiority and that women were not a distinct grouping or a *class*.

Noting that feminism had become established with no new ideas, the third wave splashed into further divisions with each being forced to identify with the liberals, the socialists, the radicals, the culturalists, or the multiracial. Embracing the third-wave philosophy as a reaction to the exclusivity of the second wave, women of color began to form "interlocking oppressions" coalitions. Although they called the movement a "redefinition" not a departure from historical roots, the third wave moved in ever widening circles away from any type of cohesion and toward multiple perspectives. Opinions were so divergent on so many issues that a common expression became "I'm not a feminist but. . ."

As feminism became more fragmented, it also became more of a boon for the economy as women took their place in a capitalistic society. Many of the third wavers, like Naomi Wolf and Camille Paglia, offered that oppression was merely a state of mind and that the solution was not to fight capitalism, a bastion of the patriarchy, but to join it as a full-fledged consumer. At long last, the definitive definition of feminism was delivered by black feminist leader Barbara Smith, who said, "Feminism is the political theory and practice to free all women: women of color, working-class women, poor women, physically challenged women, lesbians, old women, as well as white economically privileged heterosexual women. Anything less than this is not feminism, but merely female self-aggrandizement." That definition should have unified all factions.

In 1992, the American Association of University Women published research on "how schools shortchange girls," which led indirectly to a congressional resolution dedicating March as Women's History Month. In 1995, the United Nations sponsored the Fourth World Conference on Women in Beijing, China, producing a declaration that listed the issues yet to be addressed for the international rights of women. Notable among the points in the declaration was the statement that the group was "determined to advance the goals of equality, development and peace for all women everywhere in the interest of all humanity." Although many battles were unchanged from Elizabeth Cady Stanton's Declaration of Sentiments, the issues that dominated the woman's movement of the 1990s were reproductive rights, enrollment in military academies, service in active combat, women in the church leadership, pornography, sexual harassment, surrogate motherhood, gender roles, and social security benefits for homemakers.

By the twenty-first century, many young women had little knowledge of the struggles of generations that came before them. They took voting for granted; some offering that they had never voted or had *no interest* in politics. They assumed that they could enter the workforce in any field they chose and achieve success through both promotion and monetary reimbursement. They knew they had the right to control their own reproduction and had the right to accept or decline male advances. Although many were still actively functioning as watchdogs for the movement, most young women simply assumed their rights as women would continue and passively went about their day.

On the other hand, women's studies, as major or minor fields of learning and research, were peppering college campuses, nationwide. Although the critics decried the inclusion of one more *frivolous* discipline into an already overburdened curriculum, many young people, both men and women, were signing up for the courses. Other detractors insisted that if there were a course on women's studies, there should also be a course on men's studies. They were assured that course already existed—it was called "his-story."

ANNA PAULINE MURRAY
(1910–1985)

A feminist activist attorney, Pauline "Pauli" Murray journeyed through a variety of professional incarnations during her career from teaching to practicing law to becoming the first African American Episcopalian priest. In many ways she served as a peacemaker, working to pull together the divergent factions of the movement.

The granddaughter of a slave and the great-granddaughter of a slave owner, Pauli was born in Baltimore, Maryland, on November 20, 1910. Her mother, Agnes, died of a cerebral hemorrhage when Pauli was four years old and her father, William, a graduate of Howard University and a teacher, was unable to care for his six children alone. As the youngest, Pauli was sent to live with her maternal grandparents in Durham, North Carolina. There, she gained multiple mothers as three of her aunts took an interest in her upbringing, training her in courage, honesty, and the value of hard work. One of the aunts, a schoolteacher, eventually legally adopted the young woman when her father died of typhoid fever in 1923.

After graduating with honors from Hunter College in New York City, Murray accepted a short stint as a writer for *Opportunity* magazine before being hired by the Works Progress Administration, a federal work relief program designed to offer employment to those affected by the devastation of the Great Depression. In that capacity, Pauli aided in worker reeducation and taught remedial reading. She also aided the National Urban League, a nonpartisan organization for civil rights, and the Workers Defense League, concerned with protection of workers, particularly those in the military.

Her work on the periphery of the legal profession whetted Murray's appetite for the justice system and she began applying to schools of law. In 1938, she applied to the University of North Carolina and was refused admission because of her race; thus, she applied to Harvard University and was denied admission because she was a woman. Consequently, wedged between biases,

Murray determined to tear down the barriers of both race and gender as she entered Howard University School of Law in Washington, DC.

While a student at Howard, Murray took part in many of the civil rights protests and activist groups of the early 1940s. She participated in lunch counter sit-ins in the nation's capitol and was arrested in Virginia for refusing to move to the back of a bus transporting her from a visit in North Carolina back to Washington. She was an active member of the fledgling civil rights group the Fellowship of Reconciliation and in 1942, she aided in founding the Congress of Racial Equality, a group dedicated to changing the status quo through nonviolence. Throughout the period, she wrote and published articles and essays on the Civil Rights Movement, including reporting on the Harlem race riots for the *New York Call* in 1943.

After receiving her law degree from Howard University, where she discovered she was still a victim of gender discrimination, she commented that she had initially entered law school to dismantle segregation but left wanting to dismantle sexism. Murray completed a master's degree in law at the University of California Berkeley and passed the California bar exam in 1945. Her first position as a lawyer was with the district attorney's office, where she was assigned to combat the racial discrimination faced by Asians.

In 1952, she was denied a position at Cornell University because her references, including Eleanor Roosevelt, Thurgood Marshall, and Philip Randolph, were considered too radical. She continued her work with the Civil Rights Movement, while spending four years compiling and writing the semiautobiographical *Proud Shoes: The Story of an American Family* (1956), which traced the roots of her slave grandparents. After the publication of the memoir, she joined a New York City law firm for four years and spent one year teaching at the Ghana School of Law.

Only nine years after she was denied the Cornell post, Murray was appointed to John F. Kennedy's President's Commission on the Status of Women, as chair of the Committee on Civil and Political Rights. Through her work on the Commission, Murray compiled a list of laws that discriminated against women, identifying their inability to serve on juries and lack of educational opportunities as the greatest impediments. Part of her assignment was to reconcile the pro- and anti-Equal Rights Amendment factions growing in the women's movement and the country at large and to recommend means of improving the legal and political status of women. Murray underscored the point, often repeated in the past, that there was an identifiable link between women's issues and civil rights. She was one of the first to employ the equal protection clause of the Fourteenth Amendment as a tool against discrimination based on race and was convinced the amendment should be used as an umbrella for a variety of gender biases as well, rather than dealing with one law at a time. The findings of that committee, published as *American Women: Report of the President's Commission on the Status of Women* (1963), were presented to the governors of the individual states, encouraging them to review state statutes and policies on the treatment of women. Discouraged by her findings, Murray's activist spirit was renewed on both fronts and she participated in the 1963 Civil Rights March on Washington, highlighted by Martin Luther King's famous "I Have a Dream" speech.

After serving as a tutor to help cover her tuition, Murray received her doctorate in law in 1965 from Yale University, the first African American woman to be awarded that degree. She penned an early law review article on gender discrimination.

In 1966, she joined Betty Friedan and thirty other women to found the National Organization for Women, which she called the National Association for the Advancement of Colored People for women. The initial goal of the group was to insist that the government enforce the antigender provisions of the Civil Rights Act of 1964, prohibiting discrimination on the basis of race, religion, or sex. Murray coauthored the purpose statement for the group and chaired the Committee on Structure and Principles.

The following year, Pauli Murray taught in the African American Studies department at Brandeis University and accepted a seat on the Equality Committee of the American Civil Liberties Union (ACLU). While in the latter position, she sought revision of the ACLU policy on gender discrimination.

At sixty-two years of age, Murray's career embarked on yet another path and she enrolled in the General Theological Seminary in New York to avail herself of the newly created decision by the Episcopal Church that permitted women to become deacons. She became a deacon in 1976 and was ordained as a priest in 1977. She voiced her opinion that religion might serve as a means to unite white women and black women in their struggle.

Pauli Murray died of cancer on July 1, 1985, in Pittsburgh, Pennsylvania. Her autobiography, *Song in a Weary Throat: An American Pilgrimage* (1987), was published posthumously. In 1990, the Human Relations Commission in Orange County, North Carolina, her ancestral home, created the Pauli Murray Award to be given annually to a recipient who built "bridges from tolerance to acceptance."

FOR FURTHER READING

Murray, Pauli. *Proud Shoes: The Story of an American Family.* New York: Harper & Row, 1978; ———. *Song in a Weary Throat: An American Pilgrimage.* New York: Harper & Row, 1987.———. *Pauli Murray: The Autobiography of a Black Activist, Feminist, Lawyer, Priest and Poet.* Knoxville: The University of Tennessee Press, 1989.

BELLA ABZUG (1920–1998)

One of the first radical feminists to gain national public office, Bella Abzug took her seat in the ninety-second House of Representatives in January 1971, where she served three terms. Known, not always affectionately, as "Battling Bella" or "Mother Courage," Abzug was a strong advocate for women's issues, a strong opponent of the war in Vietnam, and a force for human equality and political alliances worldwide.

Born in the Bronx, a New York City borough, on July 24, 1920, Bella was the daughter of Emanuel Savitsky and Esther Tanklefsky Savitsky, both Russian Jews. Her father was a butcher, the owner of the Live and Let Live Meat Market. As a child, Bella was a tomboy, using the city streets as her playground. Her first sense of the power of community organizing came during those days as the young Jewish children of the borough banded together for outings and to raise money for Israel. Her maternal grandfather, Wolf Tanklefsky, served as her babysitter and early instructor in Hebrew. Music was integral to the family and although Bella became an accomplished violinist, her true passion was playing poker.

When the young woman was thirteen, her father died and her mother was forced to find work as a department store clerk in order to support her family, including one other daughter, Helene. During her father's funeral service, Bella was reprimanded for praying in the synagogue, a privilege forbidden to women, an event that would set the tone for the majority of her adult endeavors. A stellar student who served as class president, Bella added to the family finances by tutoring Hebrew students while she was still in high school.

At Hunter College of New York, she majored in political science, was elected president of the student council, and took an active part in the American Student Union. Based on her academic and leadership potential, Bella was offered a scholarship to Columbia University's School of Law, where she edited the *Law Review*. After receiving her degree in 1947, she did postgraduate work at the Jewish Theological Seminary of America and was admitted to the New York State Bar Association.

While visiting relatives in Miami after college, Bella met and married Maurice Abzug, a partner in a shirt manufacturing company who eventually became a stockbroker and novelist. She agreed to the marriage provided he would not object to her continuing to work. The couple had two daughters, Eve Gail in 1949 and Isobel Jo in 1952, and lived in Mt. Vernon, New York, an integrated suburb selected specifically to expose the young girls to diversity. When the children were older, they relocated to Greenwich Village, a Bohemian section of New York City.

Her first professional position was with a law firm that specialized in labor law. Forwarding the interests of the company, Abzug worked with labor unions, offered pro bono representation for civil rights cases and aided clients recommended by the American Civil Liberties Union. She was also a standard bearer on behalf of many of those who were unjustly accused of having communist leanings by Senator Joseph McCarthy and his loyalty hearings. While at the law firm, she was frequently mistaken for one of the office staff only because she was a woman. As a consequence, she began wearing her trademark oversized hats to show professionalism and to differentiate herself from the secretaries.

Abzug continued to champion the downtrodden throughout the 1950s but the next decade brought new challenges. In 1961, Bella founded and lobbied for Women's Strike for Peace, a group that fought for a nuclear test ban treaty and protested the war in Indochina. The group eventually grew to over fifty thousand members. She campaigned against Lyndon Baines Johnson in 1962 and protested the Vietnam War in 1965, adding her name to Richard Nixon's *black list* in the process. Later as a congresswoman, she was the first member of that group to call for his impeachment. Abzug served as president of the Women's Foreign Policy Council through which she attended several international women's conferences and founded the Women's Environmental and Developmental Organization, a group who labeled themselves ecofeminists.

Having gained a reputation as an activist, Abzug was asked to run for Congress in 1970. She was elected with 55 percent of the vote and, in 1971, she took office as a member of the ninety-second Congress, becoming the twelfth woman in the House of Representatives, the only one of Jewish descent, and the first woman who was elected on a woman's rights platform. She served for three terms. Her first official act as a congresswoman was a resolution calling for the immediate withdrawal of troops from Vietnam; her second, abolition of the selective service, the military draft. Although she requested a seat on the Armed Services Committee, that placement was denied and she was assigned to the Committee on Public Works and Transportation. Through that assignment, she negotiated over six million dollars for her New York District to improve sewage treatment and mass transit and to add ramps to busses for the elderly and disabled. Having been an active member of the National Organization for Women, she joined Shirley

Chisholm, Betty Friedan, and Gloria Steinem to found the National Women's Political Caucus in 1971, a group created to advocate for women's issues and to support women candidates running for public office. In addition, she led the congressional caucus on women's issues and served as a strategist for the Democratic Women's Committee.

Throughout her tenure in Congress, Bella championed legislation that would forward her feminist agenda. She was a strong supporter of the Equal Rights Amendment, voted for childcare legislation, worked against gender discrimination in federal employment, encouraged a woman's right to an abortion on military bases, and lobbied for privacy on public records that would no longer require persons to indicate a gender-based title, such as Miss or Mrs. She wrote law banning discrimination in obtaining credit based on gender, introduced bills to implement social security for homemakers, and encouraged family planning. As chairperson of the subcommittee on government information and individual rights, she coauthored the Freedom of Information Act, which opened sealed government records, including many that had been previously classified as top secret, and made them available for public scrutiny.

In 1973, Bella initiated congressional and presidential support for a national Women's Equality Day to be celebrated annually on August 26th, the anniversary of the passage of the amendment guaranteeing women the right to vote. Four years later, she secured over a million dollars in federal support to convene a National Women's Conference in Houston, Texas. During the period, she also took an active role in various international women's meetings from Mexico City in 1975 to Copenhagen in 1980 and Nairobi in 1985. One of the first in Congress to support the rights of gays and lesbians, Bella introduced an amendment to the Civil Rights Act to protect the civil liberties of those persons in 1975.

President Jimmy Carter created the National Advisory Committee on Women in 1976, naming Abzug as cochair. Never having been one to temper her opinion, however, she was removed from the committee for criticizing the administration's passive support for abortion rights and the Equal Rights Amendment as well as its economic policies. Ironically perhaps, the next year she was named the third most influential member of the House of Representatives and noted as one of the twenty most influential women in the world in a Gallup poll.

In 1976, Bella mounted a campaign to run for a seat in the Senate but lost to Patrick Moynihan. Following that defeat, she ran for mayor of New York in 1977 and made two attempts to return to Congress in 1978 and 1986. Under the growing conservatism permeating the political arena, she lost each of the elections. Not one to stop forwarding her agenda, however, Abzug moved into the international arena, creating the Women's Foreign Policy Council and working with the United Nations to elicit concern for human rights, economic development, economic justice, and population and environmental issues. She worked with fifteen hundred women from eighty-three nations who met in Miami to produce the Women's Action Agenda for the Twenty-first Century, a document encouraging universal empowerment of women. The product of that meeting was used during the UN Fourth World Conference on Women held in Beijing, China in 1995. President George Bush, Sr. reportedly noted his pity for the Chinese with Bella running around Beijing.

Having published her autobiography, *Bella!*, in 1972, Abzug returned to writing, offering a journal of her first year in Congress, *Bella: Ms. Abzug Goes to Washington* (1982) and *Gender Gap: Bella Abzug's Guide to Political Power for American Women* (1984).

Between 1993 and 1995, Abzug chaired the New York City Commission on the Status of Women and working with the environmental activist group, Greenpeace, she aided grassroots awareness through a campaign called "Women, Cancer and the Environment: Action for Prevention." Unfortunately, the campaign did little to halt her own demise; she died of breast cancer and heart disease on March 31, 1998.

FOR FURTHER READING

Abzug, Bella. *Bella! Ms. Abzug Goes to Washington*. New York: Saturday Review Press, 1972; Hyman, Paula, and Deborah Dash Moore, eds. *Jewish Women in America*. New York: Routledge, 1997; Levine, Suzanne, and Mary Thom. *Bella Abzug: How One Tough Broad from the Bronx Fought Jim Crow and Joe McCarthy, Pissed Off Jimmy Carter, Battled for the Rights of Women and Workers, Rallied against War and for the Planet, and Shook Up Politics along the Way*. New York: Farrar, Straus and Giroux, 2007.

BETTY NAOMI GOLDSTEIN FRIEDAN (1921–2006)

Called the founding mother of feminism's second wave, Betty Friedan was the creator and first president of the National Organization for Women (NOW). Her seminal work, *The Feminine Mystique* (1963), lit the fire of the modern women's movement and was widely regarded as one of the most influential books of the twentieth century.

The daughter of Miriam Horowitz and Harry Goldstein, a jeweler, Betty was born on February 4, 1921, in Peoria, Illinois, the eldest of three children in the Jewish middle-class family. She developed both a talent for writing and an inclination toward social consciousness at an early age. At Smith College, a women's only institution in Northampton, Massachusetts, she served as editor of the campus newspaper and was graduated, *summa cum laude,* in 1942. After attending a summer course at Highlander Folk School in Tennessee, a training ground for grassroots activism, Betty attended graduate school in psychology at the University of California in Berkeley. While there, she dated David Bohm, a physicist on the Manhattan Project, a government installation created to design and build nuclear bombs, and befriended members of the Communist Party of the United States. Although she was offered a scholarship to continue her studies, she opted for a career in journalism.

After returning east, she took a position as a reporter for the Federated Press, a leftist news service in New York City. She published a series of articles supporting union efforts and against corporate greed, racism, and sexism. After she was terminated in order to be replaced by a male reporter, Betty used her union expertise to land a staff reporter slot for *UE News,* the newsletter of the United Electrical, Radio and Machine Workers of America. In that position, she addressed the hardships suffered by working class and African American women.

In 1947, she married Carl Friedan, a theater producer, with whom she had three children. The marriage lasted for twenty years despite mutual allegations of physical abuse, noted in her memoir, *Life So Far* (2000).

In 1952, her last year with *UE News,* Friedan published a landmark pamphlet, *UE Fights for Women Workers,* an exposé of corporate America's exploitation of women workers. After being fired again, this time because she was pregnant, Friedan spent eleven years as a suburban housewife but continued to submit freelance writing to women's magazines and to teach part time at New York University and the New School for Social Research, where she advocated experimentation in cooperative living.

While attending a Smith College reunion, Friedan's path was altered dramatically when she discovered that the majority of her classmates were as dissatisfied with their lives as she was. After formalizing those conversations in interview format, adding other interviews from women across the country and coupling those with social and psychological research, she produced *The Feminine Mystique* (1963), which debunked the myth of suburban domestic fulfillment. Marketed as merely "a simple housewife revealing the truth of her existence," the book proclaimed that millions of American homemakers were victims of a culture that allowed them to exist only as appendages of their husbands and children. Although criticized for acknowledging only the liberal middle class and ignoring the lives of minority and working class women, the book sold more than three million copies and was translated into multiple languages. Proclaimed as one of the most influential nonfiction books of the twentieth century, the work launched Friedan as head of the new woman's movement.

In 1966, Friedan, with activist Pauli Murray and others, founded NOW. As the first national civil rights organization for women, the group was dedicated to achieving equal opportunity in all arenas. After growing into the largest feminist organization in the country under Friedan's leadership, NOW members forced airlines to alter their policies regarding married flight attendants, brought about an executive order prohibiting hiring discrimination by federal contractors and endorsed legalized abortion.

Two years after its creation, NOW, with Friedan still at the helm, became embroiled in controversy, first over the Bill of Rights for Women adopted by NOW at its national conference in 1967 and then over the organization's support for the Equal Rights Amendment. The Bill of Rights for Women consisted of eight stipulations, that (1) equal opportunities for employment should be provided to all without regard to gender; (2) employers should be required to provide maternity leave and to rehire women following those births; (3) home care and childcare tax credits should be required; (4) impoverished women should have the same access to training and housing as their male counterparts; (5) the welfare system should be reformed; (6) publicly funded daycare centers should be established; (7) laws limiting contraception and abortion should be revoked; and (8) Congress should immediately pass the Equal Rights Amendment. It was the last two items that spurred national debate and created uproar among both men and women.

The Equal Rights Amendment was drafted in 1923 by suffragist Alice Paul, who noted that merely having the right to vote would not guarantee an absence of discrimination. However, the amendment was not approved for almost fifty years; although it had previously passed House muster, it failed in the Senate. In 1972, however, the ninety-second Congress finally agreed and sent the amendment to the states for ratification. Although the amendment was intended to provide equal rights for Americans regardless of gender, opponents argued that traditional gender roles would be blurred or obliterated. Some even expressed concern over the possible integration of same-sex classrooms, sports, and even rest rooms, while others feared that it would justify women having to serve in combat or that the amendment would be used to mandate universal recognition of same-sex marriages. Despite NOW's political clout and Friedan's name recognition, the amendment failed to be ratified with only three state short of the required majority.

On August 26, 1970, two years before the equal right amendment's passage by Congress, Friedan aided in organizing the "Women Strike for Equality Day" to celebrate the fiftieth anniversary of the passage of the Nineteenth Amendment guaranteeing women the right to vote. Women joined marches in over ninety cities and, in New York City, nearly fifty thousand participated in the celebration with Friedan acting as grand marshal.

With the aid of other like-minded activists, such as Gloria Steinem, Shirley Chisholm, and Bella Abzug, Friedan created the National Women's Political Caucus in 1971. The group was designed to identify and support women candidates for public office as well as men candidates who were sympathetic to a feminist platform. In addition, they envisioned new approaches to divorce laws, abortion reform, and educational and employment opportunities. During the 1970s, she also served as a visiting professor of sociology at Temple University, Yale University, the New School for Social Research, and Queens College. She was named Humanist of the Year by the American Humanist Association in 1975 and awarded an honorary doctorate of humane letters from Smith College.

In the mid-1970s, Friedan resigned from NOW, the organization she had founded, in the midst of yet another heated debate, the "lesbian issue." Friedan expressed her belief that lesbian feminists, a group she labeled the "Lavender Menace," wanted to alter the mission of the organization and she was opposed to their anti-male sexual politics. Although many resented her negative depiction of her lesbian sisters, Friedan proclaimed that she was not *straitlaced* or made uneasy by homosexuality; instead, she vowed that she wanted a faction that would represent all women. She felt that a movement that would change society for the better was radical enough.

After leaving NOW, Friedan continued to write and appear on the college lecture circuit. In 1976, she published her memoir of the movement, *It Changed My Life*. She was a delegate to the White House Conference on

Families in 1980 and cochair of Women, Men and Media, an organization researching gender bias in various forms of media.

In 1981, she completed *The Second Stage* in which she chastised the women's movement for replacing the word "feminine" with "men versus women" and "women versus women." In the work, she argued that women who wanted traditional wife and mother roles should be allowed to assume them without criticism from feminist leaders. Many of her former colleagues and followers thought she had betrayed the movement and she was labeled as a reactionary.

Her last major work, *The Fountain of Age* (1993), was produced under a Ford Foundation grant, which allowed her to work as a senior research associate at the Center for Social Sciences at Columbia University. The book probed changing gender roles and the impact of aging on women.

Friedan died on her eighty-fifth birthday in 2006 of congestive heart failure. Although some modern radical feminists discounted her work as dated and no longer relevant, they failed to realize that her transformative crusading laid the groundwork for many of the advances in gender equity that they continued to enjoy.

FOR FURTHER READING

Boucher, Joanne. "Betty Friedan and the Radical Past of Liberal Feminism." *New Politics* 9 (Summer 2003): 3; Friedan, Betty. *The Feminine Mystique.* New York: Norton, 1963; ———. *It Changed My Life: Writings on the Women's Movement.* New York: Random House, 1976; Horowitz, Daniel. *Betty Friedan and the Making of the Feminine Mystique: The American Left, the Cold and Modern Feminism.* Amherst: University of Massachusetts Press, 1998.

GLORIA STEINEM (1934–)

Because she was attractive, charismatic, and politically savvy, Gloria Steinem, activist, author, and publisher, became a media icon and the *unofficial* symbol of second-wave feminism. Often negatively referred to as the "glamour girl" of the women's liberation movement, Steinem was the founding editor of *Ms.* magazine and one of the women responsible for initiating the National Women's Political Caucus.

Born March 25, 1934 in Toledo, Ohio, Gloria was the daughter of Leo Steinem, a ne'er-do-well dreamer of Jewish descent, and Ruth Nuneviller from French Huguenot stock. Her mother graduated from Oberlin College and worked as a journalist prior to her marriage. Her father, a part-time dealer in antiques and seasonal manager of a summer resort, was fond of get-rich-quick schemes that never quite produced as promised. Consequently, Gloria spent most of her childhood traveling from place to place in a house trailer. She did, however, have a good hereditary role model for her activism. Her paternal grandmother, Pauline, served as the president of the Ohio Woman's Suffrage Association from 1908 to 1911 and was one of only two American delegates to the International Council of Women in 1908.

In 1946, her parents divorced and Gloria and her sister journeyed back to Toledo with their mother. Perhaps frail from the outset or worn down by the years of scrabbling for a living, Ruth was beset by anxiety and depression, eventually leading to a nervous breakdown. Although she was able to attend school full time for the first time in her life, Gloria's home situation in a rat-infested basement of a rundown apartment building in an undesirable part of the city was less than pleasing but it was all they could afford because her mother was unable to work. Eventually, her sister, Susanne, moved away and Gloria became her mother's full-time caretaker, while simultaneously attending high school and entering local talent contests to earn expenses.

In her senior year of high school, Gloria moved to Washington, DC to live with her sister. She applied to and was accepted at Smith College, graduating *magna cum laude* in government in 1956. After graduation, she had the opportunity to study in India, taking classes at both the University of Delhi and the University of Calcutta. While in India, Steinem became aware of the lack of equality among the classes in that country and joined a group labeled "radical humanists" that traveled throughout southern India offering aid to the impoverished and attempting to quiet the social unrest. As a consequence of her travels within the country, she was contracted by the government in New Delhi to create a national guidebook, *A Thousand Indias*.

Following her return to the United States in 1958, Steinem was hired as the director of the Independent Research Service, a division of the National Student Association in Cambridge, Massachusetts. As part of her position, she recruited American students to travel to Europe to attend Communist youth festivals in various countries. It was later revealed that the endeavor was funded, in part, by the Central Intelligence Agency, a fact that would be of future use to those who wished to discredit Steinem and her work with the women's movement.

In 1960, the activist moved to New York City, writing political satire for *Help!* magazine. During the period, she submitted her writing to various other publications, including *Esquire* that published her piece titled "The Moral Disarmament of Betty Coed," her depiction of the sexual revolution. Based on her stylistic flair in the *Esquire* article, *Show* magazine contracted Steinem to go undercover as a Playboy bunny in order to create an exposé of the behind-the-scenes activities in Hugh Hefner's Playboy Club in Manhattan. After the work was published, Gloria became an overnight celebrity, leading to contributions of popular culture fluff in *Vogue*, *Glamour*, *McCalls*, and *Cosmopolitan*, dubbed by critics as "girl reporting," and scriptwriting for the television series, "That Was the Week That Was," a satiric examination of the news and the news media that ran from 1964 to 1965. By 1968, Steinem had worked her way into a regular column for *New York* magazine, "The City Politic." During the period, she joined farm workers organizer Caesar Chavez's Poor Peoples March; served as treasurer of the legal defense fund for African American activist and radical feminist, Angela Davis; campaigned for the presidential candidacy of Robert Kennedy; and supported the issues raised by The Black Panthers and the plight of minorities and indigenous peoples.

Initially as research for her writing, Steinem attended a consciousness-raising meeting of the Redstockings, claiming afterward that the group had awakened her feminism. During the meeting, predicated on the sharing of information among the members, she admitted that she had an abortion in her younger years. After the gathering, she scoured bookstores, newsstands, and libraries and devoured everything she could find on the woman's movement. Her first piece of feminist writing was "After Black Power, Women's Liberation." Following that, she successfully undertook fundraising for the woman's movement, using the influence she had gathered in covering politicians and celebrities, and booked speaking appearances on television talk shows. She expressed, "the political problem is that men, consciously or unconsciously, perpetuate the subjugation of women for economic and social gain."

Having aligned her voice with those of Betty Friedan and Bella Abzug, Steinem became a speech writer and spokesperson for the movement. In 1970, she aided Friedan in planning the August Woman's Strike for Equality, the first national demonstration, and the two, joined by Abzug and Shirley Chisholm, founded the National Women's Political Caucus in 1971 to encourage women to seek public office and women voters to support candidates with women's issues agendas. The same year, Steinem founded the Women's Action Alliance, a national information center concerned with educating children in a nonsexist, multiracial fashion, combating social and economic ills and attacking "the problems of dependence, discrimination and lack of alternatives" for women.

In 1972, Steinem initiated *Ms.* magazine that rapidly became the mouthpiece for the second-wave women's movement, although it was later considered too feminine for many of the feminists. The periodical, fully owned, operated, and edited by women, sold over three hundred thousand copies in only eight days and ran under her leadership for fifteen years before merging with and being published by the Feminist Majority Foundation. Steinem continued to serve as consulting editor.

Later in 1972, she went on a speaking tour, lobbying state legislatures for passage of the Equal Rights Amendment. Steinem told the Gloria-hungry media that domestic abuse was the major cause of injury to women, that passivity was frequently rewarded as feminine behavior, and that equality was not enough without recognizing the humanity in all peoples. As a speaker and author, she persistently expressed her view that gender roles and child abuse were the roots of domestic violence and advocated nonviolent conflict resolution.

She was appointed to the National Committee on the Observance of International Women's Year by President Jimmy Carter in 1977 and founded the Coalition of Labor Union Women, Voters for Choice, Women against Pornography, Women USA, and Take Our Daughters to Work Day. In 1983, she published the semiautobiographical work, *Outrageous Acts and Everyday Rebellions,* which delved into her childhood and the time spent caring for her mother. Her *Revolution from Within: A Book of Self-Esteem,* published in 1992, topped the best-seller list and was translated into eleven languages.

Consistently concerned with self-esteem issues in younger women, Steinem founded the Ms. Foundation for Women to create social change by empowering young women and girls. As a result of those efforts, *Parenting* magazine presented her with its Lifetime Achievement Award for her work in promoting girls' self-esteem and *Biography* magazine named her as one of the twenty-five most influential women in America.

A critic of the academic community, Gloria was irritated by what she called the "careerism" of academic feminist writing that dealt primarily with theory and the *gobbledygook* of creating lack of understandability through using convoluted language. She recommended a better exchange between activism and academia, wherein professors researched real-world problems. To that end, she worked with the Sophia Smith Collection at Smith College to document the grassroots origins of the women's movement in the United States.

In 2000, Steinem married South African animal rights activist David Bale in a traditional Cherokee wedding ceremony. After his death in 2003, Steinem returned to New York City to begin chronicling her thirty years as an organizer for feminist issues.

Always politically active, Steinem was involved in the campaigns of Eugene McCarthy, Shirley Chisholm, and George McGovern, among others. In 2004, she was back on the campaign trail to discuss issues of relevance to women, calling it the most important election of her lifetime. She was an advocate of participatory democracy, believing that real, sustainable change was brought about on a grassroots level and not through the political system. While some considered Steinem a transformational leader, others were put off by her media presence, calling it "self-promotion at the expense of the feminist agenda."

FOR FURTHER READING

Heilbrun, Carolyn G. *The Education of a Woman: The Life of Gloria Steinem.* New York: Dial Press, 1995; Steinem, Gloria. *Outrageous Acts and Everyday Rebellions.* New York: New American Library, 1983; Whittier, Nancy. "Persistence and Transformation: Gloria Steinem, the Women's Action Alliance, and the Feminist Movement." *Journal of Women's History* 14 (Summer 2002): 148–51.

BILLIE JEAN KING (1943–)

Although best known as the top ranked athlete on the tennis courts of the world for over ten years, Billie Jean King also served as a role model for the empowerment of women to *make it in a man's world*. She was a women's rights pioneer in sport, outspoken against sexism in both sport and society and an activist for gay rights.

Billie Jean Moffitt was born on November 22, 1943, in Long Beach, California. Her parents were conservative and traditional; her father, Bill, served as a fireman in the community and her mother stayed at home. Athletic ability was obviously in the family genes, however, for her brother, Randy, also entered professional sports as a major league pitcher for various baseball franchises.

While attending Long Beach Polytechnic High School, Billie Jean won the women's doubles title at Wimbledon in her first effort and met her future husband, attorney Lawrence King. In 1970, King was the first woman athlete to demand and receive prize monies topping $100,000 and helped to found the Virginia Slims professional tour for women. Three years later, she organized a union for women tennis players, the Women's Tennis Association, which she served as first president. Over her athletic career, she took home twenty Wimbledon titles and turned women's tennis into not only a media event but also a legitimate sport. She was the first woman to receive *Sports Illustrated*'s coveted "Sportsperson of the Year" award.

As a radical feminist, King became a symbol for gender equality in sport. Although her initial focus was to secure equal prize money for women, her efforts extended beyond the financial into areas of self-esteem for and empowerment of young women athletes. In 1971, King was the first prominent American athlete to come out as openly gay and, in 2000, she received an award from the Gay and Lesbian Alliance Against Defamation, a group whose mission was to reduce discrimination against homosexuality. The award was presented to her for "furthering the visibility and inclusion of the community in her work" and for her activities with several AIDS charities.

Although that one particular event paled beside her other accomplishments, King gained a universal reputation for her participation in

"The Battle of the Sexes." Tennis hustler, Bobby Riggs, announced that he wanted "to take down a noted libber" and invited King to a match. She turned down his first offer but when he bested his second choice, Margaret Court, Billie Jean knew she had no choice but to recoup for her gender. By the appointed date in 1973, the Houston Astrodome was packed with over thirty thousand spectators and television coverage added more than ninety million viewers in thirty-seven countries, producing the largest audience ever to witness a tennis match. Always the proverbial showman, Riggs staged the event: Billie Jean was carried into the arena on a Cleopatra-type Egyptian litter lifted by several muscular men; Riggs entered in a drawn rickshaw. At center court the two exchanged gifts; King received a Sugar Daddy and she presented Riggs with a live baby pig, both symbols of the slang of the era. King smashed through three sets, winning each by at least two points. She said if she had not won, it would have set women back fifty years and affected the self-esteem of all women. Thus, considered a win for equality and women's rights, the match produced a trickle-down effect in various areas of society as well as enhancing the image of women's sports. The bottom-line message was that a woman could succeed in a man's world where it was then safe to be a feminist.

In 1974, King worked as the player/coach of the Philadelphia Freedoms of World Team Tennis, a team she founded with her husband. She also created tennis clinics for children from impoverished neighborhoods and set up a foundation to aid in building self-esteem for women through sports. In addition, she served as the first woman commissioner in the history of professional sports.

For her work in empowering women and educating men, King received the 1998 Elizabeth Blackwell Award presented to one whose life exemplified outstanding service to humanity. She was named one of the one hundred most important Americans of the twentieth century by *Life* magazine.

FOR FURTHER READING

King, Billie Jean, and Frank Deford. *The Autobiography of Billie Jean King*. London: Granada, 1982; Roberts, Selena. *A Necessary Spectacle: Billie Jean King, Bobby Riggs, and the Tennis Match That Leveled the Game*. New York: Crown Publishers, 2005.

ALICE MALSENIOR WALKER (1944–)

Activist and author, Alice Walker was credited with coining the term "womanist," to denote black feminism in particular and to preserve an identity distinctly different from the white, middle-class majority prevalent in the early woman's movement. Among other works, she was the author of the Pulitzer Prize winning, *The Color Purple*.

Alice was born on February 9, 1944 in Eatonton, Georgia, the youngest of the eight children of Willie Lee and Minnie Tallulah Grant. Her father was a sharecropper and dairy farmer, whose meager income was proof of his lack of success at both. Her mother supplemented his income by working as a maid as well as helping out in the fields, often taking Alice along to help pick cotton. When the young girl was four years old, she was allowed to attend school, using books and wearing clothing donated by her teachers.

Alice admired her mother's strength and both of her parents' ability to weave stories. At a young age, she began to record the stories in her diary as well as adding poetry of her own often born of her unhappiness. When she was eight, she was accidentally shot in the eye with a BB from her brother's gun. Because the family had no means of transportation, there was no way to take the young girl to a doctor. By the time they finally reached the hospital, she was permanently blinded in that eye. The situation caused her to become shy, self-conscious, and withdrawn. Because the house was filled with people, Alice spent much of her time wandering the fields and woods near the property, seeking solitude in which to write and read. When she entered high school, it was discovered that her blindness was primarily the result of scar tissue and once it was removed, the young woman blossomed. She became valedictorian and queen of her senior class.

Due to her academic record and her disability, Alice was awarded a full scholarship to Spellman College, a black woman's institute in Atlanta. In 1961, her neighbors raised the money to cover her bus fare. At Spellman, she was pulled almost immediately into the heart of the Civil Rights Movement, including registering black voters in Liberty County. Upset by the reaction of the Spellman administrators to the movement activities and by the dismissal of her favored professor, Walker left the university and accepted a scholarship to Sarah Lawrence College, at the time a progressive, liberal arts girls' school in Bronxville, New York. During the summer of 1964, she traveled to Africa; on returning, she discovered she was pregnant and had an abortion. Her first published book of poems was about the experience. She was graduated from Sarah Lawrence in 1965.

After college, she worked for the Welfare Department in New York City and wrote at night. In 1966, however, she was awarded a writing fellowship, quit the job she had grown to dislike, and spent the summer registering voters in Mississippi. While there, she met Melvyn Rosenman Leventhal, a Jewish civil rights attorney, whom she married on March 17, 1967. Also, in 1967, her essay "The Civil Rights Movement: What Good Was It" was published in the *American Scholar* and won three hundred dollars in its annual essay contest. Because Melvyn needed to be close to the movement, the couple moved permanently to Jackson, Mississippi, becoming the first legally married interracial couple in the community. They stayed seven years, during which time he fought for school desegregation and she worked as a writer-in-residence at both Jackson State College and Tougaloo College, while taking care of their infant daughter, Rebecca.

In 1973, Walker was offered a lectureship in literature at Wellesley College and the University of Massachusetts in Boston, which she accepted, while Melvyn continued his work in Jackson. In 1974, they relocated to New York City, where she became a contributing editor for *Ms.* magazine and completed her novel, *Meridian,* noted as "one of the finest novels to come out of the Civil Rights Movement." Partly attributed to the success of that work, Walker won a National Endowment grant in 1969, which allowed her to pursue her writing full time. Walker and her husband of eleven years were divorced in 1976 and in 1978, after being awarded a Guggenheim fellowship, she moved to California, once again seeking solitude for her writing.

In 1982, Walker published what would become her legacy to the world of letters. *The Color Purple* was on the *New York Times* best-seller list for over twenty-five weeks and earned a Pulitzer Prize the year after its publication. Although there was critical controversy over her negative portrayal of black men, her use of dialect and her lesbian characters, the book was an enormously popular success. Warner Brothers purchased the film rights for $350,000 and the movie, directed by Steven Spielberg and starring Whoopi Goldberg and Oprah Winfrey, was released in 1985. The work was important to the women's movement because it revealed the transformation of the main character through her relationships with other women.

Although she had her share of critics, Walker claimed her work was "grounded in spirituality, not politics." Her writing dealt with the themes of rape, violence, isolation, sexism, and racism, but they also revealed the essence of community, family, and religion in the lives of African American women. Between 1989 and 1992, Walker penned two books on the custom of female circumcision in Africa. Although the works were well received by most critics, others accused the author of cultural imperialism, the tendency to impose one's own cultural values on another culture.

Her use of the word womanist to depict her feminism was, in part, a reaction to the white, middle-class origins of the woman's movement that often shunned black members and overlooked the issues of women of color. She cited that the word was derived from black dialect to indicate a teenage female who acted "too grown up." The expression, for her, revealed a desire for universal healing for the entire community and became an all-encompassing term that blended both race and gender.

FOR FURTHER READING

Walker, Alice. *In Search of our Mothers' Gardens: Womanist Prose.* Orlando, FL: Harcourt, 2004; White, Evelyn C. *Alice Walker: A Life.* New York: Norton, 2004.

KATE MILLETT (1934–)

Although it was not her intention when she turned her dissertation into the influential work, *Sexual Politics* (1970), Kate Millett is credited with providing the cannon that fired the initial shot of second-wave feminism and of altering the perceptions of thousands of women.

Katherine Murray Millett was born in St. Paul, Minnesota, on September 14, 1934, the middle child of three daughters. Her father James Albert, an engineer, abandoned her mother, Helen Feely, and his children when Kate was fourteen. Although her mother was college educated, she had difficulty finding a position with sufficient salary to support the family.

Kate was graduated *magna cum laude* from the University of Minnesota in 1956. With financial assistance from an aunt, she opted for graduate study in England. In 1958, she was awarded a master's in English literature from St. Hilda's College of Oxford University and became the first American woman to receive a postgraduate degree with honors from that institution.

After briefly teaching in North Carolina, Millet moved to New York City in 1959 to study painting and sculpting. In 1961, in an effort to improve her artistic style, she relocated to Tokyo, Japan, where she spent two years practicing her art and teaching English at Waseda University. The first showing of her paintings was at the Minami Gallery in 1963.

On returning to the United States in 1964, Millett took a teaching post at Barnard College for Women in New York City and plunged headlong into the Civil Rights Movement, becoming an active member of the Congress of Racial Equality. The following year she married Japanese sculptor Fumio Yoshimura. Although it was likely a marriage in name only, undertaken to avoid his deportation, the two remained legally joined for twenty years.

In the late 1960s, while she was pursuing a doctorate at Columbia University, Millett joined the National Organization for Women (NOW), became a member of the New York Radical Women and initiated a women's liberation group on campus. As a NOW committee member, she announced her bisexuality, which reinforced the media stereotype of the organization as being composed of lesbians. Although some NOW members became her staunch defenders, others wanted to squash the entire issue and to close membership to professed lesbians.

Millett's dissertation grew from a position paper she wrote on the relationship between feminism and sexuality, "Sexual Politics: A Manifesto for Revolution." The subsequent dissertation and the book created from it served as a critique of the patriarchy prevalent in Western society and literature. In the work, she identified patriarchy "as a socially conditioned belief system masquerading as nature." When the book was first published, she was a relatively unknown sculptor and activist, living in poverty in the Bowery district of New York City. Within a matter of weeks, *Sexual Politics* hit the best-seller list and Millett was lauded as laying the foundation for feminist scholarship and for *creating* feminist literary criticism that attacked classic misogynist writers like Norman Mailer and D.H. Lawrence.

Nearly overnight, Millett became a media darling and one of the most eminently quotable of the era's feminists. She advocated an end to romantic love and monogamous marriage and called for sexual revolution. Dubbed the "High Priestess" of feminism, Millett became an unwilling spokesperson for the women's movement despite some resentment among those who felt she failed to represent *every* woman. Although she changed the perceptions of thousands of women, *Time* magazine referred to her as the "Mao Tse-tung of Women's Liberation."

In an effort to remove herself from the spotlight, Millett left Barnard for Bryn Mawr and writing. Using the funds from her published work, Millett began purchasing and restoring the fields of a former Christmas tree farm near Poughkeepsie, New York and in 1971, she opened the Women's Art Colony Farm, a summer commune for women artists. Continuing to write, she published the autobiographical *Flying* (1974), which highlighted her marriage to Yoshimura and discussed her various affairs with women. She also penned several works on prostitution and *The Loony-Bin Trip* (1990), a graphic description of her battle with bipolar disorder and multiple suicide attempts. In 1979 Millett, in an attempt to broaden her message into the international arena, traveled to Iran to work for woman's rights. She was summarily expelled and asked not to return to the country.

Millett seemingly disappeared into the obscurity from which she came. The media darling and popular speaker who *didn't want to be a leader* because she felt it was against the spirit of the movement was eclipsed by others. Although she continued to write—her most recent endeavor *Mother Millett* was published in 2001—she was no longer clamored after by the fickle public and rumor-hungry media.

FOR FURTHER READING

Millett, Kate. *Sexual Politics*. Garden City, NY: Doubleday, 1970; ———. *Flying*. New York: Knopf, 1974; ———. *Going to Iran*. New York: Coward, McCann & Geoghegan, 1982.

SHIRLEY ST. HILL CHISHOLM (1924–2005)

Through her work in the political arena, Shirley Chisholm altered public perception regarding the abilities of both women and of African Americans. As the first African American woman elected to Congress, she was a strong advocate for human rights, became a national symbol of liberal politics, and was the first woman seriously considered as a candidate for president of the United States.

Born in Brooklyn, New York, Shirley was the daughter of Charles St. Hill, a factory worker from British Guiana, and Ruby, a seamstress, originally from Barbados. When she was three years old, she was sent to Barbados to live with her grandmother in order for her parents to save enough money to support the family. She returned to New York City in 1934 and enrolled at the Girls High School in Brooklyn.

After high school, the young woman was offered scholarships to both Vassar College and Oberlin University but she could not afford the incidental and living expenses connected with relocation. Consequently, she enrolled at Brooklyn College, majoring in sociology and excelling in debate. Racism was rampant at the time and when she was denied admission to a college social club, Shirley set up an alternative group for black students at the school. She graduated *cum laude* in 1946.

Following many rejections for employment, she took a position as a teacher's aide at the Mt. Calvary Childcare Center in Harlem, where she was eventually promoted to teacher. In that environment, she was exposed daily to the problems faced by the poor of all races and she became determined to better their situation. As others, she believed change could be manifested through providing education to the underserved. Consequently, she reentered school, gaining a master's degree in elementary education from Columbia University Teacher's College. In 1949, she met and married Jamaican Conrad Chisholm, a private investigator with whom she had no children.

Because the plight of the poor formed the crux of her political conscience, Chisholm founded the Bedford-Stuyvesant political league to facilitate change in the living conditions of that community as well as working with the League of Women Voters. Through her continuing efforts with day care and her insistence that early education was essential, she was named educational consultant for the Division of Day Care of the New York City Bureau of Child Welfare, a position she held from 1959 to 1964. Despite being told that *politics was a man's job,* Chisholm started the Unity Democratic Club to mobilize African American and Hispanic voters.

In 1964, she ran for and was elected to the New York State General Assembly, serving four years in the Albany legislature. During that time, she sponsored bills for state funding for daycare centers, increased school funding appropriations, especially for disadvantaged students, gained unemployment insurance for domestic workers, and negated discrimination against pregnant school teachers.

In 1968, Chisholm was invited to campaign for a seat in the House of Representatives from the Twelfth Congressional District. Although she was labeled as "uppity" for her nerve to run for office as a black woman, she garnered 80 percent of the vote, defeating Republican James Farmer, the former director of the Congress of Racial Equality, who attacked her credentials for the office based on her gender. To combat his negative campaign, she organized the women voters in the district and won the congressional seat, becoming the first African American woman to achieve that distinction. Her campaign slogan "unbossed and unbought" became the title of her 1970 autobiography and once in office, Chisholm hired an all woman staff. From the outset of her career in Washington, she advocated for civil rights, women, and the poor and was an avid opponent of the war in Vietnam. Although she was initially placed on the House Forestry Committee, where she could do little damage, she resigned the post, calling it *a waste of time* and irrelevant to her urban district. Her next assignment was on the Veterans' Affairs Committee and she was then moved to the Education and Labor Committee.

In 1969, Chisholm helped form the Congressional Black Caucus and she was elected to a second term in 1970. She was a cofounder of the National Organization for Women (NOW) and became a diligent champion and watchdog for the feminist coalition, reprimanding the group when they neglected issues of importance to the poor. In addition, she was one of the group of women that initiated the National Women's Political Caucus.

On January 25, 1972, Chisholm announced her candidacy for president of the United States. The Democratic Convention, held in Miami, Florida, represented the first such gathering to consider a woman for serious nomination to the office. With NOW support, Chisholm received 151 votes from the delegates, representing an ethnically diverse group, but lost to South Dakota senator George McGovern. Chisholm noted that being a woman was a larger obstacle to her nomination than being black, that "sexism ha[d] no color line" but that, even through defeat, her campaign had created a *catalyst for change.*

Chisholm added to her national press coverage by visiting Governor George Wallace after the assassination attempt on his life in 1972. Although she was criticized in the African American community, she felt an obligation since the other candidates were visiting Wallace. The visit was beneficial; Wallace encouraged southern support for minimum wages for domestic workers, a bill for which she was lobbying. Chisholm continued to push for persons living in the inner city and to recommend increased funding for education and health care, while proposing a reduction in military spending. She was divorced from Chisholm in 1972 and married Arthur Hardwick, a Buffalo, New York liquor store owner, with whom she had served in the state assembly. Shirley Chisholm served in the House of Representatives until 1982, a seven-term run.

After retiring from Congress, Chisholm was named to the Purington Chair at Mount Holyoke College in Massachusetts where she taught for four years. She was also invited to serve as ambassador to Jamaica under the Clinton administration.

Chisholm died on January 3, 2005, following a series of strokes. A 2005 documentary, "Shirley Chisholm '72: Unbought and Unbossed," featured her presidential run. The film aired on PBS and received an award at the Sundance Film Festival and the Peabody Award in 2006.

FOR FURTHER READING

Chisholm, Shirley. *Unbought and Unbossed: An Autobiography.* New York: Houghton Mifflin Company, 1970; ———. *The Good Fight.* New York: Harper & Row, 1973.

WILMA PEARL MANKILLER (1945–)

As principal chief of the Cherokee nation from 1985 to 1995, Wilma Mankiller served a population of more than one hundred forty thousand worldwide, controlled an annual budget of more than $75 million, and employed more than twelve hundred persons spread across seven thousand square miles. Her duties and range of power were equivalent to those of a head of state, such as the president of the United States, as well as those of a chief executive officer of a major corporation. Although it was a widely held belief that she had been destined for this role, it was not always readily apparent in her shy early years in rural Oklahoma.

The sixth of eleven children, Wilma Pearl Mankiller was born on November 18, 1945, in the Hastings Indian Hospital in Tahlequah, Oklahoma, the last stop on the infamous Trail of Tears (1838–1839), which forced the removal of the Cherokee from their ancestral lands in the South. Her father, Charley, was a full-blooded Cherokee and her mother, Irene, was of Dutch-Irish descent. Wilma was raised at Mankiller Flats on 160 acres allocated to her grandfather through the Dawes Act of 1887, land which is still preserved for future generations of her family.

Although the family was poor, her life was comfortable and community based. Her situation altered drastically, however, when in her tenth year, her parents agreed to a voluntary relocation program designed to assimilate Native Americans into the mainstream. The family was moved to San Francisco, California, and even though her neighborhood of Hunter's Point was racially mixed, Wilma felt like an outsider, particularly when she entered school. There was a growing climate of racial tension in California during the 1950s, and much of it was directed at Native Americans, the fastest growing minority in the state at the time.

To compensate for the lack of friends at school, Mankiller invested her free time in the San Francisco Indian Center, where she relieved her homesickness by creating bonds with other relocated Native American children. When she was seventeen, she met Ecuadorian immigrant Hector Hugo Olaya de Bardi at the Center, and they were married shortly before her eighteenth birthday. Although Hugo expected her to become a traditional wife and mother to their two daughters, Felicia and Gina, Mankiller required more challenge in her life.

Under protest from Hugo, Mankiller enrolled at San Francisco State College to study sociology. Much of her sociological training at the time, however, came not from the classroom but from her observations of the life around her. She became intrigued by the Civil Rights Movement and the involvement of the Black Panthers in the fight for freedom, as well as being impressed by the petitioning of the women's rights activists in asserting full equality.

San Francisco of the 1960s was an intriguing place, filled with peace-and-love flower children, antiwar activists, and Bohemian rebels of all types. It was also a community where women held places of prominence unfamiliar in Mankiller's world. At first, seeking a diversion, Mankiller and her daughters were merely observers of the radical behavior, but in November, 1969, the cause of activism hit home. A group of Native Americans took over the abandoned prison island of Alcatraz in San Francisco Bay, citing their right to ownership from an old treaty, which stated that any unused government land would revert to the tribe. Unable to ignore the plight of her people, she joined the protest and later asserted that her participation in the Alcatraz occupation changed her perceptions forever, not only of her role as a Cherokee but of her role as a woman as well.

In this spirit of awakening, she spent five years as a volunteer with the Pit River Tribe of northern California, establishing a legal defense fund for their battle to reclaim ancestral lands from the powerful Pacific Gas and Electric Company. This departure from her expected role further impaired her already weakened marriage, and in 1974, she and her husband of eleven years were divorced.

As a single parent and virtually without income, Mankiller felt the never-forgotten pull of her homeland more strongly and she and her daughters returned to Mankiller Flats in Oklahoma. Although she arrived with only twenty dollars, she was soon hired by the Cherokee Nation as Economic Stimulus Coordinator, and she began attending graduate classes in community planning. Eventually, she was appointed as principal organizer of a revitalization project for the Bell Community, a grant-funded program to allow the Cherokees to help themselves. In this capacity, she came under the close scrutiny of Principal Chief Ross Swimmer, who asked her to run for deputy chief during the next election. Despite hate mail, death threats, and obscene phone calls, Mankiller won the position and assumed office in 1983.

When Swimmer was invited to head the Bureau of Indian Affairs in Washington in 1985, Mankiller took over the position of principal chief, the first woman ever to head an American Indian nation. She completed Swimmer's term, and with encouragement from her family and her new husband, Charlie Soap, Mankiller ran for office in her own right in 1987, the same year she won *Ms.* magazine's Woman of the Year award. Even though resistance to placing a woman in such a position of power still existed, she was elected, then reelected in 1991, at last with a mandate from her people. She said, "Prior to my election, young Cherokee girls would never have thought that they might grow up and become chief."

During her tenure as principal chief, Mankiller worked to increase literacy for all her people and to encourage tribal women to become better educated. A civil rights activist, she used her political power to forward women's issues, to improve health care, and to secure the rights of children.

In 1993, with the aid of coauthor Michael Wallis, she composed *Mankiller: A Chief and Her People*. Although the work is a reflective overview of her life and her accomplishments as principal chief, the book is much more. It is a comprehensive history of the Cherokee people, written in a new light by one who lived it.

Preferring to give someone new an opportunity for the position, Wilma Mankiller did not seek reelection. Her official retirement took effect in July of 1995 but she continued to be a positive force in the life of her people as well as a role model for women in general. After being diagnosed with myasthenia gravis, a chronic neuromuscular disease that causes varying degrees of weakness in the voluntary muscles of the body, Mankiller dropped from public view although she continued to make occasional presentations and to advocate for her people.

FOR FURTHER READING

Janda, Sarah Eppler. *Beloved Women: The Political Lives of Ladonna Harris and Wilma Mankiller*. DeKalb: Northern Illinois University Press, 2007; Mankiller, Wilma, and Michael Wallis. *Mankiller: A Chief and Her People*. New York: St. Martin's Press, 1993.

JOAN RUTH BADER GINSBURG (1933–)

Called the "Thurgood Marshall of the Woman's Movement," Ruth Bader Ginsburg mounted the top of the judicial profession in the United States in 1993 as the 107th Supreme Court justice and only the second woman to be nominated to such a prestigious position. Throughout her tenure on the bench, Ginsburg remained true to her belief in woman's rights, gender equality, and a woman's right to choose.

Born in Brooklyn, New York on March 15, 1933, Ruth was the daughter of Nathan Bader, a furrier, and Celia Amster, both Jewish immigrants. Ruth was heavily influenced by her mother's intellect, even though Celia suppressed her abilities in order to fit the role expectations of the era. In addition to being a good student, Ruth was a cheerleader and baton twirler in high school. However, when she was due to graduate in 1950, a pall was cast over her celebration for her mother died the day before.

Ruth earned a scholarship to Cornell University, where she was awarded a bachelors degree in government with honors in 1954. Following graduation, she married a fellow student, Martin Ginsburg, and the two moved to Lawton, Oklahoma in order for him to fulfill his military tour of duty at Fort Sill. Ruth worked with the Social Security office in Lawton and frequently awarded benefits to elderly Native Americans even if they had no birth certificate but had a date of birth on their driver's license. There also, she had her first taste of discrimination for she was demoted to a lower position only because she was pregnant.

When Martin was discharged from the military in 1956, both enrolled in the Law School of Harvard University in Cambridge, Massachusetts. Ruth was one of only nine women in the class of five hundred; however, she was the one selected to edit the *Law Review*. When her husband took a position in New York City in 1958, she completed her studies at Columbia University, where she tied for academic first place in her class.

Despite her outstanding academic record, Ginsburg had difficulty finding a firm that would hire a woman attorney. She finally accepted a position as a law clerk. In 1961, however, she was hired by her alma mater and spent two years at Columbia working on a project on international legal procedure. In 1963, she became the second woman to join the faculty at Rutgers University Law School and only one of twenty in the United States to teach at any law school.

Until she read Simone de Beauvoir's *The Second Sex,* Ginsburg had not viewed discrimination in feminist terms but she suddenly realized that gender issues were present in every area of life. Because it was considered a woman's issue, the New Jersey American Civil Liberties Union (ACLU) began referring cases on sex discrimination to her and, in 1972, she served as the founding counsel for that group's Women's Rights Project. Over the period, she argued six sex-discrimination cases before the Supreme Court, winning five of the six. Ginsburg joined the faculty of Columbia University Law School in 1973 as its first tenured woman professor, while continuing to serve as general counsel to the ACLU and sitting on the organization's national board of directors.

In 1980, President Jimmy Carter appointed her to the Court of Appeals in Washington, DC, where she wrote more than three hundred opinions in thirteen years on issues such as abortion rights, gay rights, and affirmative action, among others. Ginsburg stated that abortion should be seen as a fundamental right of the equality of women, rather than as a privacy issue. When asked about her stance during the congressional hearings for her Supreme Court nomination, she replied that abortion was a decision that a woman would have to make for herself and notably refused to answer other questions on heated issues, a fact that would come to be referred to as the "Ginsburg Precedent" in future hearings.

In 1993, Ginsburg was appointed to the Supreme Court by President Bill Clinton, where she revitalized the court's interest in women's rights, including calling hostile work environments a type of sex discrimination under Title VII. She was noted as being principled, diligent, and the author of scholarly, balanced opinions.

FOR FURTHER READING

Campbell, Amy Leigh. *Raising the Bar: Ruth Bader Ginsburg and the ACLU Women's Rights Project.* Princeton, NJ: Xlibris Corporation, 2003.

PHYLLIS CHESLER (1940–)

Known for her advocacy of universal human rights, Phyllis Chesler was a popular lecturer, the author of thirteen books and thousands of articles, a psychotherapist, an expert court witness, and a professor emerita of psychology and women's studies. Although her stance on political policy in the Middle East created her share of critics, she stood firm in her belief in equality for all women.

Phyllis Chesler was born on October 1, 1940 in Brooklyn, New York, the eldest of the three children of orthodox Jewish immigrants. Her father, Leon Chesler, came to the United States from Russian-occupied Poland, where his mother was murdered by Cossacks in a tea shop she managed. Her mother, Lillian Hammer, was the only child in her family to be born in the United States.

As a child, Phyllis was exposed to the arts as well as studying Hebrew and psychoanalytic psychology. Precocious, she began writing at the age of eight and by age thirteen, she was reading the works of Sigmund Freud to satiate her growing curiosity about the human psyche.

In 1961, she married her college sweetheart, Ali, the son of an upper-class family from Kabul, Afghanistan who had been away from his home country for over fourteen years, studying in both Europe and the United States. Although he appeared to have divested himself of the belief system inherent in his country and in his Islamic past, Ali was drawn back to Afghanistan in order for his family to meet his new bride. Assuming that her life with her husband in Kabul would be similar to her life in New York, Phyllis undertook the journey without concern. When the plane landed, however, officials seized her passport, promising to return it shortly, and she was immediately swept away on the wave of Ali's family.

Once back on native soil, her new husband reverted to his upbringing, defending his father's polygamy and marital dalliances and his mother's iron rule of the household, including requiring his bride to wear a *chadari,* a culturally traditional head and face covering, if she ventured outside the home. Phyllis's wishes soon took a backseat to those of Ali's family and she realized that she was essentially a prisoner on unfamiliar soil. After befriending a group of other foreign wives, she convinced one of the women to aid in her escape by purchasing a forged passport and arranging transportation out of the country. Unfortunately, in the close-knit community, her plans were unveiled and brought to the attention of Ali's parents. Phyllis suffered repercussions for her actions; she contracted hepatitis from drinking water her mother-in-law had instructed the servants to stop boiling. As a means of saving face and ridding themselves of the problem, Ali's parents offered her safe passage out of Afghanistan to seek medical attention for her illness.

Safely back in the United States, Chesler returned to college, acquired her bachelor's degree in comparative literature and language from Bard College in 1963 and a divorce from Ali. In the mid- to late-1960s, she was involved in the North Student Movement, tutored underserved children in Harlem and supported both the Young Lords and the Black Panthers. She also became a staunch advocate for women who were imprisoned for murdering their abusers. Her experience in Kabul had stirred her feminism and her empathy for all women living under extreme conditions. In essence, she became a one-woman force, taking on cultural relativism, academia, the ethnocentrism of some feminists, and political correctness. In 1969 and 1970, she broadened her message through teaching one of the first women's studies courses in the country at City University in New York, eventually turning the course into a program that fulfilled requirements for both a college minor and a major. Her work influenced the creation of curricular self-defense classes for women as well as the addition of a rape crisis center and a child center on the campus. In 1969, she cofounded the Association for Women in Psychology, an organization that, according to the mission statement, "encourages feminist psychological research, theory and activism."

Shortly after earning a master's and a doctoral degree in psychology from the New School for Social Research, she published *Women and Madness* (1972), which became an international best seller, consistently reprinted and translated into multiple languages. The work addressed women's socialization into the mythology of being the weaker sex or frail and the consequent belief that they needed to *cure* a variety of conditions through therapy. The publication guaranteed Chesler's place among the leading feminist psychologists in the country.

In 1974, Chesler cofounded The National Women's Health Network, an organization that offered accurate and unbiased information on health care and functioned as an advocacy group for national policies. She was also a charter member of the Women's Forum, a charter member of the Veteran Feminists of America, and the founder of the International Committee for Women of the Wall.

During the ensuing years, Chesler continued to teach at the City University of New York in both psychology and women's studies, eventually retiring with emerita status. While at that institution, she participated in a class action lawsuit against the university on behalf of women. Throughout the period, Chesler served as a visiting professor at Brandeis University and taught courses in forensic psychology at the John Jay College of Criminal Justice. She continued to write, publishing thirteen volumes, to present lectures and programs on a variety of topics, especially on Islamic gender Apartheid, and organized political, legal, and human rights campaigns in the United States, Canada, Europe, the Middle East, and the Far East.

In 2003, with the publication of *The New Anti-Semitism: The Current Crisis and What We Must Do About It,* Chesler was again under attack by critics who accused her of being pro-Israel and of using her writing as a platform for that campaign. At one point she was even accused of being racist but held firmly to her belief in universal human rights rather than standards tailored to individual cultures.

In 2007, Chesler continued to write, working on a collection of her articles titled *The Islamification of America* and other books. A collection of her papers was archived at Duke University in North Carolina.

FOR FURTHER READING

Chesler, Phyllis. *Letters to a Young Feminist*. New York: Four Walls Eight Windows, 1997; ———. *The Death of Feminism: What's Next in the Struggle for Women's Freedom*. New York: Palgrave Macmillan, 2006; Jochnowitz, George. "A Conversation with Phyllis Chesler: American Feminist and Zionist Activist." *Midstream* 53 (Sept.–Oct. 2007): 9–14.

FANNIE LOU HAMER (1917–)

Those who truly believe that one person cannot make a difference have obviously never heard of Fannie Lou Hamer, often called the "Soul of the Civil Rights Movement." Rising from the most obscure beginnings, the child and wife of sharecroppers, Hamer became one of the most outspoken activists of the era, teaching and registering voters, helping to create a new political party, fighting for women's rights, and addressing national rallies.

The granddaughter of slaves, Fannie Lou Townsend was born on October 6, 1917, in Montgomery County, Mississippi, the youngest of the twenty children of Jim and Ella Townsend. Moving the family from Montgomery County to Sunflower County in 1919, the Townsends continued to sharecrop or *half*; in other words, they planted, cared for, and cultivated crops for a landowner in exchange for a theoretical half of the income once the bounty was sold. Frequently, however, their share was markedly less than half since the landowner took out deductions for expenses he claimed the family incurred throughout the year. In that period, the wealth of black sharecropping families often rested on their children's ability to aid in the procurement of income and, by the age of six, Fannie Lou had joined her brothers and sisters in the cotton fields. In addition to farm work, the young child attended school through the sixth grade, even though she was frequently without proper clothing. In the early years of the twentieth century, African American children were permitted to go to school for only four months each year and, eventually, Fannie Lou became discouraged and dropped out of school to help her family's resources by cutting corn. As a child, she also contracted polio for which vaccine had not then been discovered; consequently, she walked with a slight limp for the rest of her life.

In 1944, Fannie Lou married Perry "Pap" Hamer. The newlyweds moved to his place of employment, the Marlow plantation in Ruleville, Mississippi, and continued with the sharecropping life. Because Fannie Lou was more educated than most of the other field hands on the plantation, she was relieved of manual labor and given the job of timekeeper, a type of rudimentary bookkeeping. In addition to her other responsibilities, she and "Pap" were raising two girls, Dorothy Jean and Vergie. One of the children had been taken in from an unmarried woman who could not care for the child and the other had been badly burned and her family was too poor to provide treatment for her injuries. Fannie Lou wanted children of her own but her two pregnancies ended in stillbirths and she was given an involuntary hysterectomy, after being told she had a growth in her belly.

Although she had always wanted to do something about the plight of the plantation workers, particularly because she had watched one parent die and the other become infirm due to the conditions under which they labored, she felt powerless to make an impact. It was not until 1962, when she was forty-four years old, that she was, at long last, given the tools to create change. In August of that year, she attended a mass meeting led by the Student Non-Violent Coordinating Committee (SNCC). The SNCC volunteers were in the Ruleville area to aid black citizens in registering to vote. Until that moment, Fannie Lou Hamer was unaware that she had the Constitutional right to vote and when the SNCC workers asked who would be the first to volunteer, she silently raised her hand. Although she should have been reticent to get involved, considering the political climate of the region at the time, she was not afraid. She was noted as saying, "The only thing they could do was kill me and it seemed like they'd been trying to do that a little bit at a time ever since I could remember."

Shortly after the meeting, Fannie Lou Hamer, with seventeen others, took a bus to the county seat in Indianola and tried to register. As a safeguard against a black voting block, the registrars were instructed to require *some* potential voters to interpret the state Constitution prior to permitting them to sign up. Hamer failed to pass the test and was turned away. On their way back to Ruleville, the local police stopped the bus, claiming it was "too yellow," consequently the "wrong color." The passengers were detained but ultimately released.

News spreads quickly in small towns, however, and when her employer of eighteen years heard of her actions, he issued an ultimatum. Either Fannie Lou removed her name from the voting roll or she must leave the plantation. She chose the latter. Leaving behind her husband, children, and the only life she had ever known, the plucky soul ventured out into the world. For a short while she lodged with friends until white Night Riders fired into the house sixteen times and multiple threats were made against her life. Fearing for the safety of her friends, as well as her own life, she left the area for Tallahatchie County.

By November of 1962, she had returned to Sunflower County, transformed into an activist for civil rights. She commented at the time that she was sick and tired of being sick and tired. Deeply religious and fervently patriotic, Fannie Lou Hamer was committed to nonviolence. She often recalled her mother's instruction that hating made one as weak as those who were filled with hatred. Wearing that mantle, she became an instructor of voter-education programs run by SNCC, In December 1962, she once again attempted to register. In January, she was notified that she had passed the test and she proudly signed the voter rolls.

The year 1963 was the most violent of the Civil Rights Movement. Nine hundred thirty protests were staged in 115 cities in the South and the frustrated fervor was escalating. Although she was not highly educated or trained as a public speaker, a SNCC conference in Nashville launched Hamer's career as a orator and she toured the country with the SNCC Freedom Singers for several months, giving presentations and encouraging people to register. During the period, she also lobbied to gain welfare benefits for poor black families.

On June 3, 1963, while returning from voter-registration training in Charleston, South Carolina, Fannie Lou Hamer was arrested at a bus station in Winona, Mississippi for using the wrong rest room and for moving toward the front of the station. After she was taken to the Montgomery County Jail, a state highway patrolman and two other white officers entered her cell accompanied by two black inmates. The policemen ordered the prisoners to beat Hamer with a blackjack. Afraid not to comply with the officer's instructions, the first prisoner flayed her until he was exhausted and passed the weapon to his companion. When it was finally over, she had a blood clot in her eye that impaired her vision and an injured kidney from repeated blows to her back. She was left mercifully alone in the cell where she was forced to listen to the screams of a fellow civil rights worker under attack in the area next to hers. Over the pain of her allies, she overheard the policemen in the corridor, laughing about throwing their bodies into the Big Black River where they would never be found. Eventually, Andrew Young, then an aide to Martin Luther King, posted her bail and noted her stoicism and commitment to nonviolence during the ordeal. Although she was permanently disfigured by the beatings, her only comment was that she had to love her attackers because they were sick like the country was sick.

By September, the U.S. Justice Department had filed criminal charges against the Winona police chief, the Montgomery County sheriff, the Mississippi highway patrolman, and two others in the Winona jail-beating incident. Although she was still not well and aware she would be called on to testify, Fannie Lou was not deterred from attending a SNCC rally. In addition to her ability as a speaker, she was known throughout the movement for her powerful musical voice and was frequently asked to display her talent. In November, she went to Washington, DC to sing songs of protest during the SNCC conference.

Shortly thereafter, she helped found the Council of Federated Organizations, a consolidation of the voting rights groups who were considering recruiting one thousand college students from other states to aid in the voter registration drive. Some of the group was opposed to inviting willing white students to participate but Fannie Lou emphatically announced that if they were trying to break the bonds of segregation, they could not enforce the policy themselves. In 1964, that recruitment drive culminated in Freedom Summer, an influx of white students primarily from the northern states. While Hamer was involved in other activities, the preliminaries for the trial of the law enforcement officers continued and in December 1963, she testified in federal court in Oxford, Mississippi. The all-white jury acquitted each of the men of any wrongdoing in the incident.

Mississippi's State Sovereignty Commission was established by legislation in 1956 to protect the state's *sovereign rights* after the passage of *Brown v. Board of Education*. In early 1964 the group investigated Hamer, suspecting her of subversive activity because she was organizing a clothing drive for the poor. After escaping their scrutiny, her focus turned to the 1964 presidential election and to lobbying for more political reinforcements for open registration in the South.

In an effort to gain greater national attention for the problem of discrimination in the registration process, civil rights groups came together to form the Mississippi Freedom Democratic Party (MFDP) on April 26, 1964. The party sent a delegation to Atlantic City where the Democratic Party was holding its nominating convention for the presidency. One of those delegates was Fannie Lou Hamer. The purpose of the group was to challenge the seating of Mississippi's standard democratic delegation at the convention. The group asserted bias since those present were all white and, thus, could not fairly represent the population of the state particularly since many blacks had not even been allowed to register.

Fannie Lou Hamer spoke to the Credentials Committee of the convention about the injustice she felt was being perpetrated. She asked, "Is this America, the land of the free and the home of the brave, where we are threatened daily because we want to live as decent human beings?" Reporters swarmed through the room but the live television coverage of her speech was clipped in mid-comment, preempted by Lyndon Baines Johnson for a presidential press conference. Although many think the timing was not accidental, the national networks aired her speech in its entirety later in the evening, alerting many of the American people to the realities of life in the South.

President Johnson offered the MDFP a compromise. Although he refused to seat the entire delegation, two seats with voting rights were offered. He also proposed that in the future no delegates be allowed from any state that denied voting rights to blacks. Hamer was not overjoyed and she told Hubert Humphrey she "didn't come up here for no two seats." What the woman lacked in formal education, she more than made up for in determination. After returning to Mississippi, she put in a bid for the House of Representatives seat as the MFDP candidate from Mississippi's Second Congressional District. Although she lost the election, she did garner 33,009 votes. That fall, she traveled to Guinea in Africa with other SNCC workers, James Foreman and Julian Bond, and the entertainer Harry Belafonte.

She noted that she received better treatment from those many referred to as *savages* than she usually got in this country.

In 1965, partly because of his promised compromise, President Lyndon Baines Johnson signed the Voting Rights Act, empowering federal registrars to aid in registering African American votes in the South. Persistent still, Fannie Lou Hamer was a plaintiff in a case, *Hamer v. Campbell,* also in 1965 that resulted in overturning local election results in two Mississippi counties where blacks had not been allowed to vote.

In addition to being in demand as a speaker and entertainer, *Mississippi* magazine voted Hamer one of the six women of influence in the state in 1965. Essentially unimpressed by her own notoriety, Hamer continued to work for better conditions for the people of Mississippi by organizing grass-roots antipoverty programs. In 1969, she helped found the Freedom Farm Cooperative, an organization that purchased forty acres to be used for growing food; in addition, the group provided outreach to aid the poor in enriching their diet and to raise funds for the Pig Bank to add more meat to their diet. She attended the White House Conference on Hunger and appeared in a nationally televised documentary. During the first year, the cooperative produced and purchased enough food to share with five thousand people and, in 1970, the group expanded to include the Young World Developers who increased the holdings by 640 acres and built houses for the indigent, both black and white.

Hamer was asked to serve on the 1968 Loyalist Democratic National Committee. She was seated as a delegate at the Democratic convention in Chicago and challenged the Alabama delegation on racial bias. Her belief in the power of politics to control people's lives continued throughout her life and in 1971 she participated in the founding meeting of the National Women's Political Caucus. That fall, she made an unsuccessful bid for a seat in the Mississippi State Senate. In January of 1972, the pace and demands of her life were wearing her down and she was hospitalized for nervous exhaustion. Hamer was a difficult woman to keep silenced and made to rest, however, and by July, she was racing again as a delegate to the national convention in Miami Beach.

In addition to working on issues of poverty and politics, Hamer served on the board of directors of the Fannie Lou Hamer Day Care Centre in Ruleville that was founded in 1970 by the National Council of Negro Women and was one of the earliest members of the National Organization for Women. She received many honorary degrees and awards and the mayor of Ruleville announced the annual observance of Fannie Hamer Day at Ruleville Central High School in March of 1970.

During the latter days of her life, she worked for school desegregation, adequate child day care, and affordable low-income housing. In 1974, she was again hospitalized for exhaustion and her beloved Freedom Farm lost all but forty acres of its holdings to creditors. During her hospital stay, she began writing her autobiography, *To Praise Our Bridges*. In the spring of

1976, Hamer had surgery for the removal of breast cancer, possibly caused by the beatings she endured in Winona. Although the surgery seemed successful, she died only a year later, on March 15, 1977 of heart failure brought on by cancer, diabetes, and hypertension.

On March 20, many of those involved in the Civil Rights Movement attended her funeral, including Andrew Young, former U.S. ambassador to the United Nations and mayor of Atlanta, Georgia, who said: "Women were the spine of our movement. It was women going door to door, speaking with their neighbors, meeting in voter-registration classes together, organizing through their churches that gave the vital momentum and energy to the movement. Mrs. Hamer was special but she was also representative... She shook the foundations of this nation." Above all, Fannie Lou Hamer, the grand daughter of slaves and the daughter of sharecroppers, was best known as the woman who transformed the Civil Rights Movement.

FOR FURTHER READING

Kling, Susan. *Fannie Lou Hamer: A Biography*. Chicago: Women for Racial and Economic Equality, 1979; Mills, Kay. *This Little Light of Mine: The Life of Fannie Lou Hamer*. Lexington: University Press of Kentucky, 2007.

AUDRE LORDE (1934–1992)

Noting there were few voices for black women, Audre Lorde determined to become that voice through her poetry. According to Lorde, the primary purpose of art should be to protest the status quo and to change destructive social patterns.

Audrey Geraldine Lorde was born in New York City, the daughter of Frederick Byron and Linda Belmar, impoverished Caribbean immigrants who were living in Harlem. The third and youngest child, she was born both tongue-tied and nearsighted but overcame both disabilities by learning to speak as she was learning to read when she was four. As a child, she eliminated the "y" from her name to add rhetorical balance, an early indication of her ability as a poet and her need for self-determination.

Through her years at Hunter High School, her rebellious streak matured and she was socially ostracized by her peers. Withdrawing into her writing, Audre edited the literary section of the school arts magazine and had her first poem published in *Seventeen* magazine.

From 1951 to 1959, Audre worked her way through Hunter College as a ghost writer, a social worker, a medical clerk, and an x-ray technician. After spending a year as an exchange student at the National University of Mexico in 1954, she returned to New York and became active in the gay community of Greenwich Village. In 1961, she was awarded a master's degree in library science from Columbia University.

The year after her graduation, Lorde married Edward Ashley Rollins, an attorney, with whom she had two children, Elizabeth and Jonathan. The two were married for eight years. By 1968, Lorde began exploring professional opportunities. After receiving a National Endowment for the Arts grant and a poet-in-residence position, she began teaching at Tougaloo College, a small, historically black college in Jackson, Mississippi. It was the era of the Civil Rights Movement in the South and violence swirled around her, activity that would inform much of her later writing and activism. In Jackson, she met her longtime companion, Frances Clayton, and began to describe herself as black, lesbian, mother, warrior, and poet. Lorde noted that, without community, coalition, and freedom from oppression, there could be no liberation. As a consequence of her growing activism, she was invited to be the featured presenter at the first national march for gay and lesbian liberation in 1979.

In 1980, having survived breast cancer, Lorde published the *Cancer Journals*, the first work to underscore the viewpoint of a lesbian of color. Empowered by the success of that publication, she cofounded the Kitchen Table Women of Color Press. From 1991 to 1993, she served as the New York State poet laureate, the highest state honor bestowed on a poet.

Struggling against the label of feminist, Lorde changed her name to Gamba Adisa, meaning "Warrior: She Who Makes Her Meaning Clear." She toured as a lecturer worldwide, forming a coalition among African, German, and Dutch women. As a voice for the marginalization based on race and gender, she founded a sisterhood in South Africa and established the St. Croix Women's Coalition in the Virgin Islands.

Although she criticized the racism in the feminist movement and the sexism among African Americans, she continued to be a representative voice for women, African Americans, and lesbians. She believed that difference should be viewed as a resource rather than being perceived as a threat. After winning a fourteen-year battle against breast cancer, Lorde died of liver cancer in St. Croix on November 17, 1992.

FOR FURTHER READING

Keating, AnaLouise. *Women Reading Women Writing: Self-Invention in Paula Gunn Allen, Gloria Anzaldúa and Audre Lorde.* Philadelphia, PA: Temple University Press, 1996; Lorde, Audre. *Sister Outsider: Essays and Speeches.* Trumansburg, NY: Crossing Press, 1984.

BELL HOOKS (GLORIA JEAN WATKINS) (1952–)

Believing that the issues of race, class, and gender were inseparable, bell hooks advocated acquiring a new revolutionary consciousness that could delve to the root causes of social and discrimination problems, rather than merely treating the symptoms. She viewed each issue as a cumulative product of systems of oppression and domination and addressed those views in her writing, her teaching, and her lectures.

Born Gloria Jean Watkins on September 25, 1952, in Hopkinsville, Kentucky, hooks was the daughter of impoverished parents. Her father, Veodis Watkins, worked as a custodian and her mother, Rosa Bell, was a homemaker who cared for their seven children. Growing up poor, black, female, and physically abused created layered platforms for Gloria's later activism as well as providing much of the raw material she would use in her writing.

As a child, she attended public school in a segregated system, where her classmates and her teachers were African American; when the schools were integrated, she had difficulty adjusting to the new system and to primarily Caucasian teachers. After graduating from Crispus Attucks High School, she left Kentucky for California, earning a bachelors degree in English from Stanford University in 1973, followed by a master's from the University of Wisconsin in 1976, and a doctorate from the University of California at Santa Cruz in 1983. While working on her doctorate, she taught English and ethnic studies at the University of Southern California in Santa Cruz and at San Francisco State.

In conjunction with her teaching, she began to write poetry and when the work was published, she adopted the pen name, bell hooks, a name she borrowed from her maternal grandmother and used to honor the woman for whom she had deep admiration. She insisted on the lowercase spelling to signify that the content of the work should be looked at as more important than the author. hooks's first major publication took its title from a speech by the early abolitionist and woman's rights activist, Sojourner Truth. *Ain't I A*

Woman: Black Women and Feminism was published in 1981. She began writing the book when she was only nineteen years old; thus, she acknowledged that many of the ideas were naïve because they were penned prior to her gaining political awareness. Nevertheless, the book had an impact on feminist thought and dealt with her views on a variety of topics, such as the marginalization of black women, the disregard for race in feminism, the role of the media in creating stereotypes, the importance of education, and the white supremacist patriarchal capitalist system. From the outset, even in her youth, hooks viewed all issues of oppression as interrelated and stated that they could not be dealt with separately.

As a political and cultural critic, those themes permeated her teaching, her speaking, and her writing as she became a more sophisticated opponent of inequality. She believed educators, particularly in higher education, should be constantly challenged to view their profession as freedom in practice. In other words, she advocated teaching critical consciousness and critical thinking, demonstrating the blending of issues and providing training to attack those issues. According to hooks, the most successful method of overcoming problems came through practicing communication, building communities, providing strength in numbers, and striving for literacy for all people.

In addition to taking on academia, she was also critical of feminism, noting a definite class bias in the movement. She commented that, because of the current composition of the group as primarily white upper-class women, it was as if they were inviting others to *join in their struggle,* when rights for women were not necessarily the sole pursuit of women of color. The struggle, she said, did not begin with feminism; instead, it began with an awareness of domination in all forms. She also critiqued the sisterhood of victimization because black women did not see themselves as victims; white women, she offered, experience discrimination but black women experience oppression. She added that a woman becomes a feminist when she does away with gendered thoughts and "revolutionizes her consciousness" to accept the overlap of feminism, race, and class. According to her, the same principle should apply to men. In that regard, hooks issued a call for more black women leaders and more black men as teachers of feminism. Her 1984 work, *Feminist Theory: From Margin to Center,* launched that belief and recommended a new direction for the movement that would incorporate more of the experiences of women of color.

The media also came under her scrutiny and she expressed that the primary purpose of the mass media was the forwarding of capitalism through advertising. She noted that women, often poor women, were, unfortunately, the principal targets of those campaigns. She also cited racism and sexism as rampant in all types of media.

In the 1980s, hooks initiated a support group for black women, the Sisters of the Yam, a title that reflected the support derived from a community of like-minded women. Although the group was open to all, it was particularly for victims of psychological or physical abuse or those who were made to feel inferior by society, their position, or the media and counseling was available.

Continuing to write, hooks contributed a column to *Zeta* magazine and set a goal of publishing a book every year. In 2002, she gave the commencement address at Southwestern University in Texas and was booed off the stage. Regardless of that reception and other criticism, hooks called herself a "committed worker for freedom." She was awarded a Distinguished Professorship at Berea College in Kentucky in 2004, where she held a weekly feminist discussion group and continued to challenge the status quo in a variety of areas.

FOR FURTHER READING

Florence, Namulundah. *bell hooks' Engaged Pedagogy: A Transgressive Education for Critical Consciousness*. Westport, CT: Bergin & Garvey, 1998; hooks, bell. *Talking Back: Thinking Feminist, Thinking Black*. Toronto: Between the Lines, 1988.

ESTHER EGGERTSEN PETERSON
(1906–1997)

Awarded the Presidential Medal of Freedom in 1981, the highest civilian award for service, Esther Peterson was an activist for workers' rights for over fifty years. She also inspired and aided in the creation of the Presidential Commission on the Status of Women in the 1960s.

Born in Provo, Utah in 1906, Esther was the fifth of six children of Danish immigrants. Her father, Luther, was the state superintendent of schools for Utah and a working farmer in the Mormon community. The family was thus highly supportive of education for their children, regardless of gender.

After graduating from Brigham Young University with a degree in physical education, Esther moved to New York City to attend Columbia University Teachers College where she was awarded a master's degree. While attending Columbia, she met and married Oliver Peterson.

In 1932, the couple moved to Boston and Esther took a position with a college preparatory school, the Winsor School for Girls. In addition to her profession, she also volunteered at the Young Women's Christian Association (YWCA), teaching classes for working class young women in the evenings. At the time, two such facilities existed in Boston because the YWCA was segregated; Peterson noted the irony of forced separation by pointing out that the motto of the Y was "equality and justice." The facilities were subsequently merged due, in part, to her efforts.

While at the YWCA, Peterson gained her first awareness of gender and class inequity. One evening, a majority of her regular students, primarily factory workers, were absent. She was told they were on strike against their employer's unfair labor practices. Peterson reacted by joining her students, many of them children, on the picket line. Thus, aroused and alarmed by her discoveries, she became a voice for the empowerment of working class women. She began spending her summers at Bryn Mawr's School for Women Workers in Industry, speaking, training, and organizing as well as volunteering her time with the International Ladies Garment Workers Union.

In 1938, she took a position as a paid organizer for the American Federation of Teachers. She also gave birth to the first of four children; consequently, she was earning fifteen dollars a week from her job and paying twenty dollars a week in childcare expenses.

The following year, she began working for the Amalgamated Clothing Workers Union and by 1944, she was appointed as the union's first lobbyist in Washington, DC. Through her congressional persuasive techniques, she was instrumental in pushing through an increase in the minimum wage from forty cents to seventy-five cents per hour.

In 1948, the Department of State assigned Oliver Peterson as a diplomat to Sweden. Consequently, the couple spent ten years in Europe, where Esther was active in the International Confederation of Free Trade Unions committee for women. When her husband contracted cancer, they returned to the United States and she was offered a position as the first woman lobbyist for the American Federation of Labor and Congress of Industrial Organizations (AFL-CIO).

After campaigning for John F. Kennedy in Utah, Peterson was appointed as head of the Women's Bureau in the Department of Labor in 1961. Through a series of hearings held from coast to coast, she presented the Department with the concerns of working women, primarily equal pay for equal work and the glass ceiling that prevented promotion. Her findings helped reignite the woman's movement in the 1960s and as a consequence of the hearings, she helped establish the President's Commission on the Status of Women, finding, among other issues, a lack of day care, women in low-wage work, and a repeated plea for equal wages. The Commission laid the groundwork for the National Women's Commission on Civil Rights that allowed the voices of African American working women to be heard perhaps for the first time. Her work aided passage of the Equal Pay Act of 1963 and she was promoted to assistant secretary for Labor Standards, making her the highest ranking woman in the Kennedy Administration.

Peterson worked as a special assistant in consumer affairs under Presidents Johnson and Carter prior to becoming vice president for Consumer Affairs with the Giant Food Corporation. In that capacity she worked to pass laws that would guarantee truth in advertising and required food manufacturers to list nutrition facts and expiration dates.

In 1993, President Clinton appointed Peterson as a delegate to the UN General Assembly. She published her autobiography, appropriately titled *Restless* in 1995. Although she was never formally a member of any woman's liberation work, Peterson did more behind the scenes to alleviate the plight of the working class, both white and black, than perhaps any other woman of her generation. She died in Washington, DC in December 1997.

FOR FURTHER READING

Peterson, Esther, and Winfred Conkling. *Restless: The Memoirs of Labor and Consumer Activist Esther Peterson.* Vero Beach, FL: Caring Publishing, 1997.

ANNA ELEANOR ROOSEVELT
(1884–1962)

Known as one of the most active first ladies in American history and likely the first to be so publicly visible and vigilant, Eleanor Roosevelt served as a role model for women in politics and public life. During her lifetime and after, she was one of the most admired women in the world.

Although she was born into privilege among New York City's elite, Eleanor had an unhappy childhood. Her mother, Ann Ludlow Hall, constantly berated the child, calling her homely, and her father, Eliot Roosevelt, brother of Theodore, was an alcoholic. By the time she was ten years old, both of her parents had died and she and her two brothers were sent to live with her maternal grandmother and uncles in Tivoli, New York. Her grandmother was a strict disciplinarian and offered the child little affection; thus, it was likely a relief when she was sent away to Allenswood in England, a private finishing school for wealthy American and British young women. There, she became a favorite of the headmistress, Marie Souvestre, who became her mentor, permitting the child to accompany her on European jaunts, improving her self-confidence, and encouraging her academic excellence.

By the time she returned to the United States in 1902, Eleanor had developed a passion for social justice and a growing sense of independence. She accepted a position at Rivington House, a settlement house on the Lower East Side of Manhattan in New York City, where she taught calisthenics and dancing to immigrant women. Although many women of her social class became reformers because they felt it was the responsibility of the wealthy to aid the unfortunate, Roosevelt saw the poverty firsthand and made a lifetime commitment to eradicating it, including limiting work hours and advocating better wages. With her friend Florence Kelly, she became involved in the National Consumers League, where she worked to improve conditions for women factory workers. Accepting a seat on the compliance committee, Roosevelt advocated equal pay for equal work, minimum wages, a ten-hour work day, no child labor, and an absence of sweatshops, particularly for children. She continued to move philosophically from a charity mind-set to one devoted to social justice, understanding a need for changing the system, rather than merely treating the symptoms.

Due to her political connections through her uncle Theodore Roosevelt, Eleanor was invited to a White House reception where she was reintroduced to her fifth cousin, Franklin. Despite negative comments in the press and the disapproval of his family, the two were married on St. Patrick's Day in 1905. During World War I, when Franklin was appointed as assistant secretary of the Navy, the couple moved to Washington, DC. Eleanor was active in the Red Cross and worked to improve conditions in mental services for returning soldiers at the Naval Hospital.

After the war, the Roosevelts returned to New York City where Eleanor chaired the legislative committee of the New York State League of Women. While vacationing in New Brunswick in 1921, Franklin contracted a disease, initially thought to be polio but likely Guillain-Barré syndrome, resulting in permanent paralysis from the waist down. When the infirmity took him briefly out of the public spotlight, he used the time to educate Eleanor in the political process through editing his speeches and aiding in fundraising. At his suggestion, she joined the New York Democratic Party as a supporter of unions and an advocate of a living wage. By the mid-1920s, she had developed her own political identity, believing that politics and reform were intertwined. She noted that, if society as a whole were improved, the situation for women would improve.

Through her association with the Party, she put together planks of interest to women to be presented at the 1924 Democratic National Convention. For the first time, she saw firsthand the discrimination that permeated the politics of the era for when the committee met, she was not allowed to attend. Not discouraged, she worked to get women into the party and encouraged them to run for office.

In 1933, Franklin Delano Roosevelt took office as president of the United States and Eleanor, with her own agenda in tow, became First Lady. Although she was criticized for continuing her business and activist causes, she continued to press for the rights of working women and for African Americans. In her vocal opposition to inequality on all fronts, she permanently changed the role of the First Lady, setting benchmarks for those who would follow as advocates for their particular causes. Eleanor campaigned tirelessly against all forms of discrimination and for the rights of the disadvantaged. In that regard, she held weekly press conferences for women reporters, traveled thousands of miles, and wrote a daily newspaper column, "My Day," as well as several books. Additionally, she cochaired a national committee on civil defense and supported more opportunities for African Americans and women.

Although she was a champion of working women, Roosevelt was frequently at odds with the leaders of the woman's movement and feminism.

She was particularly vocal in her opposition to the Equal Rights Amendment, not because she saw it as unnecessary or wrong, but because she viewed it as providing protection for middle- and upper-class white women and felt it would have a negative impact on the working poor. She thought the amendment would decrease the right of individual states to pass protective legislation for women workers. Although she believed that men and women should have the same rights, she also felt that those rights for women should be protected.

After Franklin's death in 1945, Eleanor was appointed as a delegate to the United Nations by President Harry Truman. Named chair of the Human Rights Committee, she was largely responsible for creating the Universal Declaration of Human Rights. Although she felt women should not be singled out in the Declaration, which would, in essence, separate their *gender* from *human,* feminists insisted that the wording had to be incorporated. The Declaration was accepted in December 1948 and was considered her greatest achievement.

When Esther Peterson proposed the President's Commission on the Status of Women, President Kennedy appointed Roosevelt as chair. When the report was published, it reiterated that equality should be based on an acknowledgment of gender differences and not based on support of an Equal Rights Amendment.

After receiving thirty-five honorary degrees and publishing her autobiography in 1961, Roosevelt entered a new field. At the age of seventy-five, she accepted a visiting professorship in international relations at Brandeis University.

In 1960, Roosevelt was struck by a car. When she saw her physician, it was discovered that she had aplastic anemia, followed by the development of tuberculosis in her bone marrow. She died in New York City on November 7, 1962.

FOR FURTHER READING

Beck, Susan Abrams. "Eleanor Roosevelt: The Path to Equality." *White House Studies* 4, no. 4 (Fall 2004): 531–45; Freedman, Russell. *Eleanor Roosevelt: A Life of Discovery.* New York: Clarion Books, 1993; Glendon, Mary Ann. *A World Made New: Eleanor Roosevelt and the Universal Declaration of Human Rights.* New York: Random House, 2001.

CAMILLE ANNA PAGLIA (1947–)

Labeled as "the feminist other feminists love to hate," Camille Paglia was a social critic and popular culture icon. Calling herself "a classroom teacher," she attacked what she considered the pretentiousness of academia, political correctness and the *poor me* lamentations of the women's movement.

Born in Endicott, New York, on April 2, 1947, Paglia was the daughter of Pasquale Paglia and Lydia Anne Colapietro. Her father was a first-generation Italian immigrant and her mother was born in Ceccano, Italy. Although the family was not well off, her parents instilled a love of the arts in the young child, including an early appreciation of opera, a passion that would guide much of her later work. During her elementary school years, the family moved to Oxford, New York, where her father managed a working farm and taught high school at the Oxford Academy. When Camille entered the fifth grade, they moved again to Syracuse in order for her father to attend graduate school. He eventually was offered a position as a professor of romance languages at Le Moyne College. Having inherited his love for learning, Camille was a stellar student and spent the majority of her free time in the library.

Even as a child, Paglia became known for her pranks, including causing an outhouse to explode while she was at summer camp. She noted these early *cultural attacks* as defining moments for she would spend the balance of her life *looking into the latrine of culture.* The ultimate defining moment, however, came in 1963 when a friend gave Paglia a copy of Simone de Beauvoir's *The Second Sex,* which she credited for initiating her feminism. The book inspired her to pen a letter advocating equal opportunities for women, which was subsequently published in *Newsweek* magazine. Prior to her newly piqued interest in women's issues, she spent three years researching the life of her childhood hero, Amelia Earhart, with the intention of writing a biography but she dropped that project to undertake research on larger issues, primarily her budding interest in androgyny, the blending of masculine and feminine images.

While attending the State University of New York at Binghamton, she began a series of essays on sexual ambiguity, which would build the framework for her subsequent dissertation and larger published work, *Sexual Personae* (1990). Although her time at Binghamton was marred by the ridicule of her classmates because she refused to fit the prescribed gender roles of the day as well as the administration of the university that placed her on probation for her perpetual pranks, she edited the college literary magazine and graduated *summa cum laude* with highest honors in English in 1968.

Paglia entered graduate school in philosophy at Yale University, where she noted she was the only *outed* openly lesbian student in the program. While pursuing her studies, she began her ongoing tirade against many of the well-known feminists of the era, including Rita Mae Brown and Kate Millett, whom she accused of being less than thorough in her research methodology.

With master's degree in hand in 1971, Paglia undertook the doctoral program on a Woodrow Wilson Fellowship with nationally renowned intellectual Harold Bloom as her dissertation director and mentor. Through Bloom's recommendation, she was offered a teaching post at Bennington College, where she worked while completing the requirements for her degree. After clashing with colleagues over academic theory, criticizing women's studies professors for refusing to acknowledge the influence of biology as well as sociology on the plight of women and being accused of engaging in fist fights with her students, Paglia resigned from Bennington in 1980. Because the majority of her research had been focused toward the area of popular culture or in interdisciplinary studies, it was difficult to find another teaching position since she lacked a specific area of expertise. Consequently, she spent one year at Wesleyan College and the next few years teaching part time, simultaneously at Yale and the University of New Haven, where, among other subjects, she instructed off-campus night classes at the Sikorsky Helicopter plant. During the period, Paglia also created and contributed articles to the *Advocate,* a publication geared toward gay and lesbian issues.

In 1990, *Sexual Personae: Art and Decadence from Nefertiti to Emily Dickinson* was released by Yale University Press after being rejected by seven other publishers. The first of the two volumes, culled from her previous essays and her 450-page dissertation, examined sexually ambiguous representations that appeared throughout the history of both art and literature, what she called a "psychic union" between the masculine and the feminine.

In addition to her academic examination of culture in *Sexual Personae,* Paglia also renewed her attack against contemporary feminism. Among other accusations, she referred to feminists as perpetual victims and man haters and offered the view that they were totally ignorant of history. She added her aversion to affirmative action, citing that it had helped only middle-class white women, and applauded capitalism as the vehicle that had created the independent woman. As others of the era, Paglia attacked the idea of date rape as nonexistent and a theory created by the false ideas of sexual equality. She did not imply, however, that "women bring it on themselves" but affirmed their ability to say no.

Throughout the decade, Paglia continued to wage war with other feminists, especially those she implied had made feminism their religion and cultural world view. She was particularly malicious in her attack of women's studies programs because she felt those courses dwelled on teaching victim theory, in other words, in encouraging their women students to adopt a woe-is-me attitude. Continuing, she posited that the problem with higher education was political correctness; that feminists were "hostile to dissent" and mired in their own beliefs; and that government should stay out of people's personal lives.

Even though *Sexual Personae* was released by a university press, traditionally known for lower sales than commercial publishers, the book did well enough to merit a second printing and a subsequent paperback release. In 1991, the work was nominated for a National Book Critics Circle award, inched forward to become a best seller and was optioned for television. By the time her second and third works, *Sex, Art and American Culture: Essays* (1992) and *Vamps and Tramps* (1994), were released, Paglia had the name recognition to assure immediate success.

Paglia continued to write, teach, and give presentations, while becoming the adoptive parent of a baby boy born to her longtime partner, Alison Maddex. She was a columnist for salon.com and a contributing editor to *Interview* magazine, while maintaining her position as social critic, particularly and persistently of academia and feminism.

FOR FURTHER READING

Paglia, Camille. *Vamps & Tramps: New Essays*. New York: Vintage Books, 1994; ———. *Break, Blow, Burn*. New York: Pantheon Books, 2005.

SHERE HITE (1942–)

Shere Hite is the author of the "Hite Reports," a sequence of three researched studies that became controversial best sellers. To create the reports, Hite undertook a major qualitative study of men's and women's separate views on love and sexuality by asking for anonymous participation in a series of questionnaires. Her work was criticized by many as not being representative of the general population because so few people completed and returned the survey and because it appeared to be anti-male. Nevertheless, the volumes were favorably compared to the pioneering efforts of William H. Masters and Virginia E. Johnson as well as Alfred C. Kinsey, the researchers noted for their previous work on gender and sexuality.

She was born Shirley Diana Gregory on November 2, 1942 in St. Joseph, Missouri, the daughter of Paul Gregory, an air traffic controller for the military, and Shirley Hurt. After her parents divorced, her mother remarried a truck driver, Raymond Hite, who adopted the child. When that marriage also ended in divorce, the young woman moved in with her mother's parents, a conservative environment where certain topics were never discussed. In her preteen years, Hite's grandparents divorced as well and the young woman was sent to live with an aunt and uncle in Daytona Beach, Florida. In Florida, she excelled in her studies and showed promise as both a pianist and a clarinetist.

Although she wanted to become a composer of classical music, she felt the field was closed to women, thus, she opted for a university major in history. With funding from her grandfather, Hite earned her bachelors degree, *cum laude,* and a master's from the University of Florida in 1964 and 1968, respectively. Since she had performed so well academically, she applied to Columbia University in New York City and was accepted to the doctoral program in history. As one of only a handful of women in the department, Hite encountered gender prejudice, noting she felt "more or less invisible"; consequently, she withdrew from the program after only two semesters. After leaving the university, she joined the Wilhelmina modeling agency and spent several years as a top fashion model in both the United States and Europe.

Ironically, her involvement with the women's liberation movement came as a result of a National Organization for Women (NOW) protest of an advertisement in which she was featured in the early 1970s. In the advertisement, she portrayed a "secretary," touting an Olivetti typewriter that was so intelligent that its user was not required to be. Shortly after the protest, Hite joined NOW and credited the organization with improving her self-esteem.

In the early 1970s, Hite was asked to deliver a presentation to the organization, based in part on a NOW pamphlet, "The Myth of Female Orgasm." As a means of gathering information for that appearance, Hite interviewed several women about their sexual practices. The responses were so intriguing that she decided to broaden the survey and the geographic area it covered. After four years of advertising the availability of the questionnaire in local and national publications geared to women, Hite mailed out in excess of one hundred thousand copies but only a few more than three thousand were returned. Even with the small sample size, Hite determined the material of value and published the first volume in the series in 1976, *The Hite Report: A Nationwide Study on Female Sexuality.* Many agreed that, despite the small number, the essay responses illustrated a period in American history that marked the advent of the ongoing confrontation between family values and individual freedom and that her method was unique in giving women a *voice.* Although the work became a best seller in the United States, was translated into sixteen foreign languages, and Hite earned a "distinguished service award" from the American Association of Sex Educators, Counselors and Therapists, she became the focus of intense criticism for what was considered her feminist bias.

To counter some of that ridicule, she followed with the publication of *The Hite Report on Male Sexuality* in 1981, which hypothesized that men were more influenced by culture than by biology. Using the same methodology, Hite distributed a questionnaire through men's clubs, university and senior citizen venues, and advertised in publications with male readership. Despite her efforts to dispel the criticism, she was, once again, accused of male-bashing and of allowing her individual inclination toward feminism to influence her work. The third volume, *The Hite Report: Women and Love, a Cultural Revolution in Progress,* published in 1987, was noted by some reviewers as merely catering to the responses of a group of angry women.

In 1995, after receiving a series of death threats, Hite renounced her U.S. citizenship and relocated to Europe. There, she founded a Paris-based research institute, found wider acceptance for her work, and had some of her writings translated into Arabic for distribution in the Middle East.

FOR FURTHER READING

Hite, Shere. *The Hite Report on Shere Hite: Voice of a Daughter in Exile.* London: Arcadia, 1999; ———. "Why I Became a German." *New Statesman,* November 17, 2003, 25.

BARBARA SEAMAN (1935–)

Called "the first prophet of the women's health movement" by activist Gloria Steinem, Barbara Seaman single-handedly fought to have the possible side effects of the birth control pill and estrogen replacement therapy addressed by the medical community and labeled as such by the pharmaceutical companies. Her work, showing that The Pill could lead to cancer, heart disease, diabetes, and stroke, led to congressional hearings on the medication in 1970.

Born in Brooklyn, New York during the Depression, Barbara acquired an appreciation for social justice from her father, Henry Rosner, who worked for Mayor Fiorello LaGuardia to design the city's first welfare program, and a love of language from her mother, Sophia Kimels, an English teacher. Her parents met at a Young People's Socialist League picnic and politics continued to be an integral part of their home. Because her father's twin sister Sally worked to pay his way through college, he was particularly aware of the issues of women. When her aunt Sally died of cancer, induced by an estrogen-rich drug that was prescribed for menopause, Barbara was inspired to investigate women's medicine.

She was graduated from Oberlin College in 1956 as a Ford Foundation Scholar and later awarded an honorary Doctorate of Humane Letters from that institution in 1978. In addition, she studied advanced science writing at Columbia University's School of Journalism. Following graduation, Barbara worked as a freelance writer, contributing to such periodicals as *Brides* and *Ladies Home Journal,* where she published her first pieces on the dangers inherent in estrogen, particularly the amount present in the birth control pill. As a consequence of those articles, she was invited to join the Society of Magazine Writers through which she met feminist activists Betty Friedan and Gloria Steinem. In the course of those associations, she was asked to apply her journalistic skill to cover such events as the founding of the National Organization for Women and the National Association for the Repeal of Abortion Laws (NARAL Pro-Choice America) as well as being invited to join the staff of Steinem's *Ms.* magazine as a contributing editor.

Married to psychiatrist Gideon Seaman, Barbara discovered she was pregnant in 1957. Although her doctor discouraged the activity, she believed nature was the best course and insisted on breastfeeding. While she was pregnant, the same doctor prescribed a laxative for her that was subsequently transferred to her unborn son, who almost died from the medication. Once again, Seaman was mired in the controversy of the mismanagement of women's health advice. Inspired by another medical professional, who advised her against taking estrogen replacement therapy due to her family history of cancer, she wrote *The Doctors' Case Against the Pill* (1969). Even though the *Journal of the American Medical Association* called it *a strange book,* the work launched the Nelson Pill Hearings on the safety of oral contraceptive pills. Referred to as the "Boston Tea Party of the Women's Movement," Seaman and a group of women, who were seriously ill as a result of their taking the pill, interrupted the gathering but the Senate refused to listen to them. In spite of that refusal, the result of the hearings was a mandate for the pill label to include health warnings, the first such information included on any prescription drug. As a consequence of her involvement, Seaman was blacklisted by many of the publications to which she had previously contributed because the pharmaceutical lobby refused to purchase advertising in any periodical that published her work.

In 1975, Seaman cofounded the National Women's Health Network (NWHN). Through the efforts of this organization, she and other members created awareness about the hazards of hormone replacement therapy as well as the risks of birth control pills. In demonstrating, congressional hearings, and political advocacy, the group continued to work on behalf of women's health issues. Also, in 1975, in a speech at the Harvard Medical School, Seaman issued her "Four Demands," including having more women trained in obstetrics and gynecology; at the time, women represented only 3 percent of the medical professionals in those fields. As an advocate for women's participation in their own treatment, she also suggested that women should have more decision-making power in how research funds were spent.

Through her activism, Seaman helped change medicine, placing more women in the field, encouraging more university offerings in women's medicine, and establishing government offices for women's health. She was called one of the most influential women of the twentieth-century women's movement by the *Hite Report on the Family*. In 1991, she and other members of NWHN protested the Women's Health Initiative for its experimental testing of estrogen on healthy women. In 2000, she was selected by the U.S. Postal Service as an honoree for the 1970s Women's Rights Movement stamp.

FOR FURTHER READING

Seaman, Barbara. *The Doctor's Case Against the Pill.* New York: P.H. Wyden, 1969; ———. *The Greatest Experiment Ever Performed on Women: Exploding the Estrogen Myth.* New York: Hyperion, 2003.

MARY DALY (1928–)

Like some of her feminist foremothers, particularly Elizabeth Cady Stanton, Mary Daly believed that Christian theology should be revised to reflect a woman-centered belief system. Calling her views "post-Christian radical feminism," Daly believed that institutionalized sexism was too embedded to be changed, while many of her contemporaries in the National Organization for Women disagreed.

Born in Schenectady, New York, Daly was the daughter of Anna Catherine Morse and Frank X. Daly and was raised in a conservative Catholic home. She was graduated from the College of St. Rose in 1950 and the Catholic University of America in 1952. After earning a doctorate in religion from St. Mary's College at Notre Dame University in 1954, Daly discovered that no doctoral program in the United States would permit a woman to study Catholic theology. Thus, she enrolled in the University of Fribourg in Switzerland, where her classmates were all men. In 1963, she was graduated *summa cum laude* and became the first woman to receive the highest degree offered in sacred theology. In addition, she earned a third doctoral degree in philosophy in 1965.

Based on her impressive academic credentials, Daly was hired by the Jesuit-operated Boston College as an assistant professor of theology; however, following the publication of her controversial feminist critique of Catholicism, *The Church and the Second Sex* (1969), her contract was abruptly terminated. At the time, all of her students were male and they immediately launched a petition demanding academic freedom and her return to the classroom. Twenty-five hundred students signed the petition and fifteen hundred marched to the university president's home to deliver the document. With some reservation on the part of the administration, Daly was returned to her post as a full professor with tenure, a position she retained for thirty-three years.

While some considered Daly visionary and on the forefront of feminist theory, others thought she was merely unbalanced. In addition to her views on religion, she was a noted as a misandrist, a hater of men as a group, and an advocate of parthenogenesis, the development of an embryo without male fertilization, which she deemed a metaphor for "woman creating herself."

With Jane Caputi and others, Daly created an alternate feminist vocabulary that she employed in nonsequential writing and published *Websters' First New Intergalactic Wickedary of the English Language* (1994), a parody of other dictionaries that she believed were penned from a patriarchal perspective. Many writers spin tales; Daly spun language, coining words and inverting syntax.

In 1999, she refused to admit men students to her upper-division feminist classes. Although she agreed to tutor the students privately, the university insisted that the men must be allowed to attend the formal course. Daly commented that she would rather retire than succumb to their demands. Evidently, the university considered her statement an offer for when she returned to work, her office and classroom were locked and she was denied admittance. Because she was tenured, the university was required to produce just cause for her termination. The case was eventually settled out of court.

Daly continued to write, lecture, and create controversy. Of particular note were her publications, *Quintessence: Realizing the Outrageous Contagious Courage of Women, a Radical Elemental Feminist Manifesto* (1998), that depicted an Utopian society comprised of women only, *Gyn/Ecology: The Metaethics of Radical Feminism* (1990), referred to as a "leap forward in feminist theory" and *Outercourse: The Bedazzling Voyage Containing Recollections from My Logbook of a Radical Feminist Philosopher* (1992), her autobiography. Having determined that her critics were of little concern to her examination of self and philosophy, Daly humorously referred to herself as a "positively revolting hag" and noted, "There are and will be those who think I have gone overboard. Let them rest assured that this assessment is correct, probably beyond their wildest imagination, and that I will continue to do so."

FOR FURTHER READING

Daly, Mary. *Outercourse: The Bedazzling Voyage Containing Recollections from My Logbook of a Radical Feminist Philosopher.* San Francisco: Harper, 1992;
———. *Webster's First New Intergalactic Wickedary of the English Language.* San Francisco: Harper, 1994.

ANDREA DWORKIN (1946–2005)

A radical feminist, Andrea Dworkin was best known for her work against pornography, which she felt violated the civil rights of women. Through historical and literary analyses, she illustrated that women were traditionally represented as submissive and docile, which image, in turn, was used to justify their abuse at the hands of men.

Born in Camden, New Jersey on September 26, 1946, Dworkin was the daughter of Harry Dworkin, a teacher who inspired his daughter's sense of social justice, and Sylvia Spiegel, whose progressive views on birth control and legalized abortion, inspired Andrea's activism. Her childhood was brief for, at the age of nine, she was molested by an unknown man in a movie theatre. Her parents' response was to abandon the city and move the family to the small suburb of Cherry Hill Township, where Andrea, who was Jewish, was punished in grade school for refusing to sing "Silent Night."

In 1965, she attended Bennington College, where she became immediately embroiled in protesting the war in Vietnam and was subsequently arrested and mistreated in the Women's House of Detention in Lower Manhattan. When she testified about her treatment before a grand jury, the incident and Dworkin gained national and international media attention. Briefly abandoning college, she moved to Crete, the largest of the Greek islands, in order to write, publishing both poetry and fiction while there. When she returned to Bennington, she continued to participate in protest movements against the war and the student code of conduct at the institution and for the legalization of abortion and the dispersal of birth control on campus.

Following her graduation in 1969 with a degree in literature, Dworkin again traveled to Europe to interview anarchists in the counterculture movement in Amsterdam. While there, she married one of the revolutionaries who subsequently abused her. When she left him in 1971, she was poverty stricken, homeless, and desperate, for a time even supporting herself as a prostitute. Through other American ex-patriots, Dworkin was exposed to radical feminist writings of the period and discovered that she was not alone in her despair or in her beliefs. In order to gain passage to the United States, she agreed to smuggle heroin out of the country; the deal eventually fell through but she managed to retain the plane ticket.

Once safely back on her home turf, Dworkin took menial jobs and plunged into writing, publishing *Woman Hating* in 1974. The book offered a radical feminist analysis of fairy tales and other literary works, showing the women in the writing as passive and dependent, and presented her view that an androgynous society was the only route to freedom for women. Once again, she participated in protest activities against the war and Apartheid in South Africa and joined demonstrations for lesbian rights as well as becoming an organizer for radical feminist groups. In addition to protesting and organizing, Dworkin delivered impassioned public speeches, including one at the first Take Back the Night march in 1978 through the red-light district in San Francisco, and printed in *Letters from a War Zone,* published in 1988.

Dworkin's most visible and memorable campaign was her self-declared war on pornography, which she viewed as the ultimate degradation of women. In 1979, she and others, such as Shere Hite, Letty Cottin Pogrebin, Susan Brownmiller, and Gloria Steinem, formed Women against Pornography. In addition, Dworkin published *Pornography: Men Possessing Women* (1979), showing historical examples of pornography's encouragement of violence against women and advocating that victims of rape should be permitted to execute their attackers.

In 1983, Dworkin began working with feminist attorney Catharine MacKinnon on a legal route to combating pornography, citing the industry as a threat to women's civil rights under Constitutional law. MacKinnon arranged a short-term appointment for Dworkin in the Women's Studies Department of the University of Minnesota in order to have time to solidify their approach. During the period, under community pressure, the Minneapolis city government hired the women to draft an ordinance defining pornography as a civil rights violation against women and allowing women who claimed they were harmed as a result to sue producers and distributors of pornography for damages. Although the drafts of the ordinance were approved by the city council, they were vetoed by the mayor. Another version passed in Indianapolis but was overturned as unconstitutional by the Circuit Court of Appeals. In 1986, Dworkin testified before the Attorney General's Commission on Pornography (called the "Meese Commission" for Attorney General Edwin Meese), where she presented five recommendations for the control of pornography in the United States. Although the Commission agreed and for a time issued a ban on the sale of "men's magazines," their findings eventually were overturned by the courts based on the first amendment.

Dworkin continued her campaign in writing, authoring ten works of radical feminist theory, attacking pedophilia, incest, pornography, prostitution, and violence against women. She died in her sleep on April 9, 2005 in Washington, DC. A reporter once asked how she would like to be remembered, to which she replied, "In a museum, when male supremacy is dead.

I'd like my work to be an anthropological artifact from an extinct, primitive society."

FOR FURTHER READING

Dworkin, Andrea. *Men Possessing Women.* New York: E.P. Dutton, 1989; ———. *Heartbreak: The Political Memoir of a Feminist Militant.* New York: Basic Books, 2002; Dworkin, Andrea, and Catherine MacKinnon. *Pornography and Civil Rights: A New Day for Women's Equality.* Minneapolis, MN: Organizing Against Pornography, 1988.

APPENDIX: SHORT BIOGRAPHIES

Julia Ward Howe (1819–1910). Although she is best remembered for penning "The Battle Hymn of the Republic" for which she was paid five dollars, Julia Ward Howe was a champion of woman's rights.

Born in New York City into the wealthy family of Samuel Ward, Jr., a stockbroker on Wall Street, and Julia Rush, a published poet, she was educated by tutors. When Julia was five years old, her mother died of tuberculosis, causing her father to become overprotective of the young woman. In 1843, she wed Dr. Samuel Gridley Howe, the director of the Perkins Institute for the Blind. The couple had six children, the last one birthed when Julia was forty years old.

Although her husband was a staunch activist for a variety of social ills from prison and education reform to abolition, his militancy did not extend to woman's rights and he forbade Julia from entering the public sphere. Unhappy at being relegated to the home, she traveled to Italy with her children in 1850, spending the year writing and contemplating divorce. Her first collection of poetry, *Passion-Flowers,* was published in 1850 and her second, *Words for the Hour,* in 1857, both anonymously. Although she became a prolific author, one poem, the "Battle Hymn of the Republic," secured her place in literary history. Penned in 1861, while she was in Washington, DC with her husband as he distributed supplies to Union soldiers, the poem served as a call to arms during the Civil War's final years and was under consideration as the national anthem until 1931 when the "Star Spangled Banner" was selected by congressional resolution.

Having achieved some measure of fame and financial independence, Howe's long-suppressed ambition flourished, moving her further away from domesticity. She created a literary magazine, *Northern Lights,* that ran for eleven issues, wrote about her travels in Europe, published the *Woman's Journal* that became a conduit for suffrage information, and penned various other works, including a biography of Margaret Fuller in 1883.

In 1868, she founded the Northeast Woman's Club and cofounded the American Suffrage Association in 1869 with Lucy Stone. By 1870, she became president of the Massachusetts Woman Suffrage Association, an office she held for seven years. In 1881, she was elected president of the Association for the Advancement of Women, an organization she helped start to foster educational and professional opportunities for women. During the Franco-Prussian War, Howe attempted to organize women to march for peace, culminating in an 1872 day dedicated to Mothers' Peace, which was eventually replaced by Mother's Day. In 1875, she organized the first convention of women ministers. Continuing to be active in both writing and organizing, Howe lived to see her ninety-first birthday. She died in Oak Glen, Massachusetts, on October 17, 1910.

For Further Reading: Grant, Mary Hetherington. *Private Woman, Public Person: An Account of the Life of Julia Ward Howe from 1819–1868.* Brooklyn, NY: Carlson Publishing, 1994; Hall, Florence Howe. *Julia Ward Howe and the Woman Suffrage Movement.* New York: Arno, 1969.

Antoinette Louisa Brown Blackwell (1825–1921). The first woman to be ordained as a minister, Antoinette Brown was born in Henrietta, New York. At the age of eight, she indicated a desire to enter the ministry but was told that the pulpit was closed to women.

After teaching for a year, she entered Oberlin College in Ohio in a nondegree program in literature. Since Oberlin had a reputation for its liberal treatment of women, Antoinette inquired about entering the theology department. Through much protest from administrators, faculty, and male students, she was admitted to the program but had to secure special permission in order to speak in class. She completed the course work in 1850 but was not awarded a degree because of her gender.

After college, she spent two years on the woman's suffrage lecture tour and was finally ordained as a minister in 1853. In that capacity, she became the first woman to perform a wedding ceremony. That year, she was selected as a delegate to World Temperance Convention but was shouted down by the male attendees when she attempted to speak. Not discouraged, Antoinette joined forces with Susan B. Anthony and Elizabeth Cady Stanton to push for the passage of the Woman's Property Law in New York State.

Throughout 1855, she volunteered in the slums and prisons of New York City, becoming convinced in the process that the mental and social upheaval created by poverty was the cause of many of the social ills she witnessed, especially for women. She contributed a series of articles on her experience to the *New York Tribune* that were later published in book form as *Shadows of Our Social System* (1856).

In 1856, Antoinette married Samuel Blackwell, becoming a sister-in-law of suffrage activist Lucy Stone. Continuing to write and lecture, she became an advocate for women's right to work part-time, while their husbands helped with the children and the housework. She felt strongly that women should not have to choose one role over the other.

One of the few who survived to see the suffrage amendment become law, Antoinette voted in the presidential election of 1920.

For Further Reading: Cazden, Elizabeth. *Antoinette Brown Blackwell: A Biography.* Old Westbury, NY: The Feminist Press, 1983; Lasser, Carol, and Marlene Merrill, eds. *Soul Mates: The Oberlin Correspondence of Lucy Stone and Antoinette Brown, 1846–1850.* Oberlin, OH: Oberlin College, 1983.

Katherine (Kate) O'Flaherty Chopin (1850–1904). Chastised by critics and the public alike when she was first published, Kate Chopin was rediscovered by later feminists and became their literary banner carrier for decades.

Born in St. Louis, Missouri, Kate matured in the arms of strong women role models. The bulk of her education was provided by the nuns of Academy of the Sacred Heart and supplemented by her great-grandmother, who had obtained the first legal separation from her husband ever granted in Missouri. Although she was a product of Catholicism in both her schooling and her home, at an early age the young woman began to question the tenets of the church because of its stance on gender. Her mother sprang from upper-class Creole culture and her father, Thomas O'Flaherty, an Irish immigrant, was a self-made man and one of the founders of the Pacific Railroad. When a bridge collapsed on the train's inaugural trip, her father was killed, leaving Kate in the society of women. Chopin's often anthologized short story, "The Story of an Hour," may reflect her mother's mixture of grief and the joy of liberation produced by her father's death.

At nineteen, Kate married Louisiana cotton broker, Oscar Chopin, and moved to New Orleans. Following the birth of six children and the failure of his business, Oscar Chopin died, leaving Kate without funds and as the sole support of her children. She returned to Missouri, only to watch the demise of most of her family. Depressed and essentially alone, she visited a doctor who recommended she turn to writing as a means of channeling her emotions.

Her second novel, the one lauded by later feminists, *The Awakening,* published in 1899, was condemned by the critics for its sexual frankness. However, the work afforded Chopin some measure of notoriety and she began to host literary salons in her home. Over three hundred persons, primarily women, appeared for her reading of *The Awakening.* Her writing did not produce enough funds to sustain her family in her lifetime but she managed to care for her children with the profits from inherited land holdings.

After a full day at the St. Louis World's Fair in 1904, Kate Chopin died of a cerebral hemorrhage.

For Further Reading: Chopin, Kate. *The Awakening.* New York: W.W. Norton, 1993; Toth, Emily. *Unveiling Kate Chopin.* Jackson: University Press of Mississippi, 1999.

Ida Husted Harper (1851–1931). Author and suffragist, Ida Husted Harper was the person primarily responsible for gathering, collating, and compiling decades of papers that became the three-volume biography of Susan B. Anthony and for completing the *History of Woman Suffrage.* As a journalist, Harper served as chair of the National Press Bureau of the National American Woman's Suffrage Association (NAWSA), through which she supplied sixteen newspapers nationwide with news of the group's activities.

Born in Fairfield, Indiana, on February 18, 1851, Ida was the daughter of John Husted, a saddler, and Cassandra Stoddard. When she was ten years old, her family moved to Muncie, Indiana, in order for the children to attend the city school system. In 1868, Ida was admitted to Indiana University with sophomore standing but she withdrew to take a position as a high school principal in Peru, Indiana.

Ida married Thomas Winans Harper, an attorney, in 1871 and moved with him to Terre Haute. He was a political activist and served as counsel for the Union of Locomotive Firemen under the leadership of union organizer, Eugene V. Debs. Although her husband disapproved of her working, Ida began writing for the *Terre Haute Saturday Evening Mail,* employing a male pen name. She eventually gained her own column in the newspaper, under her own name, a position she held for twelve years. In 1884, Debs asked her to take over as editor of the woman's department for his union newspaper and, in 1887, she became secretary of the Indiana Suffrage Society. Since her husband continued his objections to her involvement in public life, they were divorced in 1890. Following the divorce, she became editor-in-chief of the *Terre Haute Daily News* until her daughter enrolled at Stanford University in California. Accompanying her daughter across the country, Ida too enrolled in the university but did not complete the program due to the competition for her time in the movement.

In 1897, Susan B. Anthony asked Harper to aid in writing her memoir; thus, Harper relocated to Rochester, New York, and began the arduous task of compiling Anthony's voluminous store of papers. After two years of organizing and writing, the first two volumes of the *Life of Susan B. Anthony* were published in 1898; the third volume was not published until 1908, after Anthony's death. Between 1901 and 1902, Harper aided Anthony and Elizabeth Cady Stanton with the writing of the fourth volume of the *History of Woman Suffrage* and, alone, completed the fifth and sixth volumes, published in 1922 and covering the period from 1900 to the passage of the Nineteenth Amendment.

She was a delegate to the International Council of Woman in London in 1899, wrote for *International Suffrage News,* and edited a woman's column in the *New York Sunday Sun* from 1899 to 1903. She died in Washington, DC in 1931.

For Further Reading: Harper, Ida Husted. *Suffrage: A Right.* New York: North American Review Publishing Company, 1906; ———. *How Six States Won Woman Suffrage.* New York: National American Woman Suffrage Association, 1911.

Harriot Stanton Blatch (1856–1940). Although largely overlooked in the history of the woman's movement, Harriot Stanton Blatch was bred to social activism as the daughter of Elizabeth Cady Stanton. By combining militancy and politics, Blatch revitalized the sluggish suffrage movement and brought national recognition to women's concerns by advocating direct action through civil disobedience, what some labeled "media-savvy guerilla warfare."

Born on January 20, 1856 in Seneca Falls, New York, the town considered the launching pad for the woman's movement, Harriot Eaton Stanton was exposed to activism almost from birth. Not only was her mother one of the pioneers of the woman suffrage movement, her father, Henry Brewster Stanton, was an avid abolitionist in addition to being an attorney and a state senator. The sixth of seven children, Harriot idolized her mother and frequently accompanied her to women's meetings and on her speaking tours.

After earning a bachelors degree with honors from Vassar College in 1878, she attended the Boston School of Oratory for one year prior to accepting a position as a companion and tutor for two young girls. That position took her to Germany where she met and married Britain, William H. Blatch, although she was afraid that marriage would destroy her usefulness to the movement. While living in England with her husband, Blatch undertook a statistical study on working women in English hamlets, which eventually became her master's thesis at Vassar in 1894. She was also involved with the Women's Franchise League, where she learned organizational techniques to energize the woman's movement in the United States.

After returning to the United States over a decade later, Blatch became a champion of recruiting working women into the movement, which up until then had been composed primarily of the Eastern elite. She organized the Equality League of Self-Supporting Women in 1907 that became the Women's Political Union in 1910 and was comprised of over twenty thousand factory, laundry, and garment workers on New York City's Lower East Side. A believer in stirring things up, she organized suffrage marches in New York in 1908, 1910, and 1912 and encouraged women to lobby and testify before Congress.

Blatch was one of the first to bring the "votes for women" action into the streets. She stationed confederates on street corners in New York City to discuss suffrage with anyone who would listen; the women wore sandwich boards hanging from their shoulders, stood on literal soap boxes, and demonstrated in front of store windows. In Harlem in 1908, many of the women were kicked and beaten while city police watched from the sidelines. Courting confrontation because it made news, which drew more attention to the issues, Blatch placed other suffragists in voting places as poll-watchers and was one of the first to organize suffrage parades, which many felt challenged traditional notions of femininity. In fact, some feared the parades would be hazardous to the delicate female constitution and stationed ambulances along the parade route to scoop up the fallen. Exercising her first amendment right to assembly, Blatch viewed the parades, a traditional event in American culture shared by the community to build solidarity, as vehicles for social change.

In 1913, the largest parade under her direction brought twenty thousand marchers and over fifty thousand spectators to line Fifth Avenue in New York. The parades always ended at Union Square or Carnegie Hall with a speaking platform occupied by Blatch, Anna Howard Shaw, or others prominent in the movement. For the 1913 event, she also added an all-male reviewing stand near the platform.

When her husband was accidentally electrocuted in 1915, she briefly returned to Britain to settle his estate and during World War I, she served as director of the Woman's Land Army, a group dedicated to mobilizing women to provide additional farm labor. Based on this experience, she penned *Mobilizing Woman-Power* (1918). After women won the right to vote in New York State, Blatch united the Women's Political Union and the Congressional Union, the militant group headed by Alice Paul and Lucy Burns, creating a greater push for a Constitutional amendment.

Following passage of the suffrage amendment, Blatch became a socialist and ran for controller of New York City and for the New York Assembly on the socialist party ticket but lost both elections. She was a firm advocate of both the Equal Rights Amendment and the League of Nations and believed in integrating economic and class issues and advocated mothers' pensions. In her mid-eighties, she suffered a broken hip that forced her into a nursing home in Greenwich, Connecticut, where she died on November 20, 1940.

For Further Reading: Blatch, Harriot Stanton. *Mobilizing Woman-Power.* New York: The Woman's Press, 1918; Blatch, Harriot Stanton, and Alma Lutz. *Challenging Years: The Memoirs of Harriot Stanton Blatch.* Westport, CT: Hyperion Press, 1976; Eckhaus, Phyllis. "Harriot Stanton Blatch and the Winning of Woman Suffrage." *The Nation* 265 (December 29, 1997): 28–29.

Alice Stone Blackwell (1857–1950). The only child of Lucy Stone and Henry Blackwell, Alice was literally born into the suffrage movement and became the heir to advocacy for human rights. Her efforts were instrumental in bringing together the two factions of the woman's suffrage movement.

When she was ten, her family moved from Orange, New Jersey to Boston, where Alice was graduated, *Phi Beta Kappa,* from Boston University in 1881. Following in her mother's footsteps, she served as assistant editor for the *Woman's Journal,* the official news media of the American Woman's Suffrage Association. Between 1887 and 1905, she also edited the

Woman's Column, a periodical covering additional news of the suffrage movement.

In 1890, Alice and others spearheaded the movement to reunite the American and National Woman's Suffrage Associations and she served as recording secretary of the newly formed group, NAWSA, until 1918. In addition, she was the founder of the Massachusetts League of Women Voters, associate editor of the *Ladies Home Journal,* a member of the Woman's Christian Temperance Union, the Women's Trade Union League, the National Association for the Advancement of Colored People (NAACP), and the American Peace Society. She also sat on the board of Boston University and fought to end discrimination among the students on campus and in hiring of faculty members.

As an advocate for human rights, Blackwell supported Armenian and Russian protestors who were fighting against the adverse treatment of people in those countries. She translated Armenian, Yiddish, Russian, Hungarian, and Mexican poets and created the "Friends of Armenia" Society that served to initiate the first international human rights movement. In 1896, she published her translation of the Armenian poems, which went into a second printing in a little over two weeks.

In 1930, Alice published the definite biography of her mother, *Lucy Stone: Pioneer in Women's Rights.* She was awarded an honorary doctorate from Boston University in 1945. She died on March 18, 1950 in Cambridge, Massachusetts.

For Further Reading: Merrill, Marlene Deahl. *Growing Up in Boston's Gilded Age: The Journal of Alice Stone Blackwell, 1872–1874.* New Haven, CT: Yale University Press, 1990.

Ida B. Wells (1862–1931). Straddling the intersection between race and gender, Ida B. Wells was born in Mississippi only three years after slavery was abolished. When she was sixteen, her mother, father, and one sibling were victims of a fatal yellow fever epidemic and from 1878 to 1883, Ida became the sole support of five younger siblings. Moving the family to Memphis, Tennessee, she attended the LeMoyne Institute and taught in the school system. At fifty dollars a month in salary, she was one of the area's black elite.

In 1883, Wells was told to move to a train compartment reserved for black passengers. When she refused to move, one of the conductors tried to force her into compliance but she bit his hand instead. Witnessing the incident, three other white men grabbed her and literally threw her off the train, causing her physical injury. Tired of the abuse inherent in inequality, Wells sued the railroad and won the case, which was reversed on appeal. Nevertheless, she wrote in a black church weekly, *Living Way,* "If you stand up for your rights, you'll be able to keep them."

From 1884 to 1891, Wells wrote for a variety of black newspapers across the country before purchasing an interest in the paper, *Free Speech*. The focus of her investigative reporting was twofold: lynchings of blacks and the public justification of the rape of black women. She uncovered 728 cases of lynching over a ten-year period. Before the article was published, however, her office was vandalized and all of her equipment was destroyed. Fortunately, she was out of town visiting in Philadelphia but an "order" went out for her to be hanged if she returned.

Wells continued to write for New York area newspapers under the pseudonym, "Exiled." Her most significant contribution to the woman's movement was unveiling the habitual sexual abuse of black women by white men that was prevalent in the era.

For Further Reading: Franklin, Vincent P. *Living Our Stories, Telling Our Truths: Autobiography and the Making of African American Intellectual Tradition.* New York: Oxford University Press, 1995; Miller, Erica M. *The Other Reconstruction: Where Violence and Womanhood Meet in the Writings of Ida B. Wells-Barnett, Angelina Weld Grimké, and Nella Larsen.* New York: Routledge Press, 1999; Schechter, Patricia A. *Ida B. Wells and American Reform: 1880–1930.* Chapel Hill: University of North Carolina Press, 2001.

Mary Eliza Church Terrell (1863–1954). Recognized as one of the leading women spokespersons for African Americans, Terrell founded the Colored Women's League in 1892 and became the first president of the National Association of Colored Women, from 1896 to 1901. It was her ambition to empower black women by securing enfranchisement and economic independence.

Born in Memphis, Tennessee, Terrell was the daughter of Robert Reed Church, a businessman and former slave who became the first black millionaire in the South, and Louisa Ayers, a beautician and beauty salon owner. She was graduated from Oberlin College with a bachelor's degree in classical languages, where she edited the *Oberlin Review*, in spite of encountering overt racism. Contrary to her father's objections, Terrell began a teaching career at Wilberforce College in Ohio and in 1887, she moved to Washington, DC to teach at the M Street Colored High School. While in that position, she met Robert Herberton Terrell, the chair of the language department, whom she married in 1891. In 1888, Terrell's father forgave her choice of profession and provided expenses for a two-year study and travel adventure in Europe.

In 1892, Terrell's call to activism was ignited by the lynching of her childhood friend, Thomas Moss, and she joined with segregationist leader Frederick Douglass to mount an antilynching campaign. Through her work on that endeavor, she became known as a persuasive speaker; consequently, she was invited to speak at a NAWSA meeting in 1898. A confirmed suffragist, she was the only African American delegate to the International

Council of Women held in Berlin in 1904, impressing the audience by giving her speech in fluent German.

She served two terms on the Board of Education in Washington, DC, the first black woman to hold that position. In addition, she was a charter member of NAACP, a recruiter for the Republican Party and the author of over twenty-five articles. Her autobiography, *A Colored Woman in a White World,* was published in 1940. In her waning years, she organized sit-ins and protests against segregated establishments in Washington. She died in 1954 in Highland Beach, Maryland.

For Further Reading: Jones, Beverly Washington. *Quest for Equality: The Life and Writings of Mary Eliza Church Terrell, 1863–1954.* Brooklyn, NY: Carlson Publishing, 1990; Terrell, Mary Church. *A Colored Woman in a White World.* New York: Arno Press, 1980.

Mary Jane McLoed Bethune (1875–1955). Born to former slaves, the fifteenth of seventeen children, Mary Bethune briefly considered a career as a missionary in Africa but decided that persons in the United States needed an equivalent amount of aid. As an educator, she was devoted to securing the right to equal training and freedom from discrimination for African Americans. In addition to activism for her race, Mary taught at a prison in Chicago, served mission lunches to the homeless, and counseled families living in poverty.

Following her marriage to Abertus Bethune, Mary opened the Daytona Normal and Industrial Institute for Negro Girls in Florida in 1904. Initially, the school sported five students, who paid fifty cents a week in tuition, and had an operating budget of one dollar and fifty cents. An astute fundraiser, Bethune eventually added a high school and a hospital. She served as president of the school for more than forty years and oversaw a merger with Cookman Institute in 1923 to form Bethune-Cookman College.

Politically, Bethune initiated the integration of the American Red Cross, served as president of the Florida Federation of Colored Women in 1917, became president of the National Association of Colored Women, the highest national office for a black woman, in 1924 and formed the National Council of Negro Women in 1935, a group dedicated to political activism. In 1940, she was elected vice president of NAACP.

Serving under three presidents, Coolidge, Hoover, and Roosevelt, Bethune was active on the Committee of Twelve for National Defense and worked with the National Urban League, the Association of American Colleges, and the League of Women Voters. From 1936 to 1944, she was the director of the Division of Negro Affairs for the National Youth Administration, becoming the first black woman to head a federal agency. In addition, she was consulted by the secretary of war in selecting the first women eligible for officer candidate status.

For Further Reading: Hanson, Joyce A. *Mary McLeod Bethune and Black Women's Political Activism.* Columbia: University of Missouri Press, 2003; McCluskey, Thomas, and Elaine Smith. *Mary McLeod Bethune: Building a Better World: Essays and Selected Documents.* Bloomington: Indiana University Press, 1999.

Inez Milholland Boissevain (1886–1916). Suffragist, labor attorney, and World War I correspondent, Inez Milholland Boissevain led the most dynamic suffrage parade ever mounted in Washington, DC on the day before the inauguration of Woodrow Wilson.

Having the good fortune to be born into a wealthy family in Brooklyn, New York, Inez studied in England and Germany before enrolling at Vassar College in 1909, where she became the star of the track team. While at Vassar, she was appalled that the college would not allow woman's rights speakers to appear on campus. Not being discouraged, however, she set up headquarters and organized presentations in a neighboring cemetery, inviting speakers such as Harriot Stanton Blatch and Charlotte Perkins Gilman. By the time she graduated, two-thirds of the student body had joined the suffrage group she created. Suffrage was not her only area of interest, however, and in 1910, she was arrested for marching with striking garment workers.

After graduating, she petitioned Harvard Law School, at the time an exclusively all-male institution, for admission but her application was declined. Thus, she enrolled at New York University's School of Law, receiving her degree in 1912. Although she was hired by Osborne, Lamb, and Garvan as a law clerk, she continued to lead protests for suffrage and against underpaid labor, particularly women retail clerks. As a practicing attorney, she defended labor activists and petitioned for children's rights.

Along with other like-minded activists, Inez joined a Greenwich Village group of progressive socialists that published, the *Masses,* a magazine that featured art, political commentary, and satire. She also worked with the Women's Trade Union League, NAACP, and was a speaker for the National American Woman Suffrage Association.

Although she gained a certain amount of notoriety from her law practice and her previous activism, the single act that carved her memory in the American consciousness occurred on March 3, 1913, the eve of the inauguration of Woodrow Wilson. Inez, dressed in white and carrying a floating banner, led over eight thousand women down the broad boulevard to the White House. Decked out in Grecian-style robes of her design and astride a white horse, Inez charged the gathering protestors and shouted back at them. Because she was beautiful as well as being an activist for woman's rights, she became an immediate media icon and her photograph on horseback graced the pages of national newspapers.

In 1913, she married Eugen Jan Boissevain, a Dutch citizen. Because her legal identity was considered the same as her husband's, a practice upheld until 1915, she was forced, for awhile, to forfeit not only her license to practice law but also her U.S. citizenship.

Inez objected to America's entry into World War I and joined Henry Ford's "Peace Ship," the *Oscar II*, which sailed to Europe in 1915 to attempt diplomatic negotiations to end the confrontation. She also served as a correspondent, submitting articles "from the field" to a variety of newspapers.

During a speaking tour of the West she had taken by rail in spite of medical advice that she not ignore her pernicious anemia, Inez collapsed on stage during a presentation in Los Angeles. She died a few days later. Consequently, she became a martyr for woman's suffrage, especially with her last public words recorded as "Mr. President, how long must women wait for liberty?" Her death offered Alice Paul and the Congressional Union the final push needed to secure passage of the Nineteenth Amendment. Paul demanded that lives should not be lost for the cause.

Although Boissevain was an agent for social change, the attention paid her was primarily a consequence of her physical attractiveness and her ability to offer entertainment. She was likely taken less than seriously by the movement because of her advocacy of free love and affairs. Her husband was later remarried to the poet, Edna St. Vincent Millay.

Her drive for the vote was commemorated by the actress Julia Ormond in the film "Iron Jawed Angels."

For Further Reading: Ford, Linda G. *Iron-Jawed Angels: The Suffrage Militancy of the National Woman's Party 1912–1920.* New York: University Press of America, 1991; Lumsden, Linda J. *Inez: The Life and Times of Inez Milholland.* Bloomington: Indiana University Press, 2004.

Paulina Kellogg Wright Davis (1813–1876). Born in Bloomfield, New York, and orphaned at age seven, Paulina took her place in the woman's rights movement when she was only twenty. Working with Elizabeth Cady Stanton and others, she aided in securing passage of the Married Women's Property Act in 1848.

After the death of her first husband, Paulina began studying medicine, particularly women's anatomy and physiology, on which she based a series of lectures. She is credited for encouraging many of her women listeners to pursue a career in medicine.

Paulina organized the first National Women's Rights Convention in Worcester, Massachusetts, subsequently serving as the organization's first president. Between 1853 and 1855, she published *Una,* a woman's rights newspaper, and in 1871, she penned *A History of the National Woman's Rights Movement.*

For Further Reading: Stanton, Elizabeth Cady, Susan B. Anthony, and Matilda Joslyn Gage, eds. *History of Woman Suffrage.* New York: S.B. Anthony, 1922.

Helen Gurley Brown (1922–). Although she identified herself as an unfailing feminist, Helen Gurley Brown was repeatedly criticized by others in the movement for catering to men and concentrating on sexual rather than gender issues. Moving from secretary to advertising copywriter, within two years Brown became the highest-paid woman in her position on the West Coast. At age thirty-seven, she married David Brown, a film executive at Twentieth Century Fox, who suggested she write a how-to book for single women. The subsequent *Sex and the Single Girl* (1963) became an overnight best seller, stirring national controversy due to its radical advice on affairs and seduction. By giving women "permission to be permissive," the book and Brown played a part in the sexual revolution of the era. In 1964, she sold the film rights to Warner Brothers studio at the highest price ever paid for a work of nonfiction.

In 1965, Brown took over a failing *Cosmopolitan* magazine. Under her guidance, the periodical found a new target market, women 18–34, and tripled its circulation, eventually topping three million readers. Featuring consumerism, feminism, and freedom, *Cosmopolitan* became the female counterpart of *Playboy,* even publishing a male centerfold in 1972, and the perpetual target of scorn by radical feminists.

For Further Reading: Brown, Helen Gurley. *I'm Wild Again: Snippets from My Life and a Few Brazen Thoughts.* New York: St. Martin's Press, 2000.

Mitsuye Yasutake Yamada (1923–). Mitsuye Yamada, a second-generation Japanese American, grew up in Seattle, Washington. During World War II, her father was accused of espionage and the family was placed in a concentration camp in Mindoka, Idaho. Considered nonthreatening, Mitsuye was allowed to leave the camp to attend the University of Cincinnati. She married Yoshikazu Yamada in 1950 and received a master's degree in literature from the University of Chicago in 1953.

As a poet, Yamada used her words to empower Asian American women to find their voice and speak out despite the cultural norms that required women to be silent. Although she identified herself as a feminist first, she viewed gender and race as intersections of the same problem.

For Further Reading: Wong, Nellie, Merle Woo, and Mitsuye Yamada. *3 Asian American Writers Speak Out on Feminism.* San Francisco, CA: Red Letter Press, 2003.

Phyllis Schlafly (1924–). One of the most vocal leaders of the conservative movement in the United States, Phyllis Schlafly gained national attention during her ten-year battle against the Equal Rights Amendment. Opposed to almost all of the ideology of the radical feminists, Schlafly adopted the role of the archetypal antifeminist.

Born on August 15, 1924 in St. Louis, Missouri, Phyllis McAlpin Stewart was the daughter of John Bruce Stewart, a machinist and salesman, and

Odile Dodge, a school teacher and librarian. Her father lost his job during the Great Depression and her mother provided most of the family income as well as aiding her grandparents financially and paying tuition for Phyllis to attend a private Catholic girls' school.

Intellectually precocious, Phyllis earned an undergraduate degree, *Phi Beta Kappa*, from Washington University in 1944 at the age of nineteen and a master's degree in government from Radcliffe College in 1945, as well as a doctorate from Washington University School of Law in St. Louis in 1978. She was married to attorney John Fred Schlafly for forty-four years and gave birth to six children.

Having lost several political bids, including a congressional campaign in 1952, Schlafly gained national attention with the publication *A Choice, Not an Echo* (1964), a work widely distributed during Barry Goldwater's run for the presidency. Her concentrated efforts, however, were mounted during the 1970s when she became the most visible opponent of the passage of the Equal Rights Amendment, which she felt would hurt more than help the condition of women. She founded the "Stop the ERA" movement, shortened to STOP, an acronym for "Stop taking away our privileges." Schlafly mounted a grassroots campaign against the amendment in the states that had not yet voted on ratification. Her arguments, among others, were that the amendment would force women to join the military in times of war and would lead to unisex restrooms. She was credited by some as being the force behind the ERA's lack of passage.

In 1972, Schlafly founded the Eagle Forum, as well as the Eagle Forum Education & Legal Defense Fund, which distributed information and educational modules primarily through the Web site Conservapedia, created and edited by her son, Andrew. As a prolific author of over twenty-one books, she was widely criticized for opposing sex education in public schools, federally funded day care, and reproductive rights. Gloria Steinem noted that Schlafly's advocacy of stay at home moms and family values was odd considering that Schlafly worked as an attorney, an editor, a writer, and a political activist.

For Further Reading: Critchlow, Donald T. *Phyllis Schlafly and Grassroots Conservatism: A Woman's Crusade.* Princeton, NJ: Princeton University Press, 2005; Schlafly, Phyllis. *Feminist Fantasies.* Dallas, TX: Spence Publishing, 2003.

Aileen C. Hernandez (1926–). Education and public relations director of the International Ladies Garment Workers Union for the Pacific Coast region, Hernandez was the only woman on the five-member panel appointed by President Lyndon Baines Johnson to serve on the U.S. Equal Employment Opportunities Commission in 1965. In 1967, she founded Hernandez Associates, an urban consulting firm in San Francisco.

Born in Brooklyn, New York to Jamaican immigrants, Hernandez earned a scholarship to Howard University from where she was graduated *magna cum laude* with a double major in political science and sociology. Disturbed by the racial discord in Washington, DC, she moved to California and earned a master's degree in government from California State University. She was eventually granted an honorary Doctorate in Humane Letters from Southern Vermont College.

Hernandez was the second president of the National Organization for Women (NOW) and the founder of several organizations for black women, both locally and nationally, including the group, Black Women Stirring the Waters, which published essays from forty-four of the organization's members in 1998.

Because of her view of labor, civil rights, women's rights, and human rights as interrelated, coupled with her travels throughout the world, Hernandez treated her work from a global perspective. As chair person of California Women's Agenda, a network of over six hundred organizations and one million women, she implemented the action proposed by 189 countries at the Fourth World Conference on Women held in Beijing, China in 1995 through an electronic grassroots network.

Hernandez was nominated for the Nobel Peace Prize in 2005, as one of a one thousand women's collective from 150 countries.

For Further Reading: Hernandez, Aileen C. *National Women of Color Organizations: A Report to the Ford Foundation.* New York: Ford Foundation, 1991; Rosen, Ruth. *The World Split Open: How the Modern Women's Movement Changed America.* New York: Penguin, 2006.

Marilyn French (1929–). Born in New York City into a family of Polish descent, Marilyn French was one of the two daughters of E. Charles Edwards, an engineer, and Isabel Edwards, a department store retail clerk. A bright child, Marilyn began writing in earnest before she was ten years old and by her early teens, she was devouring works by the great philosophers of the world. A year before receiving her bachelors degree, she married Robert M. French, dropped out of school and worked in a series of menial jobs to pay his way through law school. Despite her husband's objections, she returned to school in 1960, earning a master's degree from Hofstra University and accepting a teaching post there following graduation. Following her divorce in 1967, she completed a doctorate at Harvard University.

In 1977, French published *The Women's Room,* a fictionalized account that followed the lives of several Harvard coeds as they become embroiled in feminist activism. The work incorporated suburbia into the movement, provided consciousness-raising for a generation, was translated into twenty languages, and made into a television movie in 1980. Following publication, French was considered a pivotal figure in the women's movement and the novel as one of the most influential works of the feminist movement, selling more than four million copies.

The bulk of her work centered on the polarized battle between the sexes based on her thesis that women were suppressed due to a male-dominated global culture. Her next work, *Beyond Power: On Women, Men and Morals* (1985), traced the historical rise of patriarchy, which she defined as a system that values power and control above all else.

For Further Reading: French, Marilyn. *A Season in Hell: A Memoir*. New York: Knopf, 1998.

LaDonna Harris (1931–). Primarily an advocate for indigenous peoples of the world, LaDonna Harris served for decades as a dynamic advocate for Native Americans, women, children, and the mentally ill. As a member of the Comanche tribe, she founded and served as the president of Americans for Indian Opportunity, a group dedicated to securing economic welfare for Native American peoples of all tribes.

Born in Temple, Oklahoma on February 15, 1931, Harris was the daughter of a white Irish American father and a Comanche mother. As a consequence of their mixed-race union, problems arising from the couple's lack of acceptance in the community caused her father to leave the family shortly after LaDonna's birth. The child was sent to live with her grandparents on a farm near Walters, Oklahoma. Through her grandparents, she was exposed to both white and Native culture; her grandmother, although Comanche, was a Christian, while her grandfather was a tribal medicine man. Despite their different viewpoints, her grandparents proved that the two beliefs could coexist, providing positive role models for the child.

When LaDonna entered first grade, she spoke only Comanche and was forced to learn English before she could begin her studies. While she was in high school, she met Fred Harris and, although he was not Native American, the two shared similar values rooted in the adversity created by poverty. Although he was the son of a sharecropper, Fred was ambitious and wanted to attend law school as a route into politics. After they were married, LaDonna worked to put Fred through undergraduate and law school, while raising their three children.

Her labor and his studies paid off and Fred was elected first to the Oklahoma State Senate and, in 1965, to the U.S. Senate. As a citizen of two states and essentially two worlds, LaDonna developed an increased interest in issues of national concern. She also began to realize the importance of coalitions in moving those issues forward. During the part of the year the family spent in Oklahoma, she worked to unify the various tribes in the state with the goal of ending segregation. She aided in forming Oklahomans for Indian Opportunity, bringing together members from sixty tribes to work toward political unity.

While in Washington, LaDonna became the first wife of a senator to address Congress on behalf of her people. As a result of her growing public presence, President Lyndon Johnson appointed her to head the National

Women's Advisory Council of the War on Poverty in 1967 and the following year, Johnson created the National Council on Indian Opportunity, naming Harris as a council member.

In the early 1970s, Harris expanded her activism and aided in founding the National Women's Political Caucus, while assisting women in grassroots political organizing. In 1975, President Gerald Ford named her to the Commission on the Observance of National Women's Year and President Jimmy Carter appointed her to United Nations Education Scientific and Cultural Organization (UNESCO).

Concerned with not only her own people but also the welfare of indigenous peoples worldwide, Harris was intrigued with the work of the Peace Corps and when President Carter appointed her to serve as special assistant to Sargent Shriver, the director of the Office of Economic Opportunity, she had the opportunity to investigate the organization of the international volunteer group. Based on her discoveries, Harris instituted "The Peace Pipe Project"; modeled after the Peace Corps, the organization trained Native Americans to work with other indigenous peoples all over the globe.

Long an advocate of women's rights, Harris was a member of Global Tomorrow Coalition and on the board of Women for Meaningful Summits, two organizations of women concerned with environmental issues. In 1980, she was the presidential nominee on the Citizens Party ticket.

For Further Reading: Janda, Sarah Eppler. *Beloved Women: The Political Lives of Ladonna Harris and Wilma Mankiller*. DeKalb: Northern Illinois University Press, 2007.

Alix Kates Shulman (1932–). The author of multiple works, including the *Memoirs of an Ex-Prom Queen* (1970), called the first important novel to emerge from the women's liberation movement, Alix Shulman was an early member of the consciousness-raising groups, The Redstockings, the Women's International Terrorist Conspiracy from Hell, and the New York Radical Feminists.

Born in Cleveland, Ohio, Alix was the daughter of Sam Kates, an attorney, and Dorothy Kates, a community volunteer with the Works Progress Administration. Although her early interests lay in law, she enrolled in Case Western Reserve University with a double major in philosophy and math, despite the fact that both were considered male-only pursuits. After attending one year of graduate school at Columbia, she dropped out to marry another graduate student and took jobs as a receptionist, a researcher, and an encyclopedia editor. When their short-lived union was terminated, she returned to school at New York University, earning a master's degree in humanities.

In the 1960s, Shulman became a political activist for the bundled issues of the day, antiwar, civil rights, and feminism. She was instrumental in the planning of the 1968 Miss American Pageant protest in Atlantic City, New Jersey, the first national demonstration of women's liberation where the protestors crowned a sheep outside the conference hall. In addition to her novels, she penned "A Marriage Agreement" in 1970, an essay that advocated that marriage should be the shared responsibility of both genders.

In addition to other honors, Shulman received a National Endowment for the Arts fellowship in fiction in 1983 and an honorary doctorate from Case Western University.

For Further Reading: Shulman, Alix Kates. *A Good Enough Daughter: A Memoir.* New York: Schocken Books, 1999.

Susan Brownmiller (1935–). Susan Brownmiller was born in Brooklyn, New York on February 15, a birthday she shared with Susan B. Anthony. While waiting for her break as a Broadway actress, Brownmiller worked as a secretary, a waitress, and an editor for confession magazines. The Civil Rights Movement piqued her interest in activism and in the 1960s, she joined the Congress of Racial Equality, participated in a picket line at Woolworth's Drug Store in New York City and took part in Freedom Summer, a voter registration drive for African Americans in Mississippi in 1964.

In 1968, Brownmiller accepted a position as a television news writer for the American Broadcasting Company and marched against the war in Vietnam. The same year, she joined the New York Radical Women Association and coordinated a sit-in launched against the *Ladies Home Journal.* Her feminist alliances led to her seminal work, *Against Our Will: Men, Women and Rape.* Published in 1975, the work pioneered the view that rape was motivated by politics and a need for power; in other words, it was a symbolic act by one man representing the power of all men.

Brownmiller cofounded the group Women against Pornography in 1979 and published *In Our Time: Memoir of a Revolution,* a history of second-wave feminism in 1999. In addition, she served as an adjunct professor of women and gender studies at Pace University in New York City.

For Further Reading: Brownmiller, Susan. *In Our Time: Memoir of a Revolution.* New York: Dial Press, 1999.

Jane Fonda (1937–). Although known primarily as an actor and a political activist, Jane Fonda became a factor in the feminist movement in the early 1970s, an offshoot of her work in civil rights. Although she was embroiled in public hostility due to her antiwar activities, including a trip to Vietnam many considered lacking in patriotism and bordering on treasonous, and her support of The Black Panthers, among other controversial issues, Fonda also became a staunch advocate of movements to stop violence against women.

Born in New York City, Jane was the daughter of actor Henry Fonda and socialite Frances Ford Seymour, who committed suicide when Jane was twelve years old. She attended Vassar College. Having shown an interest in theatre, she was introduced by her father to acting guru Lee Strasberg and was admitted to his Actors Studio.

She was an honorary chairperson of V-Day, an antiviolence against women group inspired by the play, *The Vagina Monologues.* In 2002, she founded the Jane Fonda Center for Adolescent Reproductive Health at Emory University in Atlanta, Georgia, to aid in the prevention of teenage pregnancy. In her 2005 autobiography, *My Life So Far,* Fonda revealed her reticence to call herself a feminist because of the man-hating stereotype attached to the label. She noted that a patriarchal image could be as harmful to men as it was to women. In 2007, although ostensibly retired from the film industry, she continued to serve as an advocate for woman's rights, worldwide.

For Further Reading: Fonda, Jane. *My Life So Far.* New York: Random House, 2005.

Germaine Greer (1939–). Although not a citizen of the United States, Australian Germaine Greer provided an enormous impact on the woman's movement in America. Considered one of the most significant feminist voices of the twentieth century, Greer spearheaded the radical feminist movement.

Greer was born on January 29, 1939, near Melbourne, Australia, the eldest of the three children of Reginald Greer, a newspaper advertising executive, and Margaret May Greer. The young woman had an early talent for languages and was fluent in several before she was twelve years old. She graduated from Melbourne University, earned a master's degree from the University of Sydney, and a doctorate from Cambridge University in England in 1967.

Although it harshly criticized the actions of many feminists, Greer's 1970 work, *The Female Eunuch,* became an international best seller and a text for radical feminism in the United States. The title of the work sprang from her thesis that men had "castrated" women in order to assure their acceptance of society's imposed requirements for femininity. The book was one of the first to advocate sexual liberation and to discuss explicitly what Greer called the sexual repression of women. She criticized the National Organization for Women (NOW) as advocating for only the middle class. Describing herself as an anarchist, Greer avowed distaste for men whom she labeled "sperm factories."

In the United States, Greer became an intellectual celebrity, lauded in popular culture, and asked to cover the 1972 Democratic Convention in Miami for *Harper's* magazine. Her work over time renounced religion, denigrated marriage, and railed against imposing Western culture on indigenous peoples.

For Further Reading: Greer, Germaine. *The Whole Woman.* New York: A.A. Knopf, 1999; Wallace, Christine. *Germaine Greer: Untamed Shrew.* New York: Faber and Faber, 1998.

Letty Cottin Pogrebin (1939–). Committed to the women's movement, Letty Cottin Pogrebin was, with Gloria Steinem, one of the founding editors of *Ms.* magazine, a publication with which she was involved for over twenty years. She was also a cofounder of the National Women's Political Caucus in 1971.

Pogrebin was born in New York City on June 9, 1939, the daughter of Jacob, an attorney, and Cyral Halpern. The independence of the women in her family was ingrained; her grandmother had jumped from a window on her wedding day to elope with another man.

Letty's mother died of cancer in 1955, and Letty begged her father to allow her to be part of the service. Because he refused, she rejected her ties to Judaism for many years. In 1959, after graduating from Brandeis University, *cum laude* in English, Pogrebin joined the promotion and advertising firm of Bernard Geis Associates. In 1963, she married Bertrand Pogrebin, a labor attorney, with whom she had three children.

By 1969, she had gained the title of vice president at the advertising firm but resigned to engage in freelance writing. Between 1971 and 1981, she contributed a column to *Ladies Home Journal,* titled "The Working Woman," while working independently on several books. She published *How to Make It in a Man's World* in 1970.

The following year, she joined with Gloria Steinem and others to found the National Women's Political Caucus to encourage support for women candidates for public office and launched *Ms.* magazine, which became the national forum for women's issues and the platform of the associations. Pogrebin was particularly interested in investigating gender roles and how they influenced child rearing.

Combining her interest in both religion and feminism, she served on the advisory boards of both the Harvard Divinity School's Women in Religion program and Brandeis University's Women's Studies program. By 1975, she worked to combat anti-Semitism in the woman's movement and antifeminism within Judaism.

Pogrebin also aided actress-activist Marlo Thomas in selecting works to be included in the album "Free to Be You and Me," a collection of gender-nonspecific and nonsexist songs and stories.

For Further Reading: Pogrebin, Letty Cottin. *Family Politics: Love and Power on an Intimate Frontier.* New York: McGraw Hill, 1984; ———. *Deborah, Golda and Me: Being Female and Jewish in America.* New York: Anchor Books, 1992.

Barbara Alexander Ehrenreich (1941–). Although never directly involved in the woman's movement per se, Barbara Ehrenreich invested most of her professional and private life in working as a health and human rights activist, through which she shed light on the lack of gender equality in the medical profession.

Barbara Alexander Ehrenreich was born on August 26, 1941 in Butte, Montana, the daughter of Ben Howes Alexander, a copper miner, and Isabelle Oxley, a homemaker and active Democrat. From her parents, she inherited a tradition of both independence and atheism.

While being politically active, engaging in protests of the Vietnam War and working with the Civil Rights Movement, throughout the 1960s, Ehrenreich earned an undergraduate degree from Reed College in Portland, Oregon in 1963 in chemical physics and a doctorate in cell biology from Rockefeller University in New York City in 1968. During her time as a student, she worked to improve low income housing, to gain more educational opportunities for the poor, pushed for healthcare reform, aided in organizing union activities, and founded a student antiwar group.

In 1966, she married fellow activist, John Ehrenreich, with whom she published *Long March, Short Spring: The Student Uprising at Home and Abroad* in 1969. Between 1969 and 1971, while editing publications for the Health Policy Advisory Center, Ehrenreich focused on the inequity in the medical profession, noting that medicine was "a microcosm that mirrored and institutionalized sexism," not only through its hiring practices but also through the way women patients were diagnosed and treated. To that end, she published two pamphlets: *Witches, Midwives and Nurses: A History of Women Healers* (1972) and *Complaints and Disorders: The Sexual Politics of Sickness* (1973), addressing the male domination of the healthcare system.

In the early 1970s, she worked as an assistant professor of health sciences at the State University of New York, cochaired the Democratic Socialists of America, and edited a new magazine, *Seven Days*. In 1987, she was awarded a Guggenheim Fellowship at the Institute for Policy Studies in Washington, DC.

For Further Reading: Ehrenreich, Barbara. *The Hearts of Men: American Dreams and the Flight from Commitment*. New York: Anchor Books, 1983.

Rita Mae Brown (1944–). Prolific author and activist Rita Mae Brown was involved in the Civil Rights Movement, the anti-Vietnam war movement, the Gay Liberation Movement, and the feminist movement. Born to an unwed mother, the child was adopted and considered to be precocious, reading at three years old and having her own library card at age five. In 1955, the family moved to Fort Lauderdale, Florida, where Rita Mae earned a scholarship to University of Florida in 1962 but she was forced to relinquish the award due to her active involvement in the Civil Rights Movement and her open lesbianism. She was eventually graduated from New York University, where she founded the Student Homophile League, the first gay group on a university campus. As a gay activist, Brown participated in the Stonewall riots in New York City in 1969. The Stonewall Inn was a gay bar in

Greenwich Village that was raided by the police. The event marked the first time in modern history that a group of gay people resisted arrest.

Although she was an administrator in NOW, she resigned after Betty Friedan's remarks concerning lesbian women. Brown took a leading role in the "Lavender Menace" protest of the Second Congress to Unite Women in 1970 to dispute Friedan and the exclusion of lesbian issues from the women's movement. In 1970, she cofounded The Furies, a lesbian feminist newspaper collective that took the position that heterosexuality was the root of all oppression.

Brown was the author of multiple volumes, including the semiautobiographical best seller, *Rubyfruit Jungle,* which launched her as a spokesperson for Gay Liberation, *A Plain Brown Rapper* (1976), a collection of essays on the women's liberation movement between 1969 and 1975, and the highly popular Sneaky Pie mystery series. She also worked as a screenwriter and was nominated for an Emmy in 1982.

For Further Reading: Brown, Rita Mae. *Rita Will: Memoir of a Literary Rabble-Rouser.* New York: Bantam, 1997.

Shulamith Firestone (1945–). Nicknamed Shulie, Shulamith Firestone was a founding member of the New York Radical Women, the Redstockings, and the New York Radical Feminists. She professed that heterosexual families were established on unequal power bases because women were forced to depend on men for survival. She advocated division of labor within a household, particularly due to children's dependence on their mother.

In 1967, the New York Radical Women were split between the socialist feminists and the radical feminists, with which Firestone was associated. Following the dissolution of that group, Firestone aided in founding the Redstockings, the group noted for its consciousness-raising methodology, and then the New York Radical Feminists. She eventually disassociated from each of the groups because the members did not care for her leadership style. She was often cited as saying being called a feminist was an insult.

Firestone was awarded a bachelor of fine arts in painting from the Art Institute in Chicago, where she was the subject of a well-reviewed experimental documentary film appropriately titled "Shulie," which was rediscovered and released in 1997. While in Chicago, she was the coorganizer of the Westside Group.

In 1970, Firestone published *The Dialectic of Sex: A Case for Feminist Revolution* in which she asserted a feminist theory of politics. The work, which became a major text for the second wave of feminism, stressed that patriarchy was forced on women because of their biological differences. She suggested that reproduction should take place in a laboratory, predicted gender selection for fetuses and in vitro fertilization, and requested state financial support for child rearing. In addition, Firestone supported the abolishment of the nuclear family in favor of living in communal units.

For Further Reading: Firestone, Shulamith. *Notes from the First Year.* New York: The New York Radical Women, 1968; ———. *The Dialectic of Sex: The Case for Feminist Revolution.* New York: Morrow, 1970.

Catharine MacKinnon (1946–). Although criticized for her work with Andrea Dworkin on pornography, attorney Catharine MacKinnon worked tirelessly for the rights of women. She pioneered the legal claim against sexual harassment as a form of gender discrimination under Title VII of the Civil Rights Act of 1964.

Born to an upper-middle-class family in Minnesota on October 7, 1946, Catharine was the daughter of George E. MacKinnon, an attorney, congressman, and judge on the U.S. Court of Appeals for the Washington, DC circuit, and Elizabeth Valentine Davis. She was valedictorian of her high school, graduated in the top 2 percent of her class from Smith College, and received a National Science Foundation fellowship to attend Law School at Yale University. After earning a degree in law, she received a doctorate in political science also from Yale.

In 1979, MacKinnon published *Sexual Harassment of Women: A Case of Sex Discrimination,* which became the eighth most frequently cited American legal book published since 1978. The following year, the Equal Employment Opportunity Commission adopted her guidelines on quid pro quo, something for something like the offer of a job or a promotion for sexual favors, and hostile workplace harassment.

Inspired by activist Andrea Dworkin, MacKinnon worked to create ordinances in Minnesota that recognized pornography as not only distasteful but as a civil rights violation. In 1983, she was hired by the Minneapolis City government to create an ordinance that would allow women to sue the producers and distributors if they claimed they were harmed by pornography. The mayor vetoed the ordinance.

In 2000, she represented Bosnian women survivors of Serbian genocidal sex crimes. MacKinnon won the case, marking the first incidence of recognizing rape as an act of genocide and gaining a $745 million award for the women. She expressed that rape should be defined as "whenever a woman feels violated" and believed that politics was a theory of power.

MacKinnon worked with Equality Now in the Lawyers Alliance for Women, promoting international gender equality rights for women in places such as Mexico, Japan, Israel, and India. She was also a professor of law at the University of Michigan, where she specialized in sex equality issues.

For Further Reading: MacKinnon, Catharine. *Feminism Unmodified: Discourses on Life and Law.* Cambridge, MA: Harvard University Press, 1987; ———. *Are*

Women Human?: And Other International Dialogues. Cambridge, MA: Belknap Press of Harvard University Press, 2006.

Barbara Smith (1946–). African American lesbian feminist, Barbara Smith was successful in increasing the sustainability of black feminism but was likely best remembered for coining the definitive definition of the word. After having taught at numerous colleges and universities and being widely published, Smith reorganized the Boston chapter of the National Black Feminist Organization into the Combahee River Collective, a group concerned with the intersection of racial, gender, heterosexist, and class oppression in the lives of women of color. Together, the women worked for reproductive rights, health care and prison reform, and against violence directed toward women, including rape, involuntary sterilization, and racism within the women's movement.

In 1980, Smith, with author/activist Audre Lorde, founded and published *Kitchen Table: Women of Color Press,* which group became the first publishing firm in the United States specifically for women of color. Her article, "Toward a Black Feminist Conscience," published in 1982, was noted as a breakthrough in black women's literature and in black lesbian literature.

An advocate of coalitions, Smith penned the following definition of feminism that was widely adopted by her peers: "feminism is the political theory and practice to free all women: women of color, working-class women, poor women, physically challenged women, lesbians, old women, as well as white economically privileged heterosexual women. Anything less than this is not feminism, but merely female self-aggrandizement."

For Further Reading: Bulkin, Elly. *Yours in Struggle: Three Feminist Perspectives on Anti-Semitism and Racism/Elly Bulkin, Minnie Bruce Pratt, Barbara Smith.* Ithaca, NY: Firebrand Books, 1988; Smith, Barbara. "Barbara Smith on Black Feminism." *Sojourner: The Women's Forum,* December 1984, 13; ———. *The Truth That Never Hurts: Writings on Race, Gender, and Freedom.* New Brunswick, NJ: Rutgers University Press, 1998.

Cherríe Moraga (1952–). Lesbian activist Cherríe Moraga opened doors for women of color to express their beliefs openly. In creating a publishing venue, she unsilenced many women, repressed by their cultural mores, and created a forum for expression.

Born in Whittier, California on September 25, 1952, Moraga was the daughter of a Caucasian father, Joseph Lawrence, and a Latino mother, Elvira Moraga. Although she was a third-generation citizen of the United States, Cherrie still encountered racial prejudice as a child. She credits her ability as a writer to listening to the kitchen tales of women, as evidenced in the name of the publishing firm she founded, The Kitchen Table/Women of Color Press.

When she discovered the majority of writing by lesbian authors reflected the views of Caucasian women only, Moraga determined to avert the cultural taboos and to create work with which women of color could identify. While studying feminist writings in graduate school at San Francisco State University, she coedited a collection of writings by women of color, published as *This Bridge Called My Back: Writings by Radical Women of Color* in 1981, which served as a launching pad for her own work. Mixing English and Spanish in her work, Moraga published the semiautobiographical *Loving in the War Years* in 1983, reviewed as the first book of poetry by an openly lesbian Latino. Her work addressed the silence imposed on women by the male-centered Latino culture and criticized the racism and oppression present even in the women's movement. She also dismissed the stereotype that gender roles existed in lesbian relationships.

As a lecturer in Latino Studies at the University of California at Berkeley, a publisher and author, Moraga continued to attack racial bias, including her view of the injustice that allowed corporate America to cross the border to seek a less expensive labor market, while prohibiting Mexicans from seeking employment in the United States.

For Further Reading: Moraga, Cherrie, and Gloria Anzaldua, eds. *This Bridge Called My Back: Writings by Radical Women of Color.* Berkeley, CA: Third Woman Press, 2001; Yarbro-Bejanrano, Yvonne. *The Wounded Heart: Writing on Cherrie Moraga.* Austin: University of Texas Press, 2001.

Susan Faludi (1959–). A Pulitzer Prize winning journalist, Susan Faludi was best known for her 1992 book, *Backlash: The Undeclared War Against American Women,* that illustrated the media's negative portrayal of women and the consequent *backlash* that affected women's perceptions of themselves. Referred to as the new manifesto of feminism, the thesis of the work was that society was attacking the progress made by women through hypocritical depictions in film, on television, and in print. Faludi asserted that the concept of "feminine" was defined and redefined through cultural messages and political agendas and that she preferred not to be evaluated with such superficial value judgments.

Faludi was born in New York City, the daughter of Steven and Marilyn Faludi, a photographer and a writer, respectively. Having inherited her proclivity for the pen from her mother, a newspaper editor, she began journalistic pursuits as early as the fifth grade, interviewing her peers about the issues of the day. When the results of her study were revealed, the young woman was verbally attacked by members of the local John Birch Society who labeled her a communist.

Following graduation, *summa cum laude,* from Harvard University in 1981, Faludi geared her activism toward the written word, writing for *The Nation, The New Yorker* and the San Francisco bureau of the *Wall Street Journal* among other publications. After reading a 1986 article in *Newsweek* that implied a college-educated single woman over forty had a greater chance of being murdered by a terrorist than of finding a husband and on observing the subsequent fallout among women's belief systems, Faludi was inspired to begin work on *Backlash*. She dedicated four years to compiling research for the work, which she published in 1991.

The book soared up the best-seller lists and was quickly adopted by feminists. By demystifying studies and statistics surrounding the gender issue, Faludi revealed pervasive patterns of sexism. Faludi was considered a feminist; however, her publications were not limited to women, witnessed by the publication of *Stiffed: The Betrayal of the American Man* (1999). She viewed gender issues as intertwined and treated her profession as a means of creating social change through education and investigation.

For Further Reading: Faludi, Susan. "I'm Not a Feminist but I Play One on TV." *Ms.,* February/March 1995, 31–39; ———. *Backlash: The Undeclared War Against American Women.* New York: Three Rivers Press, 2006 (repr.).

Naomi Wolf (1963–). In her seminal work *The Beauty Myth: How Images of Beauty Are Used Against Women* (1990), Naomi Wolf castigated the popular culture view of beauty and the expectation that women had to live up to those *perfect* images projected through the media and advertising. As one of the premier voices of the third wave of feminism, Wolf proclaimed the beauty myth had undermined, perhaps purposively, the political and economic gains women achieved during the second wave by lowering their self-esteem.

Wolf was born in San Francisco, the daughter of Leonard Wolf, a professor of English Literature at San Francisco State University, and Deborah Wolf, a psychotherapist and former anthropologist in women's studies. Her grandmother, Fay Goleman, was a noted feminist. Despite strong women role models, Naomi became anorexic at age twelve and nearly died.

After receiving a bachelor of arts degree in English from Yale in 1984, she was selected as a Rhodes Scholar and invited to study for a doctorate at Oxford University. When the selection process was completed, only the women who were selected were taken aside and given instruction on how to present themselves physically, including instruction on dress, posture, and makeup. After three years at Oxford, Wolf had completed the work on her thesis. Although *The Beauty Myth* was to have been her topic, Wolf opted for publishing the work instead.

In the work, she claimed that women needed to rid themselves of the mythical preoccupation with what advertisers promote as the ideal appearance and create a new definition of beauty based on the unique qualities of each individual. Critics noted that Wolf failed to address the competitive nature of women based on their physical appearance.

Wolf advanced the theory that feminists should imitate successful businessmen and, rather than sisterhood, they should be interested in economic independence, including forming their own investment clubs and becoming professionally combative. While advocating consumerism, she attacked advertising for creating women's attraction to it.

In 1993, she married David Shipley, the executive editor of the *New Republic*. Although continuing to write, Wolf invested time in volunteering at women's shelters and manning hotlines. In response to a new role, she demystified motherhood in her *Misconceptions: Truths, Lies and the Unexpected on the Journey to Motherhood* published in 2003.

For Further Reading: Wolf, Naomi. *Fire with Fire: The New Female Power and How It Will Change the 21ˢᵗ Century*. New York: Ballentine, 1994; ———. *The Beauty Myth: How Images of Beauty Are Used Against Women*. New York: Perennial, 2002.

Katie Roiphe (1968–). Calling herself an antifeminist, Katie Roiphe was widely criticized for her views on rape, particularly date rape, and her opinion that the victimization of women was frequently self-inflicted.

Born in New York City, Katie was the daughter of Dr. Herman Roiphe, a psychoanalyst, and Anne Roiphe, an author and columnist for the *New York Observer*. Her mother was the author of *Up the Sandbox* (1970), which was widely regarded as one of the classics of feminist literature. Consequently, Katie was indoctrinated early on to believe that feminism equated freedom and individualism. She was awarded an undergraduate degree from Harvard and a doctorate in English Literature from Princeton University. Combining her parental influences, her dissertation applied Freudian psychoanalysis to American literature of the 1940s and 1950s. After graduation, she was offered a teaching post at New York University's Council for Media and Culture.

Roiphe gained notoriety with the publication of *The Morning After: Fear, Sex and Feminism* (1994), which led to an op-ed piece in the *New York Times* regarding the pamphlets disbursed by universities on avoiding date rape. She likened the advice in those pamphlets to that which was available in Victorian-era guides on proper conduct for women. Concluding that colleges were equating bad dates with rape, Roiphe castigated the institution for "breathing new life into musty stereotypes of weak, delicate women preyed upon by lewd, brutish men." According to her, being pressured into unwanted sex was not the same as being raped and that, in some ways, women should be held responsible for their actions, especially if those actions were the result of over indulgence in alcohol or drugs.

Almost immediately, the critics, including many from the woman's movement, attacked Roiphe for blaming the victim and offering approval of abuse; she countered that feminists were without humor and opposed to sex. On the other hand, some applauded, calling her views a novel way of telling women to stop being treated as fragile. The consequences included angry shouting at her public readings and hate mail that indicated the hope that she would be raped.

Her second work, published in 1997, was *Last Night in Paradise: Sex and Morals at the Century's End,* addressing the ways in which the AIDS epidemic changed the view of sexual conduct and contact in the United States. Roiphe appeared disturbed that the disease had been used to justify preaching abstinence. Ultimately, her thesis was that women should seek financial independence and stop being victims.

For Further Reading: Roiphe, Katie. *The Morning After: Sex, Fear and Feminism on Campus.* Boston: Little, Brown and Company, 1993; ———. *Last Night in Paradise: Sex and Morals at the Century's End.* Boston: Little, Brown and Company, 1997.

Rebecca Walker (1969–). Rebecca Walker was noted as "expanding feminist space to include women of color." She founded the Walker Third Wave Direct Action Corporation to aid young women in building leadership skills and to ignite their spirit of activism.

The daughter of writer Alice Walker and civil rights attorney Mel Leventhal, as a child, Rebecca lived under the double exposure of being in the shadow of her famous parents as well as being the product of a mixed-race marriage, which she addressed in her best-selling memoir, *Black, White and Jewish: Autobiography of a Shifting Self,* published in 2001. If that were not enough, she was born in the middle and in the midst of the Civil Rights Movement in Jackson, Mississippi and experienced disconnect with both sides of her heritage. As a consequence of her feelings of alienation, she turned to youthful experimentation with both sex and drugs, which experience provided impetus for part of her later work with young people.

Walker attended Yale University and was graduated, *cum laude,* in 1992. After graduation, she cofounded the Third Wave Foundation, a nonprofit that secured grant funding to provide leadership development and advocacy for women between the ages of fifteen and thirty. The program particularly addressed the intersecting issues of gender, race, economics, and social justice.

In addition to her work with the Foundation, Walker provided a voice for the third wave of the woman's movement by traveling around the country as a speaker, primarily at high schools and universities, and teaching the art of memoir in workshops. The central focus of those presentations underscored her interest in reproductive freedom, domestic violence, and sexuality. She served as a consultant on generational differences, diversity, and the impact of gender on the workplace for firms such as Sony Music, Microsoft, and Morgan Chase. With her partner Angel Williams, Walker opened the

Cybercafé in an underserved section of Brooklyn, New York to provide Internet access and education to the multicultural community.

Named by *Time* magazine as one of the fifty most influential leaders under forty in the United States, Walker received an honorary doctorate from the North Carolina School of the Arts and the "Women Who Could Be President" award from the League of Women Voters. Since 1989, she served as a contributing editor for *Ms.* magazine and was the author of *To Be Real: Telling the Truth and Changing the Face of Feminism* (1995), a work used as text in Gender Studies and Women's Studies programs around the world, *What Makes a Man: 22 Writers Imagine the Future* (2004) and *Baby Love: Choosing Motherhood after a Lifetime of Ambivalence* (2007).

For Further Reading: Walker, Rebecca. *To Be Real: Telling the Truth and Changing the Face of Feminism.* New York: Anchor Books, 1995.

SELECTED BIBLIOGRAPHY

Abzug, Bella. *Bella! Ms. Abzug Goes to Washington.* New York: Saturday Review Press, 1972.

Adams, Katherine. *Alice Paul and the American Suffrage Campaign.* Urbana: University of Illinois Press, 2007.

Addams, Jane. "If Men Were Seeking the Franchise." *Ladies Home Journal,* June 1913, 104–7, http://nationalhumanitiescenter.org/pds/gilded/power/text12/addams.pdf.

———. *Twenty Years at Hull House: With Autobiographical Notes.* Boston: Bedford/St. Martin's, 1999.

Alexander, M. Jacqui, and Chandra Talpade Mohanty, eds. *Feminist Genealogies, Colonial Legacies, Democratic Futures.* New York: Routledge, 1997.

Anthony, Susan B. *The Trial of Susan B. Anthony.* Amherst, NY: Humanity Books, 2003.

Anticaglia, Elizabeth. *12 American Women.* Chicago: Nelson-Hall Company, 1975.

Baker, Christina Looper, and Christina Baker Kline. *The Conversation Begins: Mothers and Daughters Talk About Living Feminism.* New York: Bantam Books, 1996.

Balducci, Carolyn Feleppa. *Margaret Fuller: A Life of Passion and Defiance.* New York: Bantam Books, 1991.

Balliet, Barbara J. *Women, Culture and Society: A Reader.* Dubuque, IA: Kendall/Hunt, 2004.

Banner, Lois W. *Elizabeth Cady Stanton: A Radical for Woman's Rights.* Boston: Little, Brown, 1980.

Bardwick, Judith. *In Transition: How Feminism, Sexual Liberation and the Search for Self-Fulfillment Have Altered America.* New York: Holt, Rinehart and Winston, 1979.

Barrett, Michèle. *Women's Oppression Today: The Marxist/Feminist Encounter.* London: Verso, 1988.

Barrett, Michèle, and Anne Phillips. *Destablizing Theory: Contemporary Feminist Debates.* Stanford, CA: Stanford University Press, 1992.

Barry, Kathleen. *Susan B. Anthony: A Biography of a Singular Feminist.* New York: New York University Press, 1988.

Bartlett, Elizabeth Ann. *Liberty, Equality, Sorority: The Origins and Interpretation of American Feminist Thought: Frances Wright, Sarah Grimké, and Margaret Fuller.* Brooklyn, NY: Carlson Publishing, 1994.

Beck, Susan Abrams. "Eleanor Roosevelt: The Path to Equality." *White House Studies,* Fall 2004, 531–45.

Becker, Susan. *The Origins of the Equal Rights Amendment: American Feminism between the Wars.* Westport, CT: Greenwood Press, 1981.

Belenky, Mary Field. *Women's Ways of Knowing: The Development of Self, Voice and Mind.* New York: Basic Books, 1997.

Bell, Margaret. *Margaret Fuller: A Biography.* Freeport, NY: Books for Libraries Press, 1971.

Bernard, Jacqueline. *Journey toward Freedom: The Story of Sojourner Truth.* New York: Feminist Press at the City University of New York, 1990.

Blackwell, Alice Stone. *Lucy Stone, Pioneer of Woman's Rights.* New York: Octagon Books, 1961.

Blatch, Harriot Stanton. *Mobilizing Woman-Power.* New York: The Woman's Press, 1918.

Blatch, Harriot Stanton, and Alma Lutz. *Challenging Years: The Memoirs of Harriot Stanton Blatch.* Westport, CT: Hyperion Press, 1976.

Bloomer, D. C. *Life and Writings of Amelia Bloomer.* New York: Schocken Books, 1975.

Bock, Gisela, and Susan James, eds. *Beyond Equality and Difference: Citizenship, Feminist Politics and Female Subjectivity.* New York: Routledge, 1992.

Borda, Jennifer L. "The Woman Suffrage Parades of 1910–1913: Possibilities and Limitations of an Early Feminist Rhetorical Strategy." *Western Journal of Communication,* 66 (Winter 2002): 25–52.

Bordin, Ruth. *Frances Willard: A Biography.* Chapel Hill: University of North Carolina Press, 1986.

Boucher, Joanne. *Betty Friedan and the Radical Past of Liberal Feminism. New Politics* 9 (Summer 2003): 3.

Boynick, David King. *Women Who Led the Way: Eight Pioneers for Equal Rights.* New York: Crowell, 1972 rep.

Brammer, Leila. *Excluded from Suffrage History: Matilda Joslyn Gage, Nineteenth Century American Feminist.* Westport, CT: Greenwood Press, 2000.

Brill, Alida, ed. *A Rising Public Voice: Women in Politics Worldwide.* New York: Feminist Press, 1995.

Brown, Helen Gurley. *I'm Wild Again: Snippets from My Life and a Few Brazen Thoughts.* New York: St. Martin's Press, 2000.

Brown, Olympia. *Acquaintances, Old and New, among Reformers.* Milwaukee, WI: S.E. Tate, 1911.

Brown, Rita Mae. *Rita Will: Memoir of a Literary Rabble-Rouser.* New York: Bantam Books, 1997.

Brown, Victoria Bissell. *The Education of Jane Addams.* Philadelphia: University of Pennsylvania Press, 2004.

Brownmiller, Susan. *In Our Time: Memoir of a Revolution.* New York: Dial Press, 1999.

Buechler, Steven M. *Women's Movements in the United States: Woman Suffrage, Equal Rights, and Beyond.* New Brunswick, NJ: Rutgers University Press, 1990.

Bulkin, Elly. *Yours in Struggle: Three Feminist Perspectives on Anti-Semitism and Racism/Elly Bulkin, Minnie Bruce Pratt, Barbara Smith.* Ithaca, NY: Firebrand Books, 1988

Burnett, Constance Buel. *Five for Freedom: Lucretia Mott, Elizabeth Cady Stanton, Lucy Stone, Susan B. Anthony, Carrie Chapman Catt*. New York: Greenwood Press, 1968.

Butler, Amy. *Two Paths to Equality: Alice Paul and Ethel M. Smith in the ERA Debate, 1921–1929*. Albany: State University of New York, 2002.

Butler, Judith. *Gender Trouble: Feminism and the Subversion of Identity*. New York: Routledge, 2006.

———. *Undoing Gender*. New York: Routledge, 2004.

Caine, Barbara, E. A. Grosz, and Marie de Lepervanche. *Crossing Boundaries: Feminisms and the Critique of Knowledges*. Boston: Allen & Unwin, 1988.

Campbell, Amy Leigh. *Raising the Bar: Ruth Bader Ginsburg and the ACLU Women's Rights Project*. Princeton, NJ: Xlibris Corporation, 2003.

Cazden, Elizabeth. *Antoinette Brown Blackwell: A Biography*. Old Westbury, NY: The Feminist Press, 1983.

Chesler, Ellen. *Woman of Valor: Margaret Sanger and the Birth Control Movement in America*. New York: Simon & Schuster, 1992.

Chesler, Phyllis. *The Death of Feminism: What's Next in the Struggle for Women's Freedom*. New York: Palgrave Macmillan, 2006.

———. *Letters to a Young Feminist*. New York: Four Walls Eight Windows, 1997.

Chisholm, Shirley. *The Good Fight*. New York: Harper & Row, 1973.

———. *Unbought and Unbossed: An Autobiography*. New York: Houghton Mifflin Company, 1970.

Chopin, Kate. *The Awakening*. New York: W. W. Norton, 1993.

Christensen, Hilda Romer, Beatrice Halsaa, and Aino Saarinen, eds. *Crossing Borders: Re-mapping Women's Movements at the Turn of the 21st Century*. Odense: University Press of Southern Denmark, 2004.

Clarke, Mary Stetson. *Bloomers and Ballots: Elizabeth Cady Stanton and, Women's Rights*. New York: Viking, 1972.

Cole, Alyson M. "There Are No Victims in This Class: On Female Suffering and Anti-victim Feminism." *NWSA Journal* 11 (Spring 1999): 72+.

Conway, Jill Ker. *Written by Herself: Autobiographies of American Women*. New York: Vintage, 1992.

Coote, Anna, and Beatrix Campbell. *Sweet Freedom: The Struggle for Women's Liberation*. Oxford: B. Blackwell, 1987.

Costello, Karin Bergstrom. *Gendered Voices: Readings from the American Experience*. Fort Worth, TX: Harcourt Brace College Publishers, 1996.

Cott, Nancy F. *The Grounding of Modern Feminism*. New Haven: Yale University Press, 1987.

Critchlow, Donald T. *Phyllis Schlafly and Grassroots Conservatism: A Woman's Crusade*. Princeton, NJ: Princeton University Press, 2005.

Cruea, Susan M. "Changing Ideals of Womanhood during the Nineteenth-Century Woman Movement." *American Transcendental Quarterly* 19 (September 2005): 187–205.

Daly, Mary. *The Church and the Second Sex*. Boston: Beacon, 1985.

———. *Outercourse: The Bedazzling Voyage Containing Recollections from My Logbook of a Radical Feminist Philosopher*. San Francisco: Harper, 1992.

———. *Webster's First New Intergalactic Wickedary of the English Language*. San Francisco: Harper, 1994.

Davis, Angela Y. *Women, Culture & Politics*. New York: Vintage Books, 1990.

———. *Women, Race & Class*. New York: Vintage Books, 1983.

Department of Economic and Social Affairs. *Convention on the Elimination of All Forms of Discrimination against Women, the Optional Protocol: Text and Materials*. New York: United Nations, 2000.

Dickenson, Donna. *Property, Women and Politics: Subjects or Objects?* New Brunswick, NJ: Rutgers University Press, 1997.

Donovan, Josephine. *Feminist Theory: The Intellectual Traditions*. New York: Continuum, 2000.

Doress-Worters, Paula, ed. *Mistress of Herself: Speeches and Letters of Ernestine Rose, Early Women's Rights Leader*. New York: Feminist Press at the City University of New York, 2007.

Dubois, Ellen Carol, ed. *The Elizabeth Cady Stanton-Susan B. Anthony Reader: Correspondence, Writings, Speeches*. Boston: Northeastern University Press, 1992.

Dubois, Ellen Carol. *Feminism and Suffrage: The Emergence of an Independent Women's Movement in America, 1848–1869*. Ithaca, NY: Cornell University Press, 1978.

Dubois, Ellen Carol, and Richard Cándida Smith. *Elizabeth Cady Stanton, Feminist as Thinker: A Reader in Documents and Essays*. New York: New York University Press, 2007.

Dworkin, Andrea. *Heartbreak: The Political Memoir of a Feminist Militant*. New York: Basic Books, 2002.

———. *Men Possessing Women*. New York: E.P. Dutton, 1989.

Dworkin, Andrea, and Catherine MacKinnon. *Pornography and Civil Rights: A New Day for Women's Equality*. Minneapolis, MN: Organizing Against Pornography, 1988.

Echols, Alice. *Daring to be Bad: Radical Feminism in America, 1967–1975*. Minneapolis: University of Minnesota Press, 1989.

Eckhardt, Celia Morris. *Fanny Wright: Rebel in America*. Cambridge: Harvard University Press, 1984.

Eckhaus, Phyllis. "Harriot Stanton Blatch and the Winning of Woman Suffrage." *The Nation* 265 (December 1997): 29–28.

Ehrenreich, Barbara. *The Hearts of Men: American Dreams and the Flight from Commitment*. New York: Anchor Books, 1983.

Eisenstein, Zillah. *Capitalist Patriarchy and the Case for Socialist Feminism*. New York: Monthly Review Press, 1979.

———. *The Color of Gender: Reimaging Democracy*. Berkeley: University of California Press, 1986.

Faludi, Susan. *Backlash: The Undeclared War against American Women*. New York: Three Rivers Press, 2006 (rep.).

———. "I'm Not a Feminist but I Play One on TV." *Ms.*, February/March 1995, 31–39.

Fausto-Sterling, Anne. *Myths of Gender: Biological Theories about Women and Men*. New York: Basic Books, 1992.

———. *Sexing the Body: Gender Politics and the Construction of Sexuality*. New York: Basic Books, 2000.

Firestone, Shulamith. *The Dialectic of Sex: The Case for Feminist Revolution*. New York: Morrow, 1970.

————. *Notes from the First Year*. New York: The New York Radical Women, 1968.

Flexner, Eleanor. *Century of Struggle: The Woman's Rights Movement in the United States*. New York: Atheneum, 1974.

Florence, Namulundah. *bell hooks' Engaged Pedagogy: A Transgressive Education for Critical Consciousness*. Westport, CT: Bergin & Garvey, 1998.

Fonda, Jane. *My Life So Far*. New York: Random House, 2005.

Ford, Linda G. *Iron-Jawed Angels: The Suffrage Militancy of the National Woman's Party 1912–1920*. New York: University Press of America, 1991.

Fosselman, Valery. *Everyone Is Equal in the Laundromat: The American Woman's Rights Movement, 1848–1920*. Shippensburg , PA: Shippensburg Collegiate Press, 1982.

Franklin, Vincent P. *Living Our Stories, Telling Our Truths: Autobiography and the Making of African American Intellectual Tradition*. New York: Oxford University Press, 1995

Freedman, Russell. *Eleanor Roosevelt: A Life of Discovery*. New York: Clarion Books, 1993.

Freeman, Jo. "The Origins of the Women's Liberation Movement." *American Journal of Sociology* 78 (1973): : 792–811.

French, Marilyn. *A Season in Hell: A Memoir*. New York: Knopf, 1998.

Friedan, Betty. *The Feminine Mystique*. New York: W.W. Norton, 1963.

————. *It Changed My Life: Writings on the Women's Movement*. New York: Random House, 1976.

Fuller, Margaret. *Woman in the Nineteenth Century*. Mineola, NY: Dover Publications, 1999.

Gage, Matilda Joslyn. *Woman, Church and State*. Amherst, NY: Humanity Books, 2002.

Giddings, Paula. *When and Where I Enter: The Impact of Black Women on Race and Sex in America*. Toronto: Bantam Books, 1985.

Gifford, Carolyn, ed. *Writing Out My Heart: Selections from the Journal of Frances E. Willard, 1855–96*. Champaign: University of Illinois Press, 1995

Gilman, Charlotte Perkins. *The Living of Charlotte Perkins Gilman: An Autobiography*. New York: D. Appleton-Century Company, 1935.

Glendon, Mary Ann. *A World Made New: Eleanor Roosevelt and the Universal Declaration of Human Rights*. New York: Random House, 2001.

Goldsmith, Barbara. *Other Powers: The Age of Suffrage, Spiritualism and the Scandalous Victoria Woodhull*. New York: Harper Perennial, 1998.

Gordon, Ann D. "Susan B. Anthony." In *American National Biography*. Vol. 1, edited by John Garraty and Mark Carnes. New York: Oxford University Press, 1999.

Gornick, Vivian. *The Solitude of Self: Thinking about Elizabeth Cady Stanton*. New York: Farrar, Straus and Giroux, 2005.

Grant, Judith. *Fundamental Feminism: Contesting the Core Concepts of Feminist Theory*. New York: Routledge, 1993.

Grant, Mary Hetherington. *Private Woman, Public Person: An Account of the Life of Julia Ward Howe from 1819–1868*. Brooklyn, NY: Carlson Publishing, 1994.

Gray, Carole. "Nineteenth-Century Women of Free Thought." *Free Inquiry* 15 (Spring 1995): 32–36.

Green, Karen, and Tristan Taormino, eds. *A Girl's Guide to Taking over the World: Writings from the Girl Zine Revolution.* New York: St. Martin's Press, 1997.

Greene, Dana, ed. *Suffrage and Religious Principle: Speeches and Writings of Olympia Brown.* Metuchen, NJ: Scarecrow Press, 1983.

Greer, Germaine. *The Whole Woman.* New York: Knopf, 1999.

Grimké, Sarah Moore. *Letters on the Equality of the Sexes, and the Condition of Woman.* Boston: I. Knapp, 1838.

Grosz, E.A. *Time Travels: Feminism, Nature, Power.* Durham, NC: Duke University Press, 2005.

Gurko, Miriam. *The Ladies of Seneca Falls: The Birth of the Woman's Rights Movement.* New York: Schocken Books, 1974.

Guy-Sheftall, Beverly. *Words of Fire: An Anthology of African-American Feminist Thought.* New York: New Press, 1995.

Hall, Florence Howe. *Julia Ward Howe and the Woman Suffrage Movement.* New York: Arno, 1969.

Hamilton, Roberta, and Michèle Barrett, eds. *The Politics of Diversity: Feminism, Marxism and Nationalism.* London: Verso, 1986.

Hanson, Joyce A. *Mary McLeod Bethune and Black Women's Political Activism.* Columbia: University of Missouri Press, 2003.

Hanson, Karen V., and Ilene Philipson, eds. *Women, Class and the Feminist Imagination: A Socialist-Feminist Reader.* Philadelphia, PA: Temple University Press, 1990.

Harper, Ida Husted. *How Six States Won Woman Suffrage.* New York: National American Woman Suffrage Association, 1911.

———. *The Life and Work of Susan B. Anthony.* 3 vols. Indianapolis, IN: Bowen-Merrill, 1899 and 1908.

———. *Suffrage: A Right.* New York: North American Review Publishing Company, 1906.

Hawkesworth, M.E. *Beyond Oppression: Feminist Theory and Political Strategy.* New York: Continuum, 1990.

Heath, Joseph, and Andrew Potter. "Feminism for Sale: Find Out the Real Reason the Women's Movement Is Losing Momentum, and Why Political Action Is the Only Way to Take Down the Patriarchy." *This Magazine* 38 (May–June 2005): 20–27.

Heilbrun, Carolyn G. *The Education of a Woman: The Life of Gloria Steinem.* New York: Dial Press, 1995.

Held, Virginia. *Feminist Morality: Transforming Culture, Society and Politics.* Chicago: University of Chicago Press, 1993.

Hernandez, Aileen C. *National Women of Color Organizations: A Report to the Ford Foundation.* New York: Ford Foundation, 1991.

Hewitt, Nancy, and Suzanne Lebsock, eds. *Visible Women: New Essays on American Activism.* Urbana: University of Illinois Press, 1993.

Higgins, Lisa Cochran. "Adulterous Individualism, Socialism and Free Love in Nineteenth-Century Anti-suffrage Writing." *Legacy: A Journal of American Women Writers* 21 (June 2004): 193–210.

Higginson, Thomas Wentworth. *Common Sense about Women.* London: S. Sonnenschein & Company, 1897.

Hite, Shere. *The Hite Report on Shere Hite: Voice of a Daughter in Exile.* London: Arcadia, 1999.

———. "Why I Became a German." *New Statesman,* November 17, 2003, 25.

hooks, bell. *Talking Back: Thinking Feminist, Thinking Black.* Toronto: Between the Lines, 1988.

Horowitz, Daniel. *Betty Friedan and the Making of the Feminine Mystique: The American Left, the Cold and Modern Feminism.* Amherst: University of Massachusetts Press, 1998.

Humm, Maggie, ed. *Modern Feminisms: Political, Literary, Cultural.* New York: Columbia University Press, 1992.

Huxman, Susan Schultz. "Perfecting the Rhetorical Vision of Woman's Rights: Elizabeth Cady Stanton, Anna Howard Shaw, and Carrie Chapman Catt." *Women's Studies in Communication* 23 (Fall 2000): 307–36.

Hyman, Paula, and Deborah Dash Moore, eds. *Jewish Women in America.* New York: Routledge, 1997.

Iannone, Carol. "Sex & the Feminists." *Commentary* 96 (September 1993): 51–54.

Jagger, Alison, ed. *Living with Contradictions: Controversies in Feminist Social Ethics.* Boulder, CO: Westview Press, 1994.

Jagger, Alison M., and Paula S. Rothenberg, eds. *Feminist Frameworks: Alternative Theoretical Accounts of Relations between Women and Men.* New York: McGraw-Hill, 1993.

Janda, Sarah Eppler. *Beloved Women: The Political Lives of Ladonna Harris and Wilma Mankiller.* DeKalb: Northern Illinois University Press, 2007.

Jochnowitz, George. "A Conversation with Phyllis Chesler: American Feminist and Zionist Activist." *Midstream* 53 (September–October 2007): 9–14.

Jones, Beverly Washington. *Quest for Equality: The Life and Writings of Mary Eliza Church Terrell, 1863–1954.* Brooklyn, NY: Carlson Publishing, 1990.

Katz, Esther. *The Selected Papers of Margaret Sanger, Vol. II.* Champaign: University of Illinois Press, 2007.

Keating, AnaLouise. *Women Reading Women Writing: Self-Invention in Paula Gunn Allen, Gloria Anzaldúa and Audre Lorde.* Philadelphia, PA: Temple University Press, 1996.

Keating, Cricket. "Building Coalitional Consciousness." *NWSA Journal* 17 (Summer 2005): 86–103.

Keller, Kristin Thoennes. *Carrie Chapman Catt: A Voice for Women.* Minneapolis, MN: Compass Point Books, 2006.

Kern, Kathi. *Mrs. Stanton's Bible.* Ithaca: Cornell University Press, 2001.

Kerr, Andrea Moore. *Lucy Stone: Speaking Out for Equality.* New Brunswick, NJ: Rutgers University Press, 1992.

King, Billie Jean, and Frank Deford. *The Autobiography of Billie Jean King.* London: Granada, 1982.

Kowalksi, Kathiann M. "Cady Stanton and Anthony Friends Fighting for the Cause." *Cobblestone* 21 (March 2000): 14.

Kraditor, Aileen. *The Ideas of the Woman Suffrage Movement/1890–1920.* New York: W.W. Norton, 1981.

Kramarae, Cheris, and Dale Spender. *The Knowledge Explosion: Generations of Feminist Scholarship.* New York: Teacher's College Press, 1992.

Lane, Ann J. *To Herland and Beyond: The Life and Work of Charlotte Perkins Gilman.* Charlottesville: University Press of Virginia, 1997.

Lane, Margaret. *Frances Wright and the "Great Experiment."* Manchester, England: Manchester University Press, 1972.

Lasser, Carol, and Marlene Merrill, eds. *Soul Mates: The Oberlin Correspondence of Lucy Stone and Antoinette Brown, 1846–1850.* Oberlin, OH: Oberlin College, 1983.

Lerner, Gerda, ed. *Black Women in White America: A Documentary History.* New York: Pantheon Books, 1972.

Lerner, Gerda. *The Creation of Patriarchy.* New York: Oxford University Press, 1986.

Lerner, Gerda. *The Feminist Thought of Sarah Grimké.* New York: Oxford University Press, 1998.

Lerner, Gerda. *The Majority Finds Its Past: Placing Women in History.* New York: Oxford University Press, 1979.

Levine, Suzanne, and Mary Thom. *Bella Abzug: How One Tough Broad from the Bronx Fought Jim Crow and Joe McCarthy, Pissed Off Jimmy Carter, Battled for the Rights of Women and Workers, Rallied against War and for the Planet, and Shook Up Politics along the Way.* New York: Farrar, Straus and Giroux, 2007.

Livermore, Mary Ashton Rice. *The Story of My Life or, the Sunshine and Shadow of Seventy Years.* Hartford, CT: A.D. Worthington, 1899.

Lopach, James J., and Jean A. Luckowski. *Jeanette Rankin: A Political Woman.* Boulder: University Press of Colorado, 2005.

Lorde, Audre. *Sister Outsider: Essays and Speeches.* Trumansburg, NY: Crossing Press, 1984.

Lotz, Amanda D. "Communicating Third-World Feminism and New Social Movements: Challenges for the Next Century of Feminist Endeavor." *Women and Language* 26 (Spring 2003): 2–9.

Loudermilk, Kim A. *Fictional Feminism: How American Bestsellers Affect the Movement for Women's Equality.* New York: Routledge, 2004.

Lowenberg, Bert James, and Ruth Bogin, eds. *Black Women in Nineteenth-Century American Life.* University Park: The Pennsylvania State University Press, 1976.

Lumsden, Linda J. *Inez: The Life and Times of Inez Milholland.* Bloomington: Indiana University Press, 2004.

Lutz, Alma. *Created Equal: A Biography of Elizabeth Cady Stanton.* New York, Octagon Books, 1974.

———. *Susan B. Anthony: Rebel, Crusader, Humanitarian.* Boston: Beacon, 1959.

Lynn, Susan. *Progressive Women in Conservative Times: Racial Justice, Peace and Feminism, 1945 to the 1960s.* New Brunswick, NJ: Rutgers University Press, 1992.

MacKinnon, Catharine A. *Are Women Human?: And Other International Dialogues.* Cambridge, MA: Belknap Press of Harvard University Press, 2006.

———. *Feminism Unmodified: Discourses on Life and Law.* Cambridge, MA: Harvard University Press, 1987.

Mankiller, Wilma, and Michael Wallis. *Mankiller: A Chief and Her People.* New York: St. Martin's Press, 1993.

Martin, Wendy. *The American Sisterhood: Writings of the Feminist Movement from Colonial Times to the Present.* New York: Harper & Row, 1972.

Matthews, Glenna. *The Rise of Public Woman: Woman's Power and Woman's Place in the United States, 1630–1970.* New York: Oxford University Press, 1992.

———. "Women in the Public Sphere." In *Encyclopedia of American Cultural & Intellectual History*. Vol. I, edited by Mary Kupiec Cayton and Peter W. Williams. New York: Charles Scribner's Sons, 2000.

McCammon, Holly J. "Stirring up Suffrage Sentiment: The Formation of the State Woman Suffrage Organizations, 1866–1914." *Social Forces* 80 (December 2001): 449–80.

McCluskey, Thomas, and Elaine Smith. *Mary McLeod Bethune: Building a Better World: Essays and Selected Documents*. Bloomington: Indiana University Press, 1999.

McMillan, Carol. *Women, Reason and Nature: Some Philosophical Problems with Feminism*. Oxford: Basil Blackwell, 1982.

McQuiston, Liz. *Suffragettes to She-Devils: Women's Liberation and Beyond*. London: Phaidon, 1997.

Meehan, Elizabeth, and Selma Sevenhuijsen, eds. *Equality Politics and Gender*. London: Sage Publications, 1991.

Melder, Keith. *Beginnings of Sisterhood, the American Woman's Rights Movement, 1800–1850*. New York: Schocken Books, 1977.

Merrill, Marlene Deahl. *Growing Up in Boston's Gilded Age: The Journal of Alice Stone Blackwell, 1872–1874*. New Haven, CT: Yale University Press, 1990.

Miller, Erica M. *The Other Reconstruction: Where Violence and Womanhood Meet in the Writings of Ida B. Wells-Barnett, Angelina Weld Grimké, and Nella Larsen*. New York: Routledge Press, 1999

Millett, Kate. *Flying*. New York: Knopf, 1974.

———. *Going to Iran*. New York: Coward, McCann & Geoghegan, 1982.

———. *Sexual Politics*. Garden City, NY: Doubleday, 1970.

Moraga, Cherríe, and Gloria Anzaldua, eds. *This Bridge Called My Back: Writings by Radical Women of Color*. Berkeley, CA: Third Woman Press, 2001.

Morgan, Robin. *Sisterhood Is Forever: The Women's Anthology for a New Millennium*. New York: Washington Square Press, 2003.

———. *Sisterhood Is Powerful: An Anthology of Writings from the Women's Liberation Movement*. New York: Random House, 1970.

Mott, Lucretia. *Discourse on Woman*. Philadelphia: W.P. Kildare, 1869.

Murray, Pauli. *Proud Shoes: The Story of an American Family*. New York: Harper & Row, 1978.

———. *Song in a Weary Throat: Pauli Murray: The Autobiography of a Black Activist, Feminist, Lawyer, Priest and Poet*. Knoxville: The University of Tennessee Press, 1987.

Nash, Margaret A. *Women's Education in the United States, 1780–1840*. New York: Palgrave Macmillan, 2005.

Neuman, Nancy M., ed. *True to Ourselves: A Celebration of Women Making a Difference*. San Francisco: Jossey-Bass, 1998.

Newman, Louise Michele. *White Women's Rights: The Racial Origins of Feminism in the United States*. New York: Oxford University Press, 1999.

Nies, Judith. *Seven Women: Portraits from the American Radical Tradition*. New York: Viking Press, 1977.

Noun, Louise R. *Strong-Minded Women*. Ames: Iowa State University Press, 1969.

Novarra, Virginia. *Women's Work, Men's Work: The Ambivalence of Equality*. London: M. Boyars, 1980.

Oliver, Susan. *Betty Friedan: The Personal Is Political*. New York: Pearson Long-
man, 2007.

O'Neill, William L. *Everyone Was Brave: The Rise and Fall of Feminism in America*.
Chicago: Quadrangle Books, 1969.

Paglia, Camille. *Break, Blow, Burn*. New York: Pantheon Books, 2005.

———. *Vamps & Tramps: New Essays*. New York: Vintage Books, 1994.

Peterson, Esther, and Winfred Conkling. *Restless: The Memoirs of Labor and Consumer Activist Esther Peterson*. Vero Beach, FL: Caring Publishing, 1997.

Peterson, Helen Stone. *Susan B. Anthony: Pioneer in Woman's Rights*. Champaign,
IL: Garrard Publishing Company, 1971.

Pfeffer, Paula. "Before Equal Suffrage: Women in Partisan Politics from Colonial
Times to 1920." *American Historical Review* 59, no. 1 (April 1997): 530–32.

———. "Eleanor Roosevelt and the National and World Woman's Parties." *The
Historian* 102, no. 2 (Fall 1996): 39–57.

Phillips, Anne, ed. *Feminism and Equality*. New York: New York University Press,
1987.

Pogrebin, Letty Cottin. *Deborah, Golda and Me: Being Female and Jewish in
America*. New York: Anchor Books, 1992.

———. *Family Politics: Love and Power on an Intimate Frontier*. New York:
McGraw-Hill, 1984.

Rhode, Deborah L., and Carol Sanger, eds. *Gender and Rights*. Burlington, VT:
Ashgate, 2005.

Richardson, Diane, and Victoria Robinson, eds. *Thinking Feminist: Key Concepts in
Women's Studies*. New York: Guilford Press, 1993.

Roberts, Selena. *A Necessary Spectacle: Billie Jean King, Bobby Riggs, and the Tennis Match That Leveled the Game*. New York: Crown Publishers, 2005.

Roiphe, Katie. *Last Night in Paradise: Sex and Morals at the Century's End*. Boston:
Little, Brown, 1997.

———. *The Morning After: Sex, Fear and Feminism on Campus*. Boston: Little,
Brown, 1993.

Rosen, Ruth. *The World Split Open: How the Modern Women's Movement
Changed America*. New York: Penguin, 2006

Russo, Ann, and Cheris Kramarae, ed. *The Radical Women's Press of the 1850s*.
New York: Routledge, 2001.

Rynder, Constance. "All Men and Women Are Created Equal." *American History*
33 (August 1998): 22–28.

Sandoval, Chela. *Methodology of the Oppressed*. Minneapolis: University of Minnesota Press, 2000.

Sanger, Margaret. *Margaret Sanger: An Autobiography*. New York: W. W. Norton,
1938.

Schechter, Patricia A. *Ida B. Wells and American Reform: 1880–1930*. Chapel Hill:
University of North Carolina Press, 2001.

Schlafly, Phyllis. *Feminist Fantasies*. Dallas, TX: Spence Publishing, 2003.

Scott, Anne Firor. *Natural Allies: Women's Associations in American History*.
Urbana: University of Illinois Press, 1991.

Seaman, Barbara. *The Doctor's Case against the Pill*. New York: P.H. Wyden, 1969.

———. *The Greatest Experiment Ever Performed on Women: Exploding the Estrogen Myth*. New York: Hyperion, 2003.

Seely, Megan. *Fight Like a Girl: How to Be a Fearless Feminist.* New York: New York University Press, 2007.

Shaw, Susan M., and Janet Lee. *Women's Voices, Feminist Visions: Classic and Contemporary Readings.* Mountain View, CA: Mayfield Publishing Company, 2001.

Sherr, Lynn. *Failure Is Impossible: Susan B. Anthony in Her Own Words.* New York: Times Books, 1995.

Shulman, Alix Kates. *A Good Enough Daughter: A Memoir.* New York: Schocken Books, 1999.

Slavin, Sarah. *Plow Women Rather Than Reapers: An Intellectual History of Feminism in the United States.* Metuchen, NJ: Scarecrow Press, 1979.

Smith, Barbara. "Barbara Smith on Black Feminism." *Sojourner: The Women's Forum,* December 1984, 13.

———. *The Truth That Never Hurts: Writings on Race, Gender, and Freedom.* New Brunswick, NJ: Rutgers University Press, 1998

Smith, Norma. *Jeanette Rankin: America's Conscience.* Helena, MT: Montana Historical Society Press, 2002.

Sochen, June. *The New Feminism in Twentieth-Century America.* Lexington, MA: D.C. Heath and Company, 1971.

Social Justice Group at the Center for Advanced Feminist Studies, University of Minnesota, eds. *Is Academic Feminism Dead?: Theory in Practice.* New York: New York University Press, 2000.

Somerville, Barbara A. *Votes for Women!: The Story of Carrie Chapman Catt.* Greensboro, NC: Morgan Reynolds Publishing, 2003.

Spelman, Elizabeth. *Inessential Woman: Problems of Exclusion in Feminist Thought.* Boston: Beacon, 1988.

Spender, Dale. *For the Record: The Making and Meaning of Feminist Knowledge.* London: Women's Press, 1985.

———. *There's Always Been a Women's Movement This Century.* London: Routlege and Kegan Paul, 1983.

———. *Women of Ideas: And What Men Have Done to Them.* London: Routledge and Kegan Paul, 1982.

Stanton, Elizabeth Cady. *Bible and Church Degrade Woman.* Chicago, IL: H.L. Green, 1898.

———. *Eighty Years and More.* London: T. Fisher Unwin, 1898.

———. *The Solitude of Self.* Ashfield, MA: Paris Press, 2001.

Stanton, Elizabeth Cady, Susan B. Anthony, and Matilda Joslyn Gage, eds. *History of Woman Suffrage.* New York: S.B. Anthony, 1922.

Stanton, Theodore, and Harriot Stanton Blatch, eds. *Elizabeth Cady Stanton.* New York: Arno, 1969.

Steinem, Gloria. *Outrageous Acts and Everyday Rebellions.* New York: New American Library, 1983.

Stern, Madeline B. *The Victoria Woodhull Reader.* Weston, MA: M & S Press, 1974.

Stetson, Erlene, and Linda David. *Glorying in Tribulation: The Lifework of Sojourner Truth.* East Lansing: Michigan State University Press, 1994.

Strom, Sharon Hartman. *Women's Rights.* Westport, CT: Greenwood Press, 2003.

Strossen, Nadine. *Defending Pornography: Free Speech, Sex, and the Fight for Women's Rights.* New York: New York University Press, 2000.

Tanner, Leslie B., ed. *Voices from Women's Liberation.* New York: Signet, 1970.

Terrell, Mary Church. *A Colored Woman in a White World.* New York: Arno, 1980.

Thompson, Becky. "Multiracial Feminism: Recasting the Chronology of Second Wave Feminism." *Feminist Studies* 28 (Summer 2002): 337–61.

Threlfall, Monica, ed. *Mapping the Women's Movement: Feminist Politics and Social Transformation in the North.* London: Verso, 1996.

Tilton, Theodore. "Victoria C. Woodhull, a Biographical Sketch." *The Golden Age,* Tract No. 3, 1871.

Toth, Emily. *Unveiling Kate Chopin.* Jackson: University Press of Mississippi, 1999.

Venet, Wendy Hamand. *A Strong-Minded Woman: The Life of Mary Livermore.* Amherst: University of Massachusetts Press, 2005

Walker, Alice. *In Search of Our Mothers' Gardens: Womanist Prose.* Orlando, FL: Harcourt, 2004.

Walker, Rebecca. *To Be Real: Telling the Truth and Changing the Face of Feminism.* New York: Anchor Books, 1995.

Wallace, Christine. *Germaine Greer: Untamed Shrew.* New York: Faber and Faber, 1998.

Ward, Geoffrey C., and Ken Burns. *Not for Ourselves Alone: The Story of Elizabeth Cady Stanton and Susan B. Anthony.* New York: Knopf, 1999.

Ware, Cellestine. *Woman Power: The Movement for Women's Liberation.* New York: Tower Publications, 1970.

Watson, Martha. *Lives of Their Own: Rhetorical Dimensions in Autobiographies of Women Activists.* Columbia: University of South Carolina Press, 1999.

Weed, Helena Hill. *Equal Rights Amendment: Questions and Answers on the Equal Rights Amendment, Prepared by the Research Department of the National Woman's Party.* Washington, DC: U.S. Government Printing Office, 1943.

West, Guida, and Rhoda Lois Blumberg, eds. *Women and Social Protest.* New York: Oxford University Press, 1990.

Wheeler, Marjorie Spruill, ed. *One Woman, One Vote: Rediscovering the Woman Suffrage Movement.* Troutdale, OR: New Sage Press, 1995.

White, Evelyn C. *Alice Walker: A Life.* New York: W.W. Norton, 2004.

Whitehurst, Carol. *Women in America: The Oppressed Majority.* Santa Monica, CA: Goodyear Publishing Company, 1977.

Whittier, Nancy. "Persistence and Transformation: Gloria Steinem, the Women's Action Alliance, and the Feminist Movement." *Journal of Women's History* 14 (Summer 2002): 148–51.

Wiley, Jean. "On the Front Lines: Four Women Activists Whose Work Touched Millions of Lives." *Essence* 20 (February 1990): 45–48.

Willard, Frances E. *Woman and Temperance: The Work and Workers of the Woman's Christian Temperance Union.* New York: Arno, 1972 (rep.)

Wilson, Anna. *Persuasive Fictions: Feminist Narrative and Critical Myth.* London: Associated University Press, 2001.

Wolf, Naomi. *The Beauty Myth: How Images of Beauty Are Used against Women.* New York: Perennial, 2002.

———. *Fire with Fire: The New Female Power and How It Will Change the 21st Century.* New York: Ballentine, 1994.

Wolff, Janet. *Feminine Sentences: Essays on Women and Culture.* Berkeley: University of California Press, 1990.

Wong, Nellie, Merle Woo, and Mitsuye Yamada. *3 Asian American Writers Speak Out on Feminism*. San Francisco, CA: Red Letter Press, 2003.

Woodhull, Victoria. *Freedom! Equality!! Justice!!!* New York: Woodhull, Clafin and Company, 1872.

Wright, Frances. *Biography and Notes of Frances Wright D'Arusmont*. Boston: J.P. Mendum, 1848.

Yarbro-Bejanrano, Yvonne. *The Wounded Heart: Writing on Cherrie Moraga*. Austin: University of Texas Press, 2001.

Yates, Gayle Graham. *What Women Want: The Ideas of the Movement*. Cambridge, MA: Harvard University Press, 1975.

Young, Iris. *On Female Body Experience: "Throwing Like a Girl" and Other Essays*. New York: Oxford University Press, 2005.

———. *Justice and the Politics of Difference*. Princeton, NJ: Princeton University Press, 1990.

Zink-Sawyer, Beverly A. "From Preachers to Suffragists: Enlisting the Pulpit in the Early Movement for Woman's Rights." *American Transcendental Quarterly* 14 (September 2000): 193.

INDEX

About the Author

JOYCE DUNCAN is a Lecturer of Cross-Disciplinary Studies at East Tennessee State University. She is the author of *Ahead of Their Time: A Biographical Dictionary of Risk-Taking Women* (Greenwood, 2001) and editor of *Sport in American Culture* (2004).